AF560022

DATA COMMUNICATION AND NETWORKING

DATA COMMUNICATION AND NETWORKING

Er. N.B.L. Mathur

ANMOL PUBLICATIONS PVT. LTD.
NEW DELHI-110 002 (INDIA)

ANMOL PUBLICATIONS PVT. LTD.
Regd. Office: 4360/4, Ansari Road, Daryaganj,
New Delhi-110002 (India)
Tel.: 23278000, 23261597, 23286875, 23255577
Fax: 91-11-23280289
Email: anmolpub@gmail.com
Visit us at: www.anmolpublications.com

Branch Office: No. 1015, Ist Main Road, BSK IIIrd Stage
IIIrd Phase, IIIrd Block, Bangalore-560 085 (India)
Tel.: 080-41723429 • Fax: 080-26723604
Email: anmolpublicationsbangalore@gmail.com

Data Communication and Networking

First Edition, 2010

ISBN 978-81-261-4510-2

PRINTED IN INDIA

Printed at Mehra Offset Press, Delhi.

Contents

Preface

The book Data Communications and Networking provides an introduction to the principles of modern, multi-media types of communication, which uncovers the underlying mechanisms of network concepts. As a considerable number of concepts appear in the two most prominent protocol suites, TCP/IP and ATM, Data Communications and Networking explains how concepts such as routing and quality of service apply differently to the Internet or ATM networks.

Data Communications and Networking presents the multitude of basic network concepts in an organized way that clarifies their interrelations. The importance of each concept is placed in the overall picture of a communications infrastructure. By contrasting the two main protocol suites, the different architectural viewpoints stand out, enriching a discussion on networking. Data Communications and Networking, provides a comprehensive and current introduction to networking technologies. The book is accessible to students from all backgrounds and uses hundreds of figures to visually represent concepts.

This book has been completely updated to reflect the constantly changing world of network technologies. Enhanced coverage of bluetooth, wireless, satellites, as well as chapter on security have been clearly explained. The book explains the transitioned from using the 7-layer OSI model to the 5-layer Internet Model.

Author

Chapter 1

Fundamental of Communication Systems

MODEL

MODEL OF COMMUNICATION

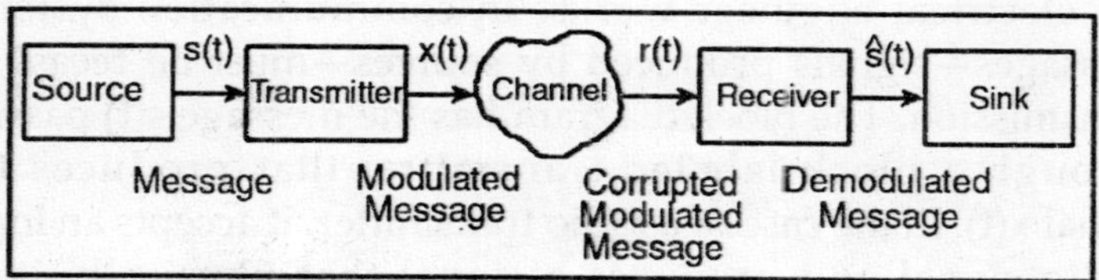

Definition of a system

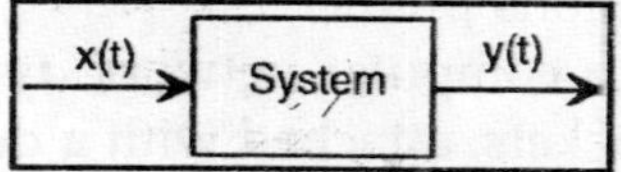

The fundamental model of communications is portrayed in Figure. In this fundamental model, each message-bearing signal, exemplified by s(t), is analog and is a function of time. A system operates on zero, one, or several signals to produce more signals or to simply absorb them. In electrical engineering, we represent a system as a box, receiving input signals (usually coming from the left) and producing from them new output signals.

This graphical representation is known as a block diagram. We denote input signals by lines having arrows pointing into the box, output signals by arrows pointing away. As typified by the communications model, how information flows, how it is corrupted and manipulated, and how it is ultimately received is summarized by interconnecting block diagrams: The outputs of one or more systems serve as the inputs to others.

In the communications model, the source produces a signal that will be absorbed by the sink. Examples of time-domain signals produced by a source are music, speech, and characters typed on a keyboard. Signals can also be functions of two variables—an image is a signal that depends on two spatial variables—or more—television pictures (video signals) are functions of two spatial variables and time.

Thus, information sources produce signals. In physical systems, each signal corresponds to an electrical voltage or current. To be able to design systems, we must understand electrical science and technology. However, we first need to understand the big picture to appreciate the context in which the electrical engineer works. In communication systems, messages—signals produced by sources—must be recast for transmission. The block diagram has the message s(t) passing through a block labeled transmitter that produces the signal x(t). In the case of a radio transmitter, it accepts an input audio signal and produces a signal that physically is an electromagnetic wave radiated by an antenna and propagating as Maxwell's equations predict.

In the case of a computer network, typed characters are encapsulated in packets, attached with a destination address, and launched into the Internet. From the communication systems "big picture" perspective, the same block diagram applies although the systems can be very different. In any case, the transmitter should not operate in such a way that the message s(t) cannot be recovered from x(t).

In the mathematical sense, the inverse system must exist, else the communication system cannot be considered reliable. (It is ridiculous to transmit a signal in such a way that no one can recover the original. However, clever systems exist that transmit signals so that only the "in crowd" can recover them. Such crytographic systems underlie secret communications.) Transmitted signals next pass through the next stage, the evil channel. Nothing good happens to a signal in a channel: It can become corrupted by noise, distorted, and attenuated among many possibilities. The channel cannot be escaped (the real world is cruel), and transmitter design and receiver design focus on how best to jointly fend off the channel's effects on signals. The channel is another system in our block diagram, and produces r(t), the signal received by the receiver. If the channel were benign (good luck finding such a channel in the real world), the receiver would serve as the inverse system to the transmitter, and yield the message with no distortion.

However, because of the channel, the receiver must do its best to produce a received message s(t) that resembles s(t) as much as possible. Shannon showed in his 1948 paper that reliable—for the moment, take this word to mean error-free—digital communication was possible over arbitrarily noisy channels. It is this result that modern communications systems exploit, and why many communications systems are going"digital. Finally, the received message is passed to the information sink that somehow makes use of the message. In the communications model, the source is a system having no input but producing an output; a sink has an input and no output. Understanding signal generation and how systems work amounts to understanding signals, the nature of the information they represent, how information is transformed between analog and digital forms, and how information can be processed by systems operating on information-bearing signals. This understanding demands two different fields of knowledge. One is electrical science: How are signals represented and manipulated electrically? The second is signal science: What is the structure of signals, no matter what their source, what is their information content, and what capabilities does this structure force upon communication systems?

COMMUNICATION LINKS

LINKS AND NETWORKING

This work package addresses various aspects related to communication links between HAPs as a central point in the network and ground nodes and satellites. Much of the activity will concentrate on the high-speed vehicle application. This demanding application will require the development of a suitable access standard, which should be based on the most suitable of the existing or developing standards with the necessary adaptations as required. The HeliNet project carried out a review of standards for the fixed broadband application, and found that IEEE 802.16 was most suitable. This work will form the starting point of this new selection process – new requirements will be taken into account such as high speed mobility and available equipment. Appropriate standards for different system segments and scenarios will be selected from the list of candidate standards offering some of the targeted characteristics (bit-rate, mobility), e.g. IEEE 802.16, IEEE 802.20,, HIPERACCESS, DVB-S, DVB-RCS, DVB-T, the critical aspects will be emphasised and possible technological constraints will be investigated, and these will form the basis of the future work.

A detailed understanding of the propagation environment is vital to the success of broadband delivery from this new architecture. Propagation measurements will concentrate on the HAP architecture specific aspects and to avoid duplication, will take into account relevant previous measurements in satellite and terrestrial links. The Heli Net project has carried out a detailed assessment of the rain attenuation mechanisms and how they affect fixed nodes. Work here will extend these analyses, looking at short-term rain outage mitigation strategies, including time diversity, and caching. The effects of scintillation will also be examined. This is of particular importance when high rate modulation schemes are used.

Short-term propagation impairments such as multipath (caused by reflections) and Doppler effect will also be investigated. Normally these are unlikely to be significant for static users with highly direction antenna at these frequencies, but may be important when antenna array technology is used on fast moving vehicles. These studies will be supported by a series of measurements taken from the system testbed throughout the project. The development of an efficient radio interface for the future high-speed application will be addressed. This will be based around existing/developing access standards, and will use work developed by HeliNet for the fixed application.

The main objective will be to illustrate what changes will be required to support this new application and architecture, and this will be input into the relevant standards/regulatory bodies by the relevant partners. Cutting edge technologies will be explored including the use of MIMO as a platform diversity technique, advanced signal processing algorithms that minimise the processing power requirements, cope with the high aggregate data rates and are computationally efficient, and with the envisaged multipath/Doppler environment. Advanced software radio signal processing techniques will be investigated in detail, concentrating specifically on aspects pertinent to an aerial platform architecture. Their performance gains achievable for aerial platform applications will be assessed through the implementation of selected algorithms on a DSP platform.

HeliNet has proposed several resource management strategies to support broadband communications to fixed users with both single and multiple platform architectures. The combination of high-speed mobility and platform movement present a significant challenge in maintaining adequate communication links in the mobile train scenario, with rapid and frequent handover required to maintain adequate quality of service for delay sensitive broadband applications.

Novel resource allocation strategies will be developed for both the user and backhaul links of a single HAP, to mitigate the effects of mobility and interference and provide both efficient spectrum utilization and adequate QoS. They will encompass resource and mobility management (interaction of channel assignment, medium access control, inter-beam and inter-platform handoff, caching, and prioritization), and will be designed to be harmonious with broadband transmission standards. The potential of multiple HAP constellations combined with highly directional user antennas to enhance capacity by means of overlapped or co-located regions of coverage will be investigated further, and this work will be extended to determine how diversity may be exploited to increase service availability. The platform constellations offering the best capacity and/or diversity benefits will be determined.

The work will additionally focus on spectrum sharing, as the present radio regulatory environment in Europe will require that the 28/31GHz frequency bands are shared with terrestrial and satellite operators. Interoperability issues will be examined to determine the viability of the coexistence of HAP systems with other wireless/satellite technologies. End-to-end networking and interworking with other technologies will be of paramount importance when delivering "Broadband for All". Users will wish to see a common set of applications, services and configurations when they are in the office, at home in a rural area, or on board a high-speed train.

These issues will be tackled here, and a network architecture that maintains diverse quality of service requirements will be developed based on existing/future standards such as IPv6. This will be based on work undertaken in HeliNet which looked at network provision for the fixed application. The purpose of this project is to understand how wireless communications links delivering data rates in excess of 1Gbps can be delivered, taking into account the system level implications of the antenna and wireless technology, propagation, and station-keeping characteristics of the HAP.

High Altitude Platforms (HAP) have the advantage of being able to deliver capacity over a wide service area, at data rates commonly found with terrestrial wireless systems. Recent developments have shown that HAPs are likely to be used to deliver spot beam islands of coverage within a service area to fill in gaps not served by other means of communications, or for specialized isolated users.

The purpose of this project is to understand how wireless communications links delivering data rates in excess of 1Gbps can be delivered, taking into account the system level implications of the antenna and wireless technology, propagation, and station-keeping characteristics of the HAP.

The project will also identify key users for the technology, for example telemedicine and video distribution. The second part of the project will then address how cognitive radio principles can be used to deliver the required amount of spectrum on an opportunistic basis in order to deliver these high capacity links. Given the scarcity of dedicated HAP spectrum this is likely to be shared with a range of other wireless communications systems, so it will be important to ensure that these new HAP systems do not cause excessive interference, and maintain fair access. The project will also aim to identify situations where it would be sensible to adopt an alternative means of delivery (e.g. terrestrial) to serve the users.

A mixture of simulation and analysis will be used. It is expected that game theory and Markov analysis will be particularly important analytical tools. This work will integrate closely with other activities within the Group.

KEY OBJECTIVES

- To understand how gigabit communication links can be delivered from HAPs, and the likely maximum service area
- To identify key applications that will benefit from these data rates
- To understand how cognitive radio can be used to assign capacity on an opportunistic basis
- To ascertain whether mixed HAP - terrestrial systems can provide seemless coverage

COMMUNICATION SYSTEM

The concept of information is central to communication. There is no precise definition of the word "information". So, instead of information, we deal with "message". Message is defined as the physical manifestation of information as produced by the sourceThere are two distinct message categories.

ANALOG

An analog message is a physical quantity that varies with time usually in a smooth and continuous fashion.

Examples of analog messages are:

- The acoustic pressure produced when you speak
- The angular position of an aircraft gyro
- The light intensity at some point in a television image.

DIGITAL

A digital message is an ordered sequence of symbols selected from a finite set of discrete elements.

Examples of digital messages are:

- Letters printed on this page
- Listing of hourly temperature readings
- The keys you press at a computer terminal.

Whether the message is analog or digital, it needs to be converted into an electrical signal. (There are only few messages, which are inherently electrical.)

INPUT AND OUTPUT

The input transducer converts the message to an electrical signal say a voltage or current. Another transducer at the destination converts the output signal to the desired message form.

Illustration

The transducers in a voice communication system could be microphone at the input and a loudspeaker at the output.

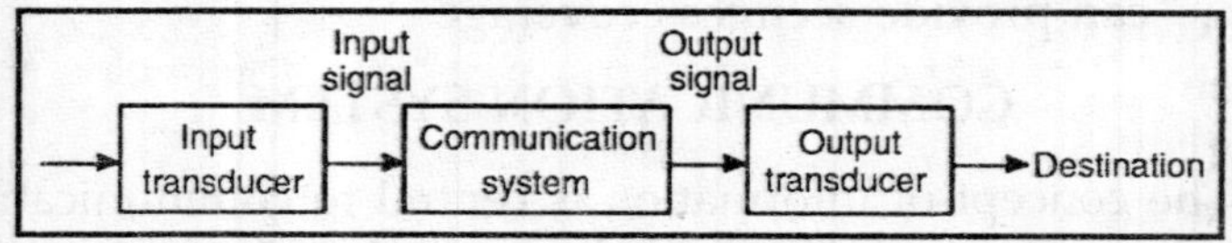

Communication system with input and output transducers

ELEMENTS OF COMMUNICATION SYSTEM

The below figure depicts the elements of a communication system. There are three essential parts of any communication system, the transmitter, transmission channel, and receiver. Each parts plays a particular role in signal transmission, as follows: The transmitter processes the input signal to produce a suitable transmitted signal suited to the characteristics of the transmission channel. Signal processing for transmissions almost always involves modulation and may also include coding.

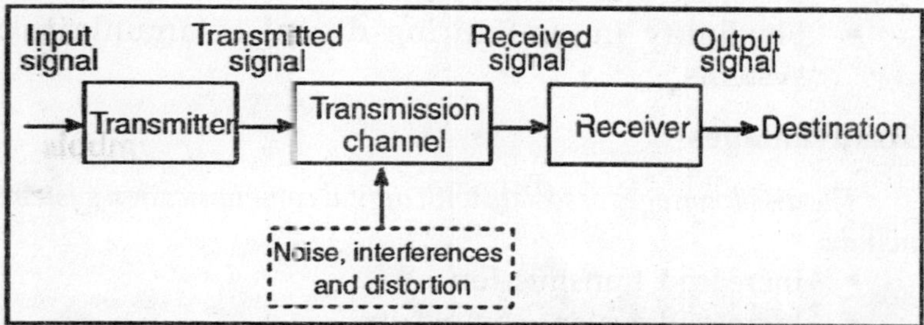

The transmission channel is the electrical medium that bridges the distance from source to destination. It may be a pair of wires, a coaxial cable, or a radio wave or laser beam. Every channel introduces some amount of transmission loss or attenuation. So, the signal power progressively decreases with increasing distance. The receiver operates on the output signal from the channel in preparation for delivery to the transducer at the destination. Receiver operations include amplification to compensate for transmission loss.

These also include demodulation and decoding to reverse the signal procession performed at the transmitter. Filtering is another important function at the receiver. The figure represents one-way or simplex (SX) transmission. Two way communication of course requires a transmitter and receiver at each end. A full-duplex (FDX) system has a channel that allows simultaneous transmission in both directions. A half-duplex (HDX) system allows transmission in either direction but not at the same time.

DIGITAL AND ANALOG COMMUNICATION SYSTEMS

Advantages

The advantages associate with digital communication systems include:

- A common format for encoding different kinds of

message signals (e.g., speech signal, video signal, computer data, etc.) for the purpose of transmission.

- An improved security of message.
- Increased immunity to noise and external interference.
- Flexibility in configuring digital communication systems.

Disadvantages

The disadvantages associate with digital communication systems include:

- Increased transmission
- Increased system complexity

Although digital communication is becoming increasingly attractive for practical use, it is a fact that analog communication systems are still in existence. Most of the broadcasting systems and a large part of telephone networks in use today are analog in nature. There are numerous ways of classifying signals depending on the requirement of study. A signal is usually described by a function of one or more independent variable. The value of the signal may be real or complex. We would consider the signal to be a function of a signal independent variable i.e. time t. Analog signals or continuous-time signals are defined for every value of time and they take on continuous values in a given time interval.

Mathematically these signals can be described by function of a continuous variable. For example, the signals.

$$s_1(t) = \cos(500\ pt)$$

$$S_2(t) = \exp(-|t|) \text{ for } -\infty < t < \infty$$

are analog or continuous-time signals. Most of the naturally occurring signals are also analog in nature.Speech, electro cardiogram(ECG), electroencephalogram(EEG) signals are some of the examples of naturally occurring analog signals.

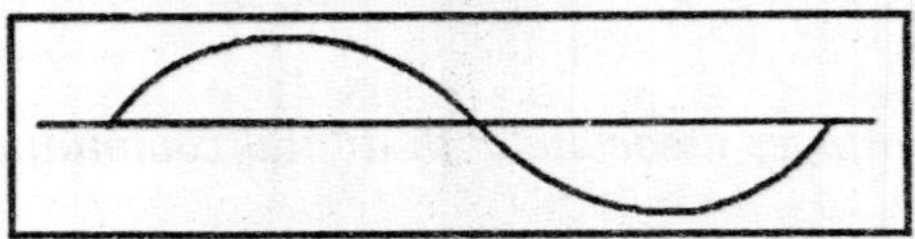

Fig. Sine Wave; Example of An analog Signal.

An analog signal is best fitted illustrated by a sine wave as shown in above figure. Notice that the sine wave is continuous. The value of the analog signal at any given instant can be anywhere within the range of the signal's extremes.

DATA COMMUNICATIONS

The distance over which data moves within a computer may vary from a few thousandths of an inch, as is the case within a single IC chip, to as much as several feet along the backplane of the main circuit board. Over such small distances, digital data may be transmitted as direct, two-level electrical signals over simple copper conductors.

Except for the fastest computers, circuit designers are not very concerned about the shape of the conductor or the analog characteristics of signal transmission. Frequently, however, data must be sent beyond the local circuitry that constitutes a computer. In many cases, the distances involved may be enormous.

Unfortunately, as the distance between the source of a message and its destination increases, accurate transmission becomes increasingly difficult. This results from the electrical distortion of signals traveling through long conductors, and from noise added to the signal as it propagates through a transmission medium.

Although some precautions must be taken for data exchange within a computer, the biggest problems occur when data is transferred to devices outside the computer's circuitry. In this case, distortion and noise can become so severe that information is lost.

Data Communications concerns the transmission of digital messages to devices external to the message source. "External" devices are generally thought of as being independently powered circuitry that exists beyond the chassis of a computer or other digital message source.

As a rule, the maximum permissible transmission rate of a message is directly proportional to signal power, and inversely proportional to channel noise. It is the aim of any communications system to provide the highest possible transmission rate at the lowest possible power and with the least possible noise.

COMMUNICATIONS CHANNELS

A communications channel is a pathway over which information can be conveyed. It may be defined by a physical wire that connects communicating devices, or by a radio, laser, or other radiated energy source that has no obvious physical presence. Information sent through a communications channel has a source from which the information originates, and a destination to which the information is delivered. Although information originates from a single source, there may be more than one destination, depending upon how many receive stations are linked to the channel and how much energy the transmitted signal possesses. In a digital communications channel, the information is represented by individual data bits, which may be encapsulated into multibit message units.

A byte, which consists of eight bits, is an example of a message unit that may be conveyed through a digital communications channel. A collection of bytes may itself be grouped into a frame or other higher-level message unit. Such multiple levels of encapsulation facilitate the handling of messages in a complex data communications network.

Any communications channel has a direction associated with it:

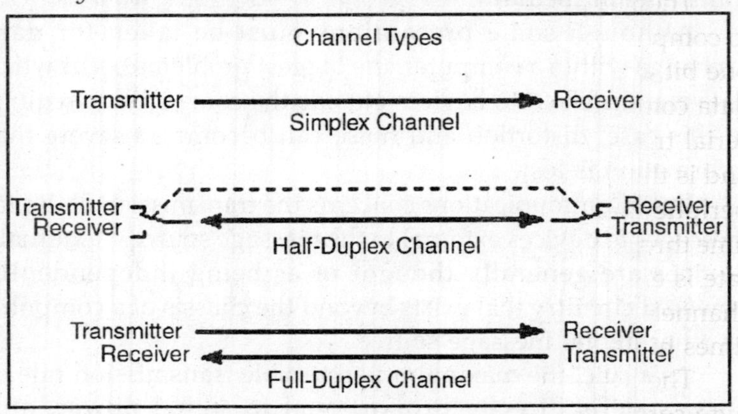

The message source is the transmitter, and the destination is the receiver. A channel whose direction of transmission is unchanging is referred to as a simplex channel. For example, a radio station is a simplex channel because it always transmits the signal to its listeners and never allows them to transmit back. A half-duplex channel is a single physical channel in which the direction may be reversed. Messages may flow in two directions, but never at the same time, in a half-duplex system. In a telephone call, one party speaks while the other listens. After a pause, the other party speaks and the first party listens. Speaking simultaneously results in garbled sound that cannot be understood. A full-duplex channel allows simultaneous message exchange in both directions. It really consists of two simplex channels, a forward channel and a reverse channel, linking the same points. The transmission rate of the reverse channel may be slower if it is used only for flow control of the forward channel.

SERIAL COMMUNICATIONS

Most digital messages are vastly longer than just a few bits. Because it is neither practical nor economic to transfer all bits of a long message simultaneously, the message is broken into smaller parts and transmitted sequentially. Bit-serial transmission conveys a message one bit at a time through a channel. Each bit represents a part of the message.

The individual bits are then reassembled at the destination to compose the message. In general, one channel will pass only one bit at a time. Thus, bit-serial transmission is necessary in data communications if only a single channel is available. Bit-serial transmission is normally just called serial transmission and is the chosen communications method in many computer peripherals. Byte-serial transmission conveys eight bits at a time through eight parallel channels. Although the raw transfer rate is eight times faster than in bit-serial transmission, eight channels are needed, and the cost may be as much as eight times higher to transmit the message.

The popular Centronics printer interface is a case where byte-serial transmission is used. As another example, it is common practice to use a 16-bit-wide data bus to transfer data between a microprocessor and memory chips; this provides the equivalent of 16 parallel channels. On the other hand, when communicating with a timesharing system over a modem, only a single channel is available, and bit-serial transmission is required. This figure illustrates these ideas.

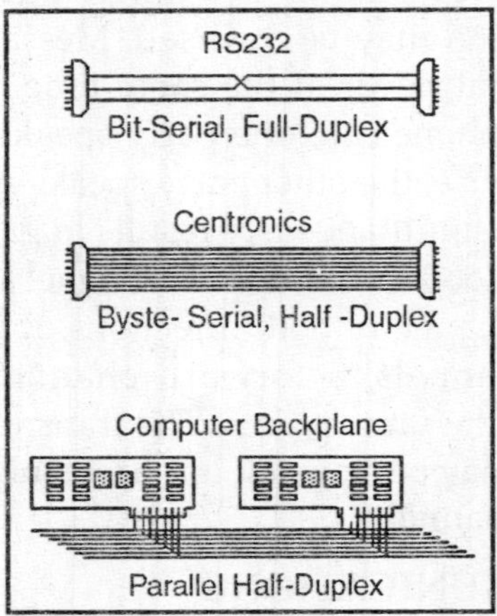

The baud rate refers to the signalling rate at which data is sent through a channel and is measured in electrical transitions per second. In the EIA232 serial interface standard, one signal transition, at most, occurs per bit, and the baud rate and bit rate are identical. In this case, a rate of 9600 baud corresponds to a transfer of 9,600 data bits per second with a bit period of 104 microseconds (1/9600 sec.). If two electrical transitions were required for each bit, as is the case in non-return-to-zero coding, then at a rate of 9600 baud, only 4800 bits per second could be conveyed. The channel efficiency is the number of bits of useful information passed through the channel per second. It does not include framing, formatting, and error detecting bits that may be added to the information bits before a message is transmitted, and will always be less than one.

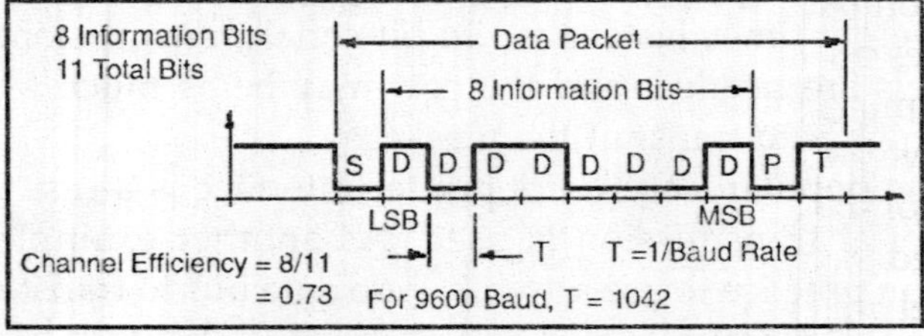

The data rate of a channel is often specified by its bit rate (often thought erroneously to be the same as baud rate). However, an equivalent measure channel capacity is bandwidth. In general, the maximum data rate a channel can support is directly proportional to the channel's bandwidth and inversely proportional to the channel's noise level.

A communications protocol is an agreed-upon convention that defines the order and meaning of bits in a serial transmission. It may also specify a procedure for exchanging messages. A protocol will define how many data bits compose a message unit, the framing and formatting bits, any error-detecting bits that may be added, and other information that governs control of the communications hardware. Channel efficiency is determined by the protocol design rather than by digital hardware considerations. Note that there is a tradeoff between channel efficiency and reliability - protocols that provide greater immunity to noise by adding error-detecting and -correcting codes must necessarily become less efficient.

ASYNCHRONOUS VS. SYNCHRONOUS TRANSMISSION

Serialized data is not generally sent at a uniform rate through a channel. Instead, there is usually a burst of regularly spaced binary data bits followed by a pause, after which the data flow resumes. Packets of binary data are sent in this manner, possibly with variable-length pauses between packets, until the message has been fully transmitted. In order for the receiving end to know the proper moment to read individual binary bits from the channel, it must know exactly when a packet begins and how much time elapses between bits. When this timing information is known, the receiver is said to be synchronized with the transmitter, and accurate data transfer becomes possible. Failure to remain synchronized throughout a transmission will cause data to be corrupted or lost.

Two basic techniques are employed to ensure correct synchronization. In synchronous systems, separate channels are used to transmit data and timing information. The timing channel transmits clock pulses to the receiver. Upon receipt of a clock pulse, the receiver reads the data channel and latches the bit value found on the channel at that moment. The data channel is not read again until the next clock pulse arrives. Because the transmitter originates both the data and the timing pulses, the receiver will read the data channel only when told to do so by the transmitter (via the clock pulse), and synchronization is guaranteed.

Techniques exist to merge the timing signal with the data so that only a single channel is required. This is especially useful when synchronous transmissions are to be sent through a modem. Two methods in which a data signal is self-timed are nonreturn-to-zero and biphase Manchester coding. These both refer to methods for encoding a data stream into an electrical waveform for transmission. In asynchronous systems, a separate timing channel is not used. The transmitter and receiver must be preset in advance to an agreed-upon baud rate. A very accurate local oscillator within the receiver will then generate an internal clock signal that is equal to the transmitter's within a fraction of a per cent.

For the most common serial protocol, data is sent in small packets of 10 or 11 bits, eight of which constitute message information. When the channel is idle, the signal voltage corresponds to a continuous logic '1'. A data packet always begins with a logic '0' (the start bit) to signal the receiver that a transmission is starting. The start bit triggers an internal timer in the receiver that generates the needed clock pulses. Following the start bit, eight bits of message data are sent bit by bit at the agreed upon baud rate. The packet is concluded with a parity bit and stop bit. One complete packet is illustrated below.

The packet length is short in asynchronous systems to minimize the risk that the local oscillators in the receiver and transmitter will drift apart. When high-quality crystal oscillators are used, synchronization can be guaranteed over an 11-bit period. Every time a new packet is sent, the start bit resets the synchronization, so the pause between packets can be arbitrarily long. Note that the EIA232 standard defines electrical, timing, and mechanical characteristics of a serial interface. However, it does not include the asynchronous serial protocol shown in the previous figure, or the ASCII alphabet described next.

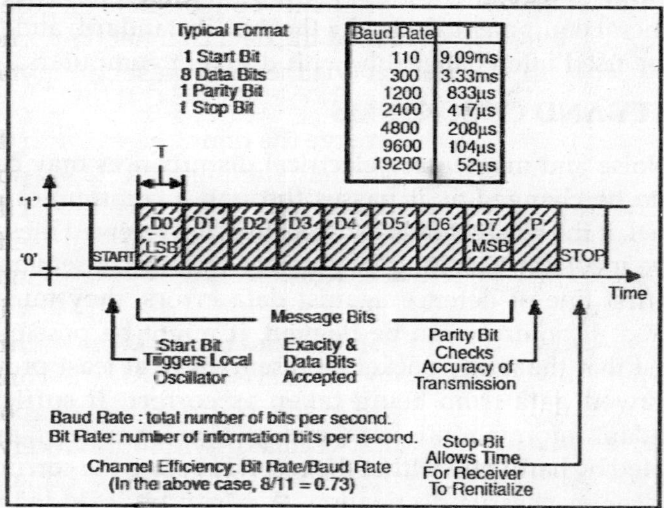

ASCII CHARACTER SET

Characters sent through a serial interface generally follow the ASCII (American Standard Code for Information Interchange) character standard:

Nonprintable Control Characters		Special Symbols	Numbers, Special Symbols	Upper-Case Alphabet		Lower-Case Alphabet	
00 NUL	10 DLE	20 SP	30 0	40 @	50 P	60 .	70 p
01 SOH	11 DC1	21 !	31 1	41 A	51 Q	61 a	71 q
02 STX	12 DC2	22 "	32 2	42 B	52 R	62 b	72 r
03 ETX	13 DC3	23 =	33 3	43 C	53 S	63 c	73 s
04 EOT	14 DC4	24 $	34 4	44 D	54 T	64 d	74 t
05 ENG	15 NAK	25 %	35 5	45 E	55 U	65 e	75 u
06 ACK	16 SYN	26 &	36 6	46 F	56 V	66 f	76 v
07 BEL	17 ETB	27 `	37 7	47 G	57 W	67 g	77 w
08 BS	18 CAN	28 (	38 8	48 H	58 X	68 h	78 x
09 HT	19 EM	29)	39 9	49 I	59 Y	69 i	79 y
0A LF	1A SUB	2A *	3A :	4A J	5A Z	6A j	7A z
0B VT	1B ESC	2B +	3B ;	4B K	5B [	6B k	7B {
0C FF	1C FS	2C ,	3C <	4C L	5C \	6D l	7C |
0D CR	1D GS	2D _	3D =	4D M	5D]	6D m	7D }
0E SO	1E RS	2E .	3E >	4E N	5E ^	6E n	7E ~
0F SI	1F VS	2F /	3F ?	4F O	5F #	6F o	7F DEL

This standard relates binary codes to printable characters and control codes. Fully 25 per cent of the ASCII character set represents nonprintable control codes, such as carriage return (CR) and line feed (LF). Most modern character-oriented peripheral equipment abides by the ASCII standard, and thus may be used interchangeably with different computers.

PARITY AND CHECKSUMS

Noise and momentary electrical disturbances may cause data to be changed as it passes through a communications channel. If the receiver fails to detect this, the received message will be incorrect, resulting in possibly serious consequences. As a first line of defence against data errors, they must be detected. If an error can be flagged, it might be possible to request that the faulty packet be resent, or to at least prevent the flawed data from being taken as correct. If sufficient redundant information is sent, one- or two-bit errors may be corrected by hardware within the receiver before the corrupted data ever reaches its destination. A parity bit is added to a data packet for the purpose of error detection. In the even-parity convention, the value of the parity bit is chosen so that the total number of '1' digits in the combined data plus parity packet is an even number.

Upon receipt of the packet, the parity needed for the data is recomputed by local hardware and compared to the parity bit received with the data. If any bit has changed state, the parity will not match, and an error will have been detected. In fact, if an odd number of bits (not just one) have been altered, the parity will not match. If an even number of bits have been reversed, the parity will match even though an error has occurred. However, a statistical analysis of data communication errors has shown that a single-bit error is much more probable than a multibit error in the presence of random noise. Thus, parity is a reliable method of error detection.

Even-Parity Computation

Data	Parity Bit
10110001	0
10000110	1

Another approach to error detection involves the computation of a checksum. In this case, the packets that constitute a message are added arithmetically. A checksum number is appended to the packet sequence so that the sum of data plus checksum is zero. When received, the packet sequence may be added, along with the checksum, by a local microprocessor. If the sum is nonzero, an error has occurred. As long as the sum is zero, it is highly unlikely (but not impossible) that any data has been corrupted during transmission.

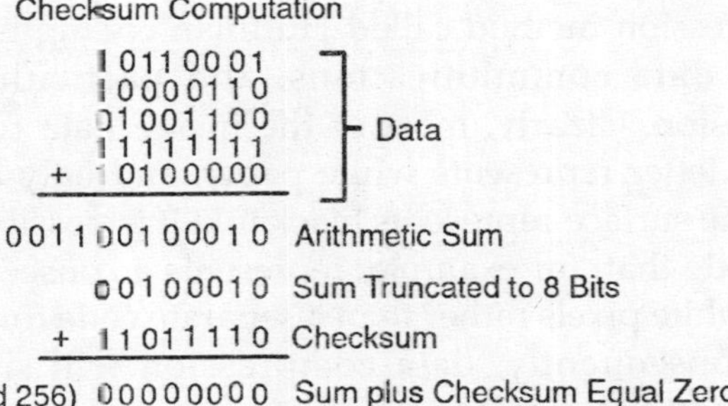

Errors may not only be detected, but also corrected if additional code is added to a packet sequence. If the error probability is high or if it is not possible to request retransmission, this may be worth doing. However, including error-correcting code in a transmission lowers channel efficiency, and results in a noticeable drop in channel throughput.

DATA COMPRESSION

If a typical message were statistically analyzed, it would be found that certain characters are used much more frequently than others. By analyzing a message before it is transmitted, short binary codes may be assigned to frequently used characters and longer codes to rarely used characters. In doing so, it is possible to reduce the total number of characters sent without altering the information in the message. Appropriate decoding at the receiver will restore the message to its original form. This procedure, known as data compression, may result in a 50 per cent or greater savings in the amount of data transmitted. Even though time is necessary to analyse the message before it is transmitted, the savings may be great enough so that the total time for compression, transmission, and decompression will still be lower than it would be when sending an uncompressed message.

Some kinds of data will compress much more than others. Data that represents images, for example, will usually compress significantly, perhaps by as much as 80 per cent over its original size. Data representing a computer programme, on the other hand, may be reduced only by 15 or 20 per cent. A compression method called Huffman coding is frequently used in data communications, and particularly in fax transmission. Clearly, most of the image data for a typical business letter represents white paper, and only about 5 per cent of the surface represents black ink. It is possible to send a single code that, for example, represents a consecutive string of 1000 white pixels rather than a separate code for each white pixel. Consequently, data compression will significantly reduce the total message length for a faxed business letter. Were the letter made up of randomly distributed black ink covering 50 per cent of the white paper surface, data compression would hold no advantages.

DATA ENCRYPTION

Privacy is a great concern in data communications. Faxed business letters can be intercepted at will through tapped phone lines or intercepted microwave transmissions without the knowledge of the sender or receiver. To increase the security of this and other data communications, including digitized telephone conversations, the binary codes representing data may be scrambled in such a way that unauthorized interception will produce an indecipherable sequence of characters. Authorized receive stations will be equipped with a decoder that enables the message to be restored. The process of scrambling, transmitting, and descrambling is known as encryption. Custom integrated circuits have been designed to perform this task and are available at low cost. In some cases, they will be incorporated into the main circuitry of a data communications device and function without operator knowledge. In other cases, an external circuit is used so that the device, and its encrypting/decrypting technique, may be transported easily.

DATA STORAGE TECHNOLOGY

Normally, we think of communications science as dealing with the contemporaneous exchange of information between distant parties. However, many of the same techniques employed in data communications are also applied to data storage to ensure that the retrieval of information from a storage medium is accurate. We find, for example, that similar kinds of error-correcting codes used to protect digital telephone transmissions from noise are also used to guarantee correct readback of digital data from compact audio disks, CD-ROMs, and tape backup systems.

DATA TRANSFER IN DIGITAL CIRCUITS

Data is typically grouped into packets that are either 8, 16, or 32 bits long, and passed between temporary holding units called registers. Data within a register is available in parallel because each bit exits the register on a separate conductor. To transfer data from one register to another, the output conductors of one register are switched onto a channel of parallel wires referred to as a bus. The input conductors of another register, which is also connected to the bus, capture the information:

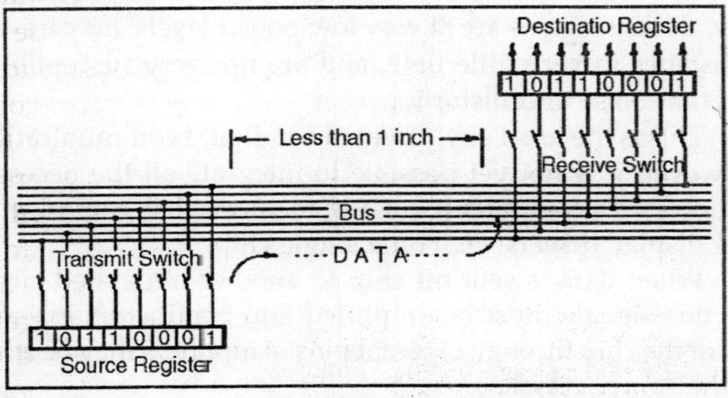

Following a data transaction, the content of the source register is reproduced in the destination register. It is important to note that after any digital data transfer, the source and destination registers are equal; the source register is not erased when the data is sent.

The transmit and receive switches shown above are electronic and operate in response to commands from a central control unit. t is possible that two or more destination registers will be switched on to receive data from a single source. However, only one source may transmit data onto the bus at any time.

If multiple sources were to attempt transmission simultaneously, an electrical conflict would occur when bits of opposite value are driven onto a single bus conductor. Such a condition is referred to as a bus contention.

Not only will a bus contention result in the loss of information, but it also may damage the electronic circuitry. As long as all registers in a system are linked to one central control unit, bus contentions should never occur if the circuit has been designed properly. Note that the data buses within a typical microprocessor are funda-mentally half-duplex channels.

TRANSMISSION OVER SHORT DISTANCES

When the source and destination registers are part of an integrated circuit (within a microprocessor chip, for example), they are extremely close (thousandths of an inch). Consequently, the bus signals are at very low power levels, may traverse a distance in very little time, and are not very susceptible to external noise and distortion.

This is the ideal environment for digital communications. However, it is not yet possible to integrate all the necessary circuitry for a computer (i.e., CPU, memory, disk control, video and display drivers, etc.) on a single chip.

When data is sent off-chip to another integrated circuit, the bus signals must be amplified and conductors extended out of the chip through external pins. Amplifiers may be added to the source register:

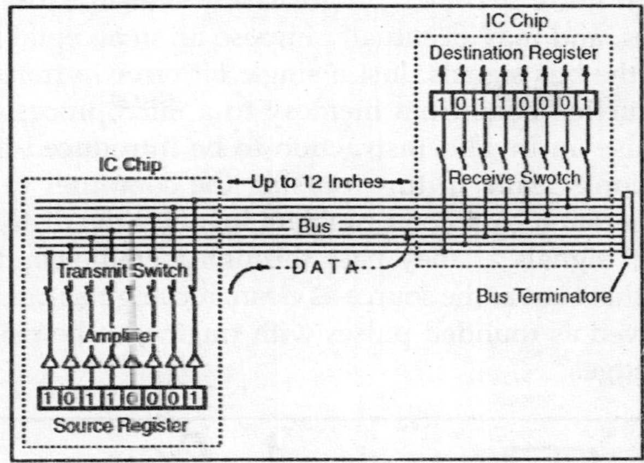

Bus signals that exit microprocessor chips and other VLSI circuitry are electrically capable of traversing about one foot of conductor on a printed circuit board, or less if many devices are connected to it. Special buffer circuits may be added to boost the bus signals sufficiently for transmission over several additional feet of conductor length, or for distribution to many other chips (such as memory chips).

NOISE AND ELECTRICAL DISTORTION

Because of the very high switching rate and relatively low signal strength found on data, address, and other buses within a computer, direct extension of the buses beyond the confines of the main circuit board or plug-in boards would pose serious problems. First, long runs of electrical conductors, either on printed circuit boards or through cables, act like receiving antennas for electrical noise radiated by motors, switches, and electronic circuits:

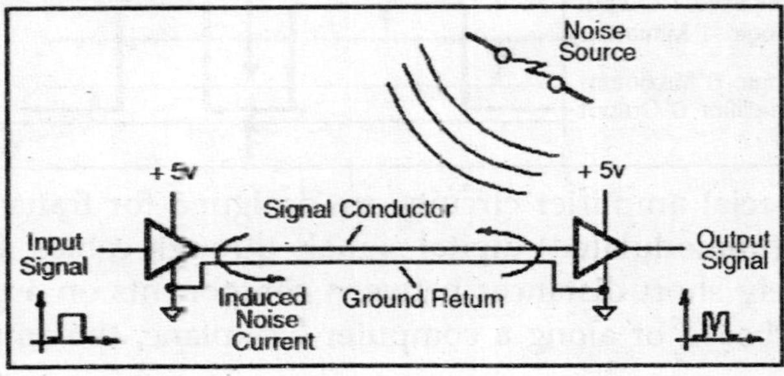

Such noise becomes progressively worse as the length increases, and may eventually impose an unacceptable error rate on the bus signals. Just a single bit error in transferring an instruction code from memory to a microprocessor chip may cause an invalid instruction to be introduced into the instruction stream, in turn causing the computer to totally cease operation. A second problem involves the distortion of electrical signals as they pass through metallic conductors. Signals that start at the source as clean, rectangular pulses may be received as rounded pulses with ringing at the rising and falling edges:

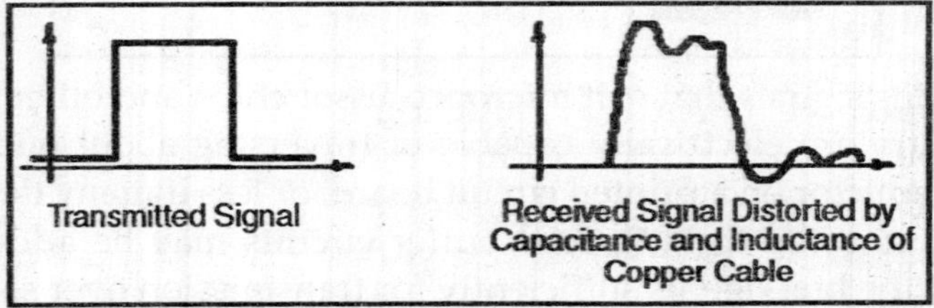

These effects are properties of transmission through metallic conductors, and become more pronounced as the conductor length increases. To compensate for distortion, signal power must be increased or the transmission rate decreased.

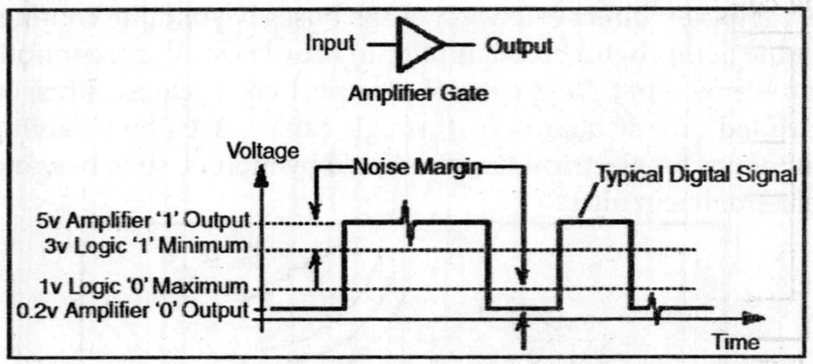

Special amplifier circuits are designed for transmitting direct (unmodulated) digital signals through cables. For the relatively short distances between components on a printed circuit board or along a computer backplane, the amplifiers are in simple IC chips that operate from standard +5v power. The normal output voltage from the amplifier for logic '1' is slightly higher than the minimum needed to pass the logic '1' threshold.

Correspondingly for logic '0', it is slightly lower. The difference between the actual output voltage and the threshold value is referred to as the noise margin, and represents the amount of noise voltage that can be added to the signal without creating an error.

TRANSMISSION OVER MEDIUM DISTANCES

Computer peripherals such as a printer or scanner generally include mechanisms that cannot be situated within the computer itself. Our first thought might be just to extend the computer's internal buses with a cable of sufficient length to reach the peripheral. Doing so, however, would expose all bus transactions to external noise and distortion even though only a very small percentage of these transactions concern the distant peripheral to which the bus is connected.

If a peripheral can be located within 20 feet of the computer, however, relatively simple electronics may be added to make data transfer through a cable efficient and reliable. To accomplish this, a bus interface circuit is installed in the computer:

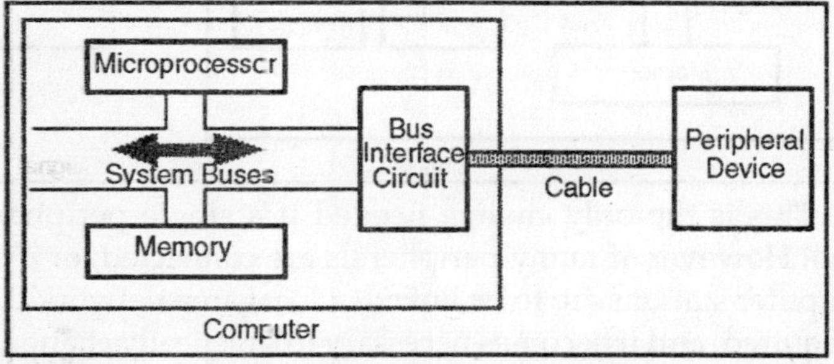

It consists of a holding register for peripheral data, timing and formatting circuitry for external data transmission, and signal amplifiers to boost the signal sufficiently for transmission through a cable. When communication with the peripheral is necessary, data is first deposited in the holding register by the microprocessor. This data will then be reformatted, sent with error-detecting codes, and transmitted at a relatively slow rate by digital hardware in the bus interface circuit. In addition, the signal power is greatly boosted before transmission through the cable. These steps ensure that the data will not be corrupted by noise or distortion during its passage through the cable. In addition, because only data destined for the peripheral is sent, the party-line transactions taking place on the computer's buses are not unnecessarily exposed to noise. Data sent in this manner may be transmitted in byte-serial format if the cable has eight parallel channels (at least 10 conductors for half-duplex operation), or in bit-serial format if only a single channel is available.

TRANSMISSION OVER LONG DISTANCES

When relatively long distances are involved in reaching a peripheral device, driver circuits must be inserted after the bus interface unit to compensate for the electrical effects of long cables:

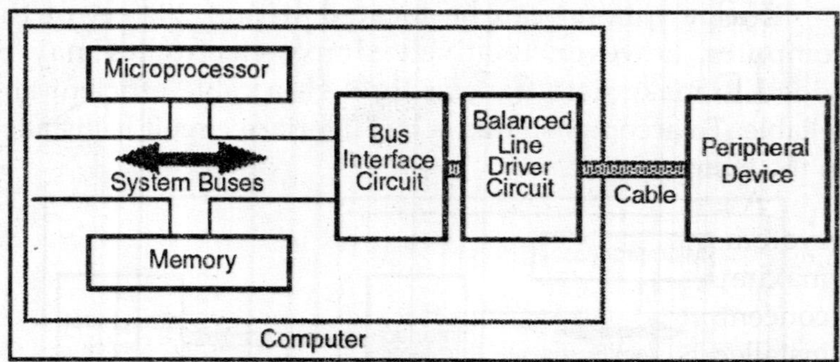

This is the only change needed if a single peripheral is used. However, if many peripherals are connected, or if other computer stations are to be linked, a local area network (LAN) is required, and it becomes necessary to drastically change both the electrical drivers and the protocol to send messages through the cable. Because multiconductor cable is expensive, bit-serial transmission is almost always used when the distance exceeds 20 feet. In either a simple extension cable or a LAN, a balanced electrical system is used for transmitting digital data through the channel. This type of system involves at least two wires per channel, neither of which is a ground. Note that a common ground return cannot be shared by multiple channels in the same cable as would be possible in an unbalanced system. The basic idea behind a balanced circuit is that a digital signal is sent on two wires simultaneously, one wire expressing a positive voltage image of the signal and the other a negative voltage image.

When both wires reach the destination, the signals are subtracted by a summing amplifier, producing a signal swing of twice the value found on either incoming line. If the cable is exposed to radiated electrical noise, a small voltage of the same polarity is added to both wires in the cable. When the signals are subtracted by the summing amplifier, the noise cancels and the signal emerges from the cable without noise:

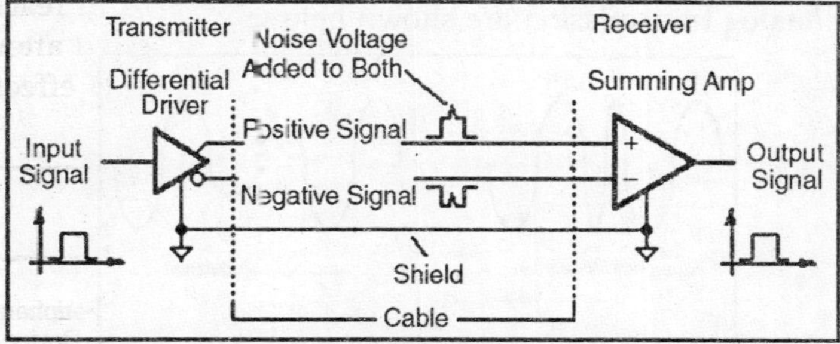

A great deal of technology has been developed for LAN systems to minimize the amount of cable required and maximize the throughput. The costs of a LAN have been concentrated in the electrical interface card that would be installed in PCs or peripherals to drive the cable, and in the communications software, not in the cable itself (whose cost has been minimized). Thus, the cost and complexity of a LAN are not particularly affected by the distance between stations.

TRANSMISSION OVER VERY LONG DISTANCES (GREATER THAN 4000 FEET)

Data communications through the telephone network can reach any point in the world. The volume of overseas fax transmissions is increasing constantly, and computer networks that link thousands of businesses, governments, and universities are pervasive. Transmissions over such distances are not generally accomplished with a direct-wire digital link, but rather with digitally-modulated analog carrier signals. This technique makes it possible to use existing analog telephone voice channels for digital data, although at considerably reduced data rates compared to a direct digital link.

Transmission of data from your personal computer to a timesharing service over phone lines requires that data signals be converted to audible tones by a modem. An audio sine wave carrier is used, and, depending on the baud rate and protocol, will encode data by varying the frequency, phase, or amplitude of the carrier. The receiver's modem accepts the modulated sine wave and extracts the digital data from it. Several modulation techniques typically used in encoding digital data for analog transmission are shown below:

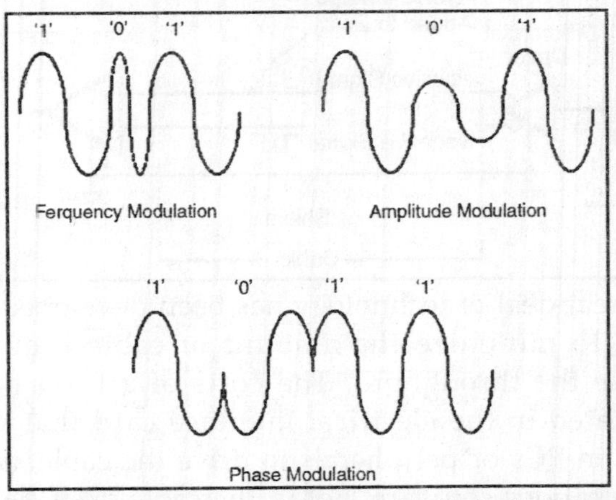

Similar techniques may be used in digital storage devices such as hard disk drives to encode data for storage using an analog medium

DIGITAL DATA RATE

DIGITAL DATA

In a CD (and any other digital recording technology), the goal is to create a recording with very high fidelity (very high similarity between the original signal and the reproduced signal) and perfect reproduction (the recording sounds the same every single time you play it no matter how many times you play it).

To accomplish these two goals, digital recording converts the analog wave into a stream of numbers and records the numbers instead of the wave. The conversion is done by a device called an analog-to-digital converter (ADC). To play back the music, the stream of numbers is converted back to an analog wave by a digital-to-analog converter (DAC). The analog wave produced by the DAC is amplified and fed to the speakers to produce the sound.

The analog wave produced by the DAC will be the same every time, as long as the numbers are not corrupted. The analog wave produced by the DAC will also be very similar to the original analog wave if the analog-to-digital converter sampled at a high rate and produced accurate numbers.

You can understand why CDs have such high fidelity if you understand the analog-to-digital conversion process better. Let's say you have a sound wave, and you wish to sample it with an ADC. Here is a typical wave (assume here that each tick on the horizontal axis represents one-thousandth of a second):

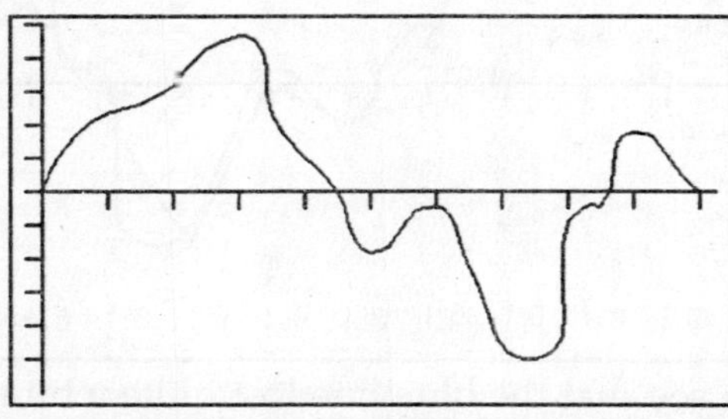

When you sample the wave with an analog-to-digital converter, you have control over two variables:

- *The sampling rate*: Controls how many samples are taken per second.
- *The sampling precision:* Controls how many different gradations (quantization levels) are possible when taking the sample.

In the following figure, let's assume that the sampling rate is 1,000 per second and the precision is 10:

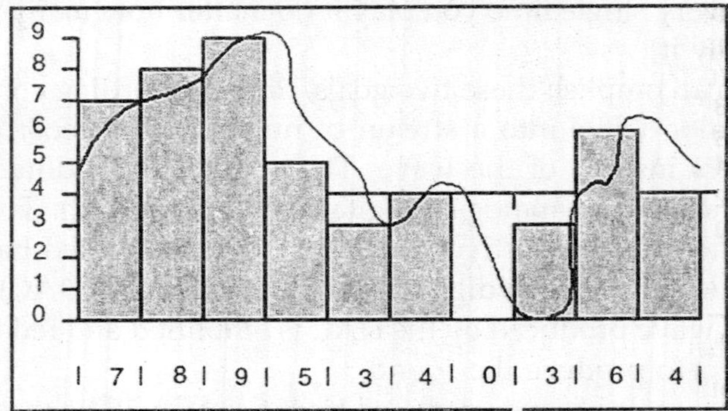

The green rectangles represent samples. Every one-thousandth of a second, the ADC looks at the wave and picks the closest number between 0 and 9. The number chosen is shown along the bottom of the figure. These numbers are a digital representation of the original wave. When the DAC recreates the wave from these numbers, you get the blue line shown in the following figure:

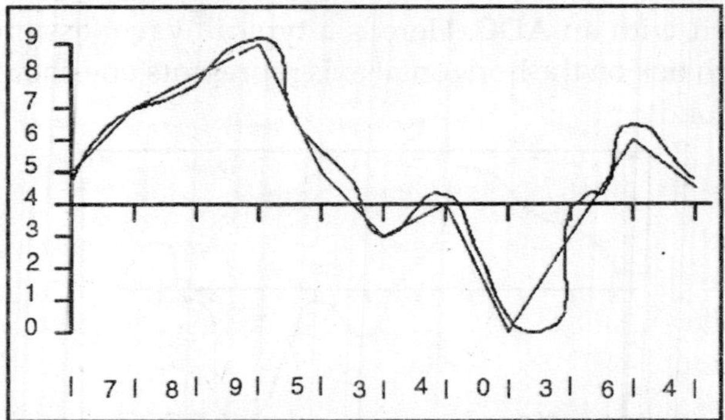

You can see that the blue line lost quite a bit of the detail originally found in the red line, and that means the fidelity of the reproduced wave is not very good. This is the sampling error.

You reduce sampling error by increasing both the sampling rate and the precision. In the following figure, both the rate and the precision have been improved by a factor of 2 (20 gradations at a rate of 2,000 samples per second):

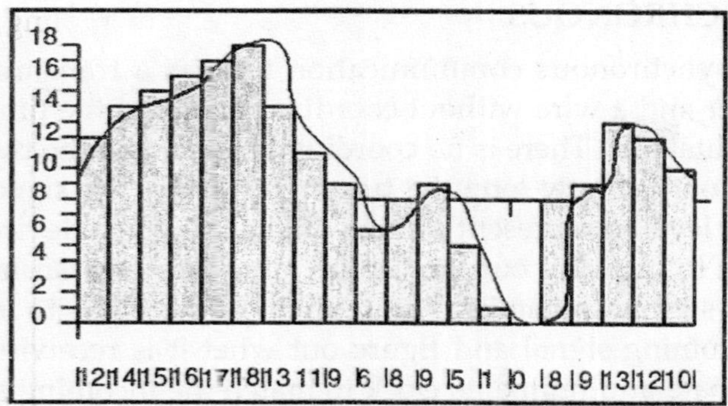

In the following figure, the rate and the precision have been doubled again (40 gradations at 4,000 samples per second):

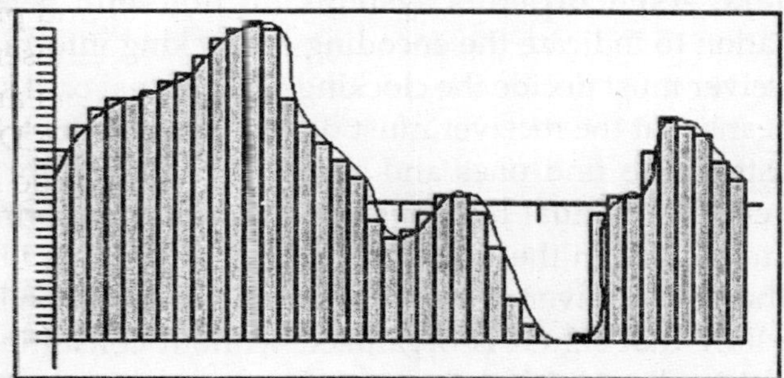

You can see that as the rate and precision increase, the fidelity (the similarity between the original wave and the DAC's output) improves.

In the case of CD sound, fidelity is an important goal, so the sampling rate is 44,100 samples per second and the number of gradations is 65,536. At this level, the output of the DAC so closely matches the original waveform that the sound is essentially "perfect" to most human ears.

ASYNCHRONOUS AND SYNCHRONOUS

Most communications circuits perform functions described in the physical and data link layer of the OSI Model. There are two general strategies for communicating over a physical circuit: Asynchronous and Synchronous. Each has it's advantages and disadvantages.

ASYNCHRONOUS

Asynchronous communication utilizes a transmitter, a receiver and a wire without coordination about the timing of individual bits. There is no coordination between the two end points on just how long the transmiter leaves the signal at a certain level to represent a single digital bit. Each device uses a clock to measure out the 'length' of a bit. The transmitting device simply transmits. The receiving device has to look at the incoming signal and figure out what it is receiving and coordinate and retime its clock to match the incoming signal.

Sending data encoded into your signal requires that the sender and receiver are both using the same enconding/ decoding method, and know where to look in the signal to find data. Asynchronous systems do not send separate information to indicate the encoding or clocking information. The receiver must decide the clocking of the signal on it's own. This means that the receiver must decide where to look in the signal stream to find ones and zeroes, and decide for itself where each individual bit stops and starts. This information is not in the data in the signal sent from transmitting unit.

When the receiver of a signal carrying information has to derive how that signal is organized without consulting the transmitting device, it is called asynchronous communication. In short, the two ends do not synchronize the connection parameters before communicating.

Asynchronous communication is more efficient when there is low loss and low error rates over the transmission medium because data is not retransmitted and no time is spent setting negotiating the connection parameters at the beginning of transmission. Asynchronous systems just transmit and let the far end station figure it out. Asynchronous is sometimes called "best effort" transmission because one side simply transmits, and the other does it's best to receive.

SYNCHRONOUS

Synchronous systems negotiate the communication parameters at the data link layer before communication begins. Basic synchronous systems will synchronize both clocks before transmission begins, and reset their numeric counters for errors etc. More advanced systems may negotiate things like error correction and compression. It is possible to have both sides try to synchronize the connection at the same time. Usually, there is a process to decide which end should be in control. Both sides can go through a lengthy negotiation cycle where they exchange communications parameters and status information.

Once a connection is established, the transmitter sends out a signal, and the receiver sends back data regarding that transmission, and what it received. This connection negotiation process takes longer on low error-rate lines, but is highly efficient in systems where the transmission medium itself (an electric wire, radio signal or laser beam) is not particularly reliable.

EXPLANATION

Asynchronous transmission uses start and stop bits to signify the beginning and end of a transmission. This means that an 8 bit ASCII character would actually be transmitted using 10 bits e.g.: A would become 1 0100 0001 0. The extra one (or zero depending on parity bit) at the start and end of the transmission tells the receiver first that a character is coming and secondly that the character has ended. This method of transmission is used when data is sent intermittently as opposed to in a solid stream. In the following example the start and stop bits are in bold. The start and stop bits must be of opposite polarity. This allows the receiver to recognise when the second packet of information is being sent.

Synchronous transmission uses no start and stop bits but instead synchronises transmission speeds at both the receiving and sending end of the transmission using clock signals built into each component. A continual stream of data is then sent between the two nodes. Due to there being no start and stop bits the data transfer rate is quicker although more errors will occur, as the clocks will eventually get out of sync, and the receiving device would have the wrong time that had been agreed in protocol (computing) for sending/receiving data, so some bytes could become corrupted (by losing bits). Ways to get around this problem include re-synchronisation of the clocks and use of check digits to ensure the byte is correctly interpreted and received.

Asynchronous and synchronous communication refers to methods by which signals are transferred in computing technology. These signals allow computers to transfer data between components within the computer or between the computer and an external network. Most actions and operations that take place in computers are carefully controlled and occur at specific times and intervals. Actions that are measured against a time reference, or a clock signal, are referred to as synchronous actions. Actions that are prompted as a response to another signal, typically not governed by a clock signal, are referred to as asynchronous signals.

Typical examples of synchronous signals include the transfer and retrieval of address information within a computer via the use of an address bus . For example, when a processor places an address on the address bus, it will hold it there for a specific period of time. Within this interval, a particular device inside the computer will identify itself as the one being addressed and acknowledge the commencement of an operation related to that address.

In such an instance, all devices involved in ensuing bus cycles must obey the time constraints applied to their actions-this is known as a synchronous operation. In contrast, asynchronous signals refer to operations that are prompted by an exchange of signals with one another, and are not measured against a reference time base.

Devices that cooperate asynchronously usually include modems and many network technologies, both of which use a collection of control signals to notify intent in an information exchange. Asynchronous signals, or extra control signals, are sometimes referred to as handshaking signals because of the way they mimic two people approaching one another and shaking hands before conversing or negotiating. Within a computer, both asynchronous and synchronous protocols are used. Synchronous protocols usually offer the ability to transfer information faster per unit time than asynchronous protocols. This happens because synchronous signals do not require any extra negotiation as a prerequisite to data exchange. Instead, data or information is moved from one place to another at instants in time that are measured against the clock signal being used.

This signal is usually comprised of one or more high frequency rectangular shaped waveforms, generated by special purpose clock circuitry. These pulsed waveforms are connected to all the devices that operate synchronously, allowing them to start and stop operations with respect to the clock waveform.

In contrast, asynchronous protocols are generally more flexible, since all the devices that need to exchange information can do so at their own natural rate-be these fast or slow. A clock signal is no longer necessary; instead the devices that behave asynchronously wait for the handshaking signals to change state, indicating that some transaction is about to commence. The handshaking signals are generated by the devices themselves and can occur as needed, and do not require an outside supervisory controller such as a clock circuit that dictates the occurrence of data transfer. Asynchronous and synchronous transmission of information occurs both externally and internally in computers.

One of the most popular protocols for communication between computers and peripheral devices, such as modems and printers, is the asynchronous RS-232 protocol. Designated as the RS-232C by the Electronic Industries Association (EIA), this protocol has been so successful at adapting to the needs of managing communication between computers and supporting devices, that it has been pushed into service in ways that were not intended as part of its original design.

The RS-232C protocol uses an asynchronous scheme that permits flexible communication between computers and devices using byte-sized data blocks each framed with start, stop, and optional parity bits on the data line. Other conductors carry the handshaking signals and possess names that indicate their purpose-these include data terminal ready, request to send, clear to send, data set ready, etc. Another advantage of asynchronous schemes is that they do not demand complexity in the receiver hardware. As each byte of data has its own start and stop bits, a small amount of drift or imprecision at the receiving end does not necessarily spell disaster since the device only has to keep pace with the data stream for a modest number of bits. So, if an interruption occurs, the receiving device can re-establish its operation with the beginning of the arrival of the next byte. This ability allows for the use of inexpensive hardware devices.

Although asynchronous data transfer schemes like RS-232 work well when relatively small amounts of data need to be transferred on an intermittent basis, they tend to be sub-optimal during large information transfers. This is so because the extra bits that frame incoming data tend to account for a significant part of the overall inter-machine traffic, hence consuming a portion of the communication bandwidth .

An alternative is to dispense with the extra handshaking signals and overhead, instead synchronizing the transmitter and receiver with a clock signal or synchronization information contained within the transmitted code before transmitting large amounts of information. This arrangement allows for collection and dispatch of large batches of bytes of data, with a few bytes at the front-end that can be used for the synchronization and control.

These leading bytes are variously called synchronization bytes, flags, and preambles. If the actual communication channel is not a great distance, the clocking signal can also be sent as a separate stream of pulses. This ensures that the transmitter and receiver are both operating on the same time base, and the receiver can be prepared for data collection prior to the arrival of the data.

An example of a synchronous transmission scheme is known as the High-level Data Link Control, or HDLC. This protocol arose from an initial design proposed by the IBM Corporation. HDLC has been used at the data link level in public networks and has been adapted and modified in several different ways since. A more advanced communication protocol is the Asynchronous Transfer Mode (ATM), which is an open, international standard for the transmission of voice, video, and data signals.

Some advantages of ATM include a format that consists of short, fixed cells (53 bytes) which reduce overhead in maintenance of variable-sized data traffic. The versatility of this mode also allows it to simulate and integrate well with legacy technologies, as well as offering the ability to guarantee certain service levels, generally referred to as quality of service (QoS) parameters.

SYNCHRONOUS DATA TRANSMISSION

Consider the following diagram that represents two programmes (or tasks) communicating with each other using send/receive/reply message protocol.

Task 1 sends a message to task 2. Using synchronous transmission, task 1 will not be able to continue processing until it has either received a reply from task 2 or the message transmission has failed.

The message may fail to send due to a couple of reasons. The recipient task may die which means the message will fail to be sent, or the attempt to send the message may time-out waiting for a reply. There may be a substantial time delay associated with task 2 processing the message and then sending back the reply to task 1. In the example above, task 1 is said to be 'blocked' on task 2 until it receives the reply to its original message.

In many mission critical applications, having one task blocked on another task is unacceptable because the blocked tasks are unable to perform other duties for the duration of the message transaction. Synchronous transmission is, however, a fast and reliable method of data transfer when you absolutely need to know that a message was received by the recipient, or when the sending task must have a response before it can continue processing.

CASCADE DATAHUB DATA TRANSMISSION

The Cascade DataHub works in conjunction with the qserve (queue manager) programme to provide asynchronous data transmission between tasks.

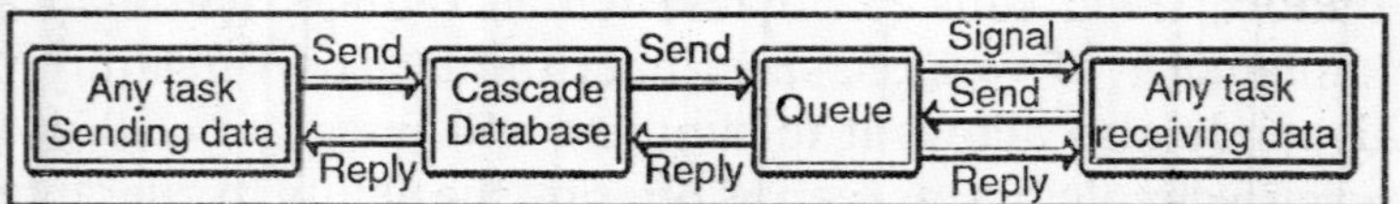

Any number of tasks can write data directly to the Cascade DataHub, because it is a non-blocking programme that is always ready to receive a message. When a programme wishes to read the point value from the DataHub, the task registers for exceptions for that point. Then, whenever the DataHub receives a new value for a particular data point, it immediately sends a message to the queue for each client programme that has registered an interest in that data point.

The queue manager then sends a signal to the client programme, informing the client that there is a message waiting on its queue. The client programme then sends a message to the queue manager requesting the message. The queue manager sends the new value for the data point in the reply to the client.

There are three ways in which a client can register for exceptions from the DataHub:

- A client registers for exceptions on a point-by-point basis. Each time one of the registered points changes value in the DataHub, a message is sent to the client.
- A client can register for exceptions for all points currently in the DataHub. Any change to the value of a data point that is placed in the DataHub after this registration will not be sent to the client.
- A client can register for exceptions for any point that ever appears in the DataHub. All data change events in the DataHub will be broadcast to the client even if the point is created in the DataHub subsequent to the client's registration.

When a DataHub client tries to register for exceptions for points that do not exist in the DataHub, the point is created in the DataHub and any further value changes are reported. The number of points in the DataHub is only limited by system resources. The DataHub has been tested with over 65,000 points and simply grows in size to meet the need of the application.

TYPES OF SIGNALS IN DATA COMMUNICATION

SIGNAL GENERATORS

Engineers, technicians and scientists use many kinds of signal generators in their work. Audio signal generators are the most common type, used for testing sound equipment and to run scientific experiments. Communications and broadcast technicians use radio frequency (RF) generators for radio and television. Telephone and radar engineers use microwave signal generators. And digital engineers use logic generators to develop computer circuits. For complex applications, such as digital television, technicians may use different kinds of signal generators at the same time.

Audio

It has a selection of fixed waveforms, including sine, triangle, square and sawtooth. The best signal generators have waveforms of very high purity to look for harmonic distortion. Noise generators produce a random, static-like signal covering the entire audio bandwidth.

White noise gives equal probability to all frequencies in its range. Pink noise has equal energy per octave; it's white noise with low-pass filtering. These are used to test the frequency response of audio circuits and room acoustics.

Radio

Radio signal generators cover a higher frequency range than audio, to hundreds of megahertz or more. They're used to test radio broadcast equipment. Generating radio frequencies with precision is more difficult than audio, so these signal generators are more expensive. Since radio broadcasts use modulation, a signal generator will produce two signals, the carrier frequency and a modulating signal. The signal generator will have amplitude and frequency modulators built in, to test different kinds of broadcast gear.

Microwave

These signal generators produce frequencies into tens of gigahertz. They're used to test communications equipment and radar. As the frequencies are even higher than for radio, and since the equipment is more specialized, it's more expensive.

Logic

Engineers who build computer-related equipment need logic signal generators. These produce a variety of high-frequency pulses modulated by data. Since data is specific to an application, the signal generators relate to external data sources.

Arbitrary

A traditional signal generator produces a fixed set of waveforms, such as sine and sawtooth. An arbitrary signal generator lets you create and programme a waveshape, which is then produced at the frequency you set. These generators are digital in nature, creating the waveshapes from a data table.

AM AND FM

AM is amplitude Modulation, and FM is Frequency Modulation. With both AM and FM, a carrier wave must be broadcasted. And it is just that... A carrier wave for the information. A greyhound bus for the information you are trying to tune in. (music, etc.). The carrier wave is at a particular frequency, which is singled out as you tune in your radio station. All other frequencies are filtered out.

EXPLANATION

The difference is how the "information" rides on that carrier frequency. And the names give it away. In AM or Amplitude Modulation, the information is added to the amplitude of the carrier signal. When your receiver receives the signal, it does an analog sample of the wave to determine it's average strength, then demodulates the differences in the amplitude to pull out the original information. This is the worst and most inaccurate way of demodulation, for the signal strength is continuously changing, with the analog demodulator always working "behind the times".

This is why it took so many years for the occurance of AM Stereo. It's hard enough to accurately pull one stream of info out of the carrier wave. Try pulling two distinct signals out of one carrier wave that is Amplitude modulated. How in the world do you do that? (But they do have AM stereo now, yet not very popular) The reason it came first, is it is very easy to mix amplitudes, and no complicated circuitry was required in the old days to pull in the correct carrier wave.

They couldn't do frequency modulation at first cause uncle sam wouldn't let commercial businesses transmit on high enough frequencies to pull out the original information. Also since AM carrier waves have relatively low frequencies, they can travel quite a distance. In Frequency Modulation, the information is added to the frequency of the carrier wave.

The amplitude of the incoming signal is a mute point as long as it is strong enough where your receiver can lock onto the carrier wave. Carrier frequencies in high ranges were released for commercial use, so they could transmit in the MegaHertz range. Since all information needed in the hearing range is commonly in the 20 to 20KiloHertz range, it was easy to pull the signal in.

The information didn't cause enough of a difference in the signal to cause the tuner to filter it out. And since the original carrier frequency is known, and locked in, it was extremely easy to pull out the original information. In fact, you could add 6 or 8 different information signals if you wanted to. Complex, but achievable. Since the demodulation is so accurate, this gives it better clarity, and the ability to modulate 2 separate signals for stereo. However, since the carrier frequency is so high, it bounces off obstacles instead of going through them, thus reducing range.

AM and FM are two very popular and very different methods of sending information over the airwaves. AM is amplitude modulation while FM is frequency modulation. But what is modulation? It is the act of modifying a certain aspect of the carrier frequency in accordance to the information being sent. It is then clear that AM modifies the amplitude of the carrier frequency while FM modifies its frequency.

AM is the older an easier of the two technologies to implement. The receiver detects the changes in the carrier frequency's amplitude and amplifies it to drive a speaker. The simplicity of the technology made it easy to build radio receivers in great quantities.

The main problem associated with AM broadcasting is the fact that it is very susceptible to various weather conditions that deteriorate and distort the signal. The simplicity of the design also limits the broadcast to a single audio channel, making it inadequate for stereo sound.

FM is a development over AM broadcasting and it provides a lot of substantial benefits thus it is much more complex compared to AM. The first and most substantial benefit is its ability to send out two channels of information at the same time with the use of advanced algorithms. This allows the station to broadcast left and right audio channels for full stereo sound.

Since most environmental factors that distort radio waves only affect its amplitude and not the frequency where FM stores the actual voice signal, the data in the FM signal doesn't degrade as easily as AM. This also means that FM signal quality doesn't degrade linearly as you get further from the transmitting station.

Range wise, AM takes the cake with its much greater distance travelled. FM signals usually drop of at around 50 miles from the station, but AM waves can be refracted in the atmosphere resulting in greater range. The range is also one of the reasons why talk radio prefers AM even if the sound quality is not very high.

The advancement in technology also meant that the degree in complexity and price between AM and FM receivers have become moot. Most manufacturers can even manage to place the whole circuitry for both AM and FM inside a single chip, turning them into a package instead of competing against each other.

AM, FM WAVES AND SOUND

To understand some of the concepts we introduced in the last module, as well as some of the strange things that happen to broadcast signals, we need to take a look at how radio works.

First, let's look at the AM radio band (group of frequencies). AM stands for amplitude modulation, which will be explained later AM radio ranges from 535 to 1705kHz (kilohertz, or thousands of cycles per-second of electromagnetic energy). These are the numbers you see on your AM radio dial.

Note in the tan area at the left of the illustration below that AM radio waves are of a lower frequency than either FM radio or TV waves. Thus, as we will see, after being transmitted, they will behave differently.

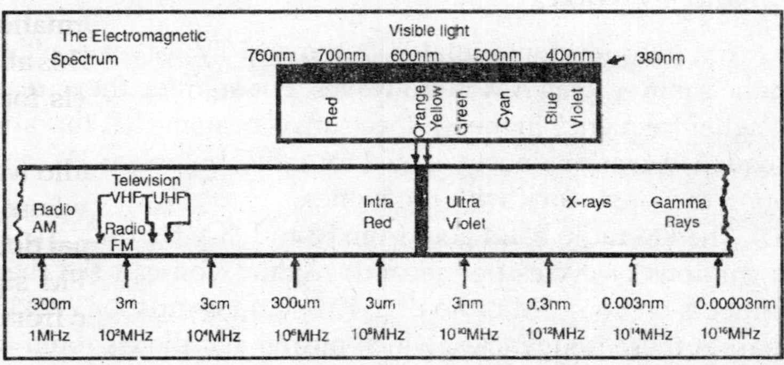

Stations can theoretically be placed every 10kHz, along the AM band. This means that there are a total of 117 different channels available for AM radio stations. If it all stopped there, things would be rather simple; but, unfortunately, other factors come into play.

First, you can't put stations on the same frequency that are too close together in a geographic area. They will interfere with each other. And for the same reason you can't have two stations close together in frequency (close to each other on the radio dial) in the same area. So these are the first things that limit the number of radio stations in an area.

The good news is that since the signals of stations tend to be limited in their range, you can use some of the frequencies many times - as long as the stations are far enough apart geographically.

This is why the United States can have nearly 5,000 AM radio stations on only 117 different frequencies. How far an AM station's signal travels depends on such things as the station's frequency (channel), the power of the transmitter in watts, the nature of the transmitting antenna, how conductive the soil is around the antenna (damp soil is good; sand and rocks aren't), and, a thing called ionospheric refraction.

The ionosphere is a layer of heavily charged ion molecules above the earth's atmosphere. Ionospheric refraction is a big issue, because AM radio waves can end up hundreds and even thousands of miles away from where they started, and in the process interfere with all other stations on the same frequency.

FM and TV Waves

FM (frequency modulated) radio and TV waves don't act in the same way as AM radio waves. For starters, they are on a higher frequency in the RF spectrum (The name RF, for radio frequency, was obviously named for radio, but when TV came along they just stuck with the name).

The FM radio band goes from 88 to 108 MHz (megahertz, or millions of cycles per second). Again, you can see these numbers on your FM radio dial. FM stations must be 200kHz apart at these frequencies, which means that there's room for 200 FM stations on the FM band.

But, unlike AM radio stations, FM stations don't end up being assigned frequencies with nice round numbers like 820 or 1240. Thus, an FM station may be at 88.7 on the dial.

You may have noticed that FM stations don't reduce power or sign off the air at sunset. Because of their higher frequency ionospheric refraction doesn't appreciably affect FM or TV signals.

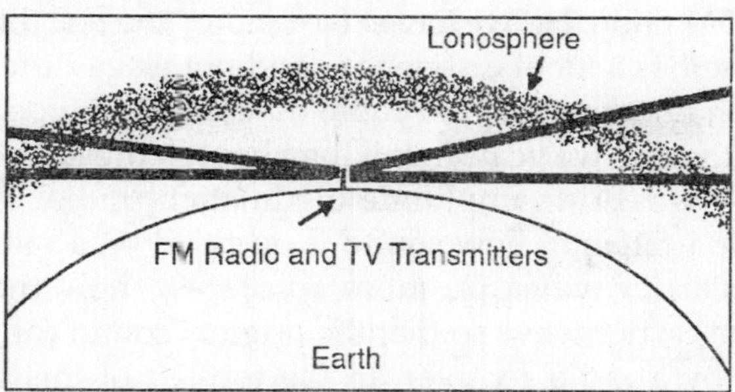

For the most part, FM and TV signals are line-of-sight. Although this means that FM stations don't interfere with each other, this characteristic creates a couple of other problems. First, these waves go in a straight line and don't bend around the earth as AM ground waves do. Thus, they can quickly disappear into space. So, the farther away from the FM or TV station you are, the higher you have to have an antenna to receive the FM or TV signal. Note that the earth is round - we hope this doesn't come as a shock to anyone - and, therefore, these signals will literally leave the earth after 50 miles or so. And, there's another problem.

Since FM and TV signals are line-of-sight, they can be stopped or reflected by things like mountains and buildings. In the case of solid objects like buildings, reflections create ghost images in TV pictures and that "swishing sound" when you listen to FM radio while driving around tall structures. Of course, the higher the FM or TV transmitter antennas are the greater area they will cover - which explains why these antennas are commonly very tall, or placed on the top of mountains. AM radio doesn't need that kind of advantage, since, as we've seen, AM radio waves don't behave in the same way. Note also from the drawing above that FM and TV signals tend to go through the ionosphere rather than being refracted form it. Again, this means that no matter what the station's power, it's signal will at some point leave the earth.

Basic Differences Between AM and FM

We need to mention a couple of other things before we leave the discussion of how radio works. We've talked about

AM and FM radio, but we haven't explained the real difference. In fact, there is a lot of difference - and not just a difference in the station numbers on your radio dial. The first type of radio service - the one we've been talking about in the last couple of modules - was AM (amplitude modulation) radio. The term modulation refers to how sound is encoded on a radio wave called a carrier wave; or, more accurately, how the sound affects the carrier wave so that the original sound can later be detected by a radio receiver. In the top-left of this drawing the RF energy (carrier wave) is not modulated by any sound. There would be silence on your radio receiver.

Sound transmitted by an AM radio station affects the carrier wave by changing the amplitude (heighı) of the carrier wave, as shown on the left. Unfortunately, this type of modulation is subject to static interference from such things as household appliances - and especially from lightening storms. AM also limits the loud-to-soft range of sounds that can be reproduced (called dynamic range) and the high-to-low sound frequency range (called frequency response, to be explained below). FM radio, which came along in the 1930s, uses a different approach than AM. It's virtually immune to any type of external interference, it has a greater dynamic range, and it can handle sounds of higher and lower frequencies. This is why music, with its much greater frequency range than the human voice, sounds better on FM radio. Note on the left that when the carrier wave of FM radio is modulated with sound that the distance between the waves, or the frequency of the carrier wave, changes. Thus, AM radio works by changing the amplitude of the carrier wave and FM radio works by changing the frequency of the carrier wave.

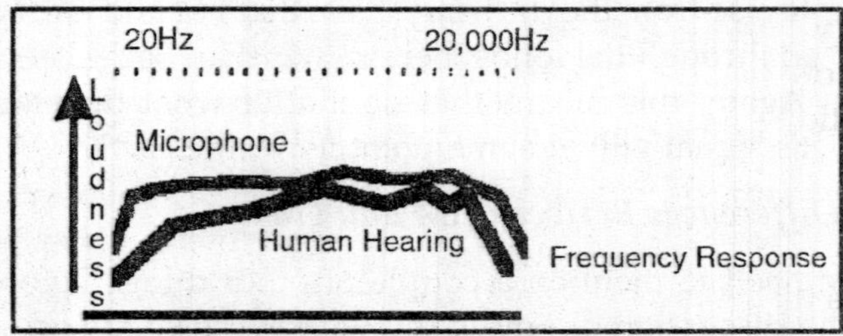

Frequency relates to the basic pitch of a sound - how high or low it is. A frequency of 20 Hz would sound like an extremely low-pitched note on a pipe organ - almost a rumble. At the other end of the scale, 20,000 Hz would be the highest pitched sound that can be imagined, even higher than the highest note on a violin or piccolo.

As we've noted, frequency is measured in Hertz (Hz) or cycles per second (CPS). A person with exceptionally good hearing will be able to hear sounds from 20-20,000 Hz. Since both ends of the 20-20,000Hz range represent rather extreme limits, the more common range used for FM radio and TV is from 50 to 15,000 Hz. (A typical AM radio signal does not cover this entire range.)

Although the 50-15,000 Hz doesn't quite cover the full range that can be heard by people with good hearing, it covers almost all naturally occurring sounds. Note in the drawing above that the ear does not hear all frequencies of sound at the same loudness, but a good microphone does.

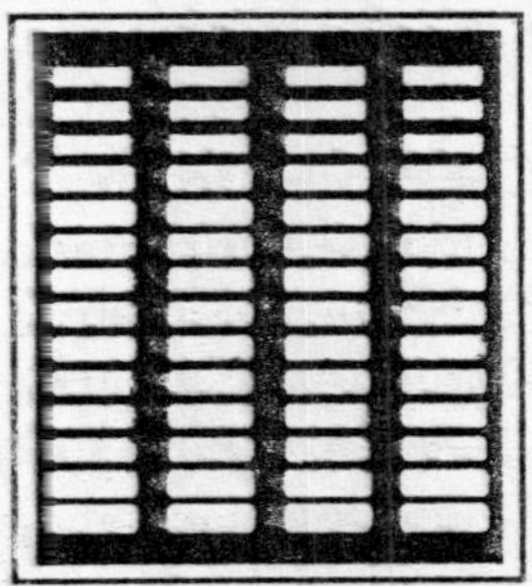

The sound level or amplitude of sound in radio and TV stations is monitored and adjusted with the help of a volume units meter (VU meter) meter.

One model is shown on the left. Audio levels must be carefully controlled in broadcasting to keep noise and distortion from reducing the quality of sound. More information on this can be found here.

PCM

The onboard computer, or Powertrain Control Module (PCM),is the brains of the engine control system, so when the brain is not functioning correctly neither is the engine or anything else that the microprocessor controls - which may include the charging system, transmission, various emission controls and communications with other onboard control modules. Once a diagnosis has been made (and we emphasize the word diagnosis), then and only then should the PCM be replaced.

Onboard Diagnostic (OBD II) diagnostic trouble codes that typically indicate a fault with the powertrain control module include:

P0600....Serial Communication Link

P0601....Internal Control Module Memory Check Sum Error

P0602....Control Module Programming Error

P0603....Internal Control Module Keep Alive Memory (KAM) Error

P0604....Internal Control Module Random Access Memory (RAM) Error

P0605....Internal Control Module Read Only Memory (ROM) Error

P0606....ECM/PCM Processor

P0607....Control Module Performance

P0608....Control Module VSS Output 'A'

P0609....Control Module VSS Output 'B'

P0610....Control Module Vehicle Options Error

If you see any of these codes when diagnosing the vehicle with a code reader or scan tool, it may mean the PCM has failed and must be replaced. Additional diagnostic tests will usually be necessary to confirm the problem is really the powertrain control module and NOT something else. Refer to the OEM diagnostic charts for what these tests are. Usually it involves checking certain inputs to the PCM to see if it outputs the correct response. No response or an incorrect response usually means the PCM is defective and needs to be replaced.

All too often, technicians tend to blame that which they understand least. If an engine is not running right and the cause is not obvious, they may blame the computer. Throwing parts at a problem in an attempt to solve it may be good for the parts business, but when a customer brings a PCM back because it failed to fix their problem, nobody wins. Warranty returns on complicated and expensive components like powertrain control modules are an ongoing problem that costs everyone money.

POWERTRAIN CONTROL MODULE RETURNS

Over 50 per cent of PCMs that are returned under warranty (either because the PCM failed to fix a performance problem or because the engine did not run properly after it was installed) have nothing wrong with them! So it is obvious a lot of people are swapping computers to see if a different PCM will fix their problem.

The trouble with returns is if the PCM has been on the car, you have no way of knowing if it is still "good" or not. Somebody may have crossed up some wires, zapped the PCM with too much voltage or who knows what? The computer needs to be tested and verified before it can go back on the shelf and be sold to somebody else.

Unfortunately, there is no easy way of doing that in a parts store. The PCM has to be hooked up to a sophisticated simulator that exercises all of the computer's input and output circuits to make sure it works correctly - which means the PCM has to go back to the supplier, be retested, and if no fault is found, repackaged and put back into stock. Be warned, though, that many parts stores have a policy of "no returns or refunds on electronic components."

POWERTRAIN CONTROL

Because there are so many different PCMs, accurate identification of the PCM and its correct replacement is absolutely essential to prevent unnecessary returns. Many PCMs appear to be exactly the same on the outside (same sized box and connectors) but may be wired or calibrated differently inside.

If the wrong PCM is installed in a vehicle, it may run but probably will not run well. Close enough is not good enough when it comes to replacing PCMs. It must be the correct replacement for the application. Accurately identifying the PCM requires not only the vehicle year, make, model and engine size, but also the OEM part number on the PCM itself. Most supplier catalogs list replacement PCMs both ways. So if in doubt, always refer to the OEM number on the PCM and look it up in the suppliers cross reference index to find their replacement part number. The calibration chip and PROM contains the programming instructions for the vehicle application.

That is why it usually does not come with the replacement PCM. There are too many different possibilities. On many newer vehicles, flash memory or "EEPROMs" (Electronically Erasable Programme Read Only Memory) are used. If the replacement PROM is not properly programmed for the application, it must be reprogrammed after it has been installed.

Unfortunately, the ability to do this type of reprogramming is not readily available to the aftermarket. The car makers do not want aftermarket technicians messing around with the calibration of their onboard computers because they are afraid doing so may alter emissions or performance. But that is another issue. One such example is Chrysler transmission modules. They must be reset with the factory DRB scan tool and dealer codes to set the "pinion factor," which controls the operation of the speedometer.

REMAN POWERTRAIN CONTROL MODULES

Because a powertrain control module can be very expensive to replace, almost all aftermarket replacement PCMs are "remanufactured" units. A PCM is not rebuilt in the same way that an alternator or water pump is rebuilt because there are no mechanical parts that wear out.

Remanufacturing in this case usually means testing the powertrain control module, isolating and repairing any faults that may be found, then retesting the powert5ain control module to make sure everything works correctly. A remanufactured PCM is typically sold one of two ways: on an exchange basis from stock, or on a custom rebuild basis. If a particular PCM is not in stock or is unavailable, you may be able to send an old PCM to a remanufacturer for repair.

Turn around time is typically a few days and the cost is about the same as an exchange unit except there is no core charge). The hard part is finding a remanufacturer who can test and repair your powertrain control module. Some PCMs, though, may not be repairable. As we said earlier, most remanufacturers will not even touch a PCM if it came out of a flooded vehicle.

PCM REPLACEMENT TIPS

Replacing a PCM is essentially a matter of swapping boxes. Accessibility can be a problem on some vehicles because the PCM is often buried under or behind other components in the instrument panel, climate control system or console. Some are located under a seat and require removing the seat. Regardless of the PCM's location, though, one thing you should do prior to removing the old PCM and installing the replacement PCM is disconnect the battery. Once the PCM has been installed and reconnected, the battery can be reconnected, too. But the job is not done yet. Many PCMs have to undergo a "relearning" procedure after they have been installed or if they have been disconnected from the battery.

On some newer vehicles, a scan tool may be required to reprogram the PCM and to reset the anti-theft system. On some applications, there may be a specific relearn procedure for establishing the base idle speed and other operating parameters. On others, it may be necessary to take the vehicle for a short test drive so the computer can adjust itself. The exact requirements will be spelled out in the vehicle service manual. The best advice here is to test drive the vehicle after the powertrain control module has been installed. A short drive cycle that includes going over 35 mph will usually reset most PCMs so they will operate properly.

The powertrain control module will also continue to learn and make small adjustments to the fuel mixture and other functions over time as the vehicle accumulates miles. If the PCM also controls the transmission, it may take awhile to relearn the driver's habits so the transmission may not shift exactly the same as before until this occurs. Finally, if the Malfunction Indicator Lamp (MIL) or Check Engine light comes back on after the PCM has been replaced, it means there is still a problem with the vehicle.

The fault is probably NOT the PCM, unless the fault code is for an internal PCM fault. The presence of fault codes means additional diagnosis is required to identify and repair the fault. And until the real problem is found and fixed, the PCM may not function normally.

If the engine control system is not going into closed loop, chances are the coolant sensor or oxygen sensor may not be working properly. If spark timing seems to be over advanced or retarded, the problem may be a faulty MAP sensor, misadjusted throttle position sensor or overly sensitive knock sensor.

And if nothing seems to work right, low charging voltage due to a weak alternator or poor battery connections may be the fault. Remember, a powertrain control module needs all its sensor inputs, proper battery voltage, a good ground and the ability to send out control signals to function normally.

CDMA AND TDMA

During this discussion I will use the generic term "CDMA" to refer to the IS-95B standard. Technically speaking, CDMA is only a means to transmit bits of information, while IS-95B is a transmission protocol that employs CDMA. You may also hear the term "TDMA" used to refer generically to the IS-136 standard.

Once again, TDMA is only a method of transmitting bits, while IS-136 is a protocol that happens to employ TDMA. I spend quite a bit of time reading the messages that flow through the various PCS newsgroups and forums on the Internet, and if one thing is abundantly clear, it is that people don't seem to know the true differences between CDMA and TDMA.

And who could blame them? There is so much hype surrounding these two competing technologies that it is difficult for a regular PCS subscriber to know who is telling the truth. I personally am NOT an RF engineer, nor do I work for any of the cellular or PCS companies.

It is however my hobby to keep up with the latest developments in mobile communication (as this web site amply demonstrates). I would like to clear the air by interjecting my own spin on this debate. I hope that by the time you finish reading this editorial you will have a better understanding of the true strengths and weaknesses of both technologies.

THE BASICS

Let's begin by learning what these two acronyms stand for. TDMA stands for "Time Division Multiple Access", while CDMA stands for "Code Division Multiple Access". Three of the four words in each acronym are identical, since each technology essentially achieves the same goal, but by using different methods. Each strives to better utilize the radio spectrum by allowing multiple users to share the same physical channel. You heard that right. More than one person can carry on a conversation on the same frequency without causing interference. This is the magic of digital technology.

Where the two competing technologies differ is in the manner in which users share the common resource. TDMA does it by chopping up the channel into sequential time slices. Each user of the channel takes turns transmitting and receiving in a round-robin fashion. In reality, only one person is actually using the channel at any given moment, but he or she only uses it for short bursts. He then gives up the channel momentarily to allow the other users to have their turn. This is very similar to how a computer with just one processor can seem to run multiple applications simultaneously.

CDMA on the hand really does let everyone transmit at the same time. Conventional wisdom would lead you to believe that this is simply not possible. Using conventional modulation techniques, it most certainly is impossible. What makes CDMA work is a special type of digital modulation called "Spread Spectrum". This form of modulation takes the user's stream of bits and splatters them across a very wide channel in a pseudo-random fashion. The "pseudo" part is very important here, since the receiver must be able to undo the randomization in order to collect the bits together in a coherent order. If you are still having trouble understanding the differences though, perhaps this analogy will help you. This my own version of an excellent analogy provided by Qualcomm: Imagine a room full of people, all trying to carry on one-on-one conversations.

In TDMA each couple takes turns talking. They keep their turns short by saying only one sentence at a time. As there is never more than one person speaking in the room at any given moment, no one has to worry about being heard over the background din. In CDMA each couple talks at the same time, but they all use a different language. Because none of the listeners understand any language other than that of the individual to whom they are listening, the background din doesn't cause any real problem.

VOICE ENCODING

At this point many people confuse two distinctly different issues involved in the transmission of digital audio. The first is the WAY in which the stream of bits is delivered from one end to the other. This part of the "air interface" is what makes one technology different from another. The second is the compression algorithm used to squeeze the audio into as small a stream of bits as possible. This latter component is known at the "Voice Coder", or Vocoder for short. Another term commonly used is CODEC, which is a similar word to modem. It combines the terms "COder" and "DECoder".

Although each technology has chosen their own unique CODECs, there is no rule saying that one transmission method needs to use a specific CODEC. People often lump a technology's transmission method with its CODEC as though they were single entities. We will discuss CODECs in greater detail later on in this article. Voice encoding schemes differ slightly in their approach to the problem. Because of this, certain types of human voice work better with some CODECs than they do with others. The point to remember is that all PCS CODECs are compromises of some sort. Since human voices have such a fantastic range of pitch and tonal depth, one cannot expect any single compromise to handle each one equally well. This inability to cope with all types of voice at the same level does lead some people to choose one technology over another.

All of the PCS technologies try to minimize battery consumption during calls by keeping the transmission of unnecessary data to a minimum. The phone decides whether or not you are presently speaking, or if the sound it hears is just background noise. If the phone determines that there is no intelligent data to transmit it blanks the audio and it reduces the transmitter duty cycle (in the case of TDMA) or the number of transmitted bits (in the case of CDMA). When the audio is blanked your caller would suddenly find themselves listening to "dead air", and this may cause them to think the call has dropped.

To avoid this psychological problem many service providers insert what is known as "Comfort Noise" during the blanked periods. Comfort Noise is synthesized white noise that tries to mimic the volume and structure of the real background noise. This fake background noise assures the caller that the connection is alive and well.

However, in newer CODECs such as EVRC (used exclusively on CDMA systems) the background noise is generally suppressed even while the user is talking. This piece of magic makes it sound as though the cell phone user is not in a noisy environment at all. Under these conditions, Comfort Noise is neither necessary, nor desirable. You can read my article on EVRC by clicking here.

CDMA

Now that we have a rudimentary understanding of the two technologies, let's try and examine what advantages they provide. We'll begin with CDMA, since this newer technology has created the greatest "buzz" in the mobile communications industry. One of the terms you'll hear in conjunction with

CDMA is "Soft Handoff". A handoff occurs in any cellular system when your call switches from one cell site to another as you travel. In all other technologies this handoff occurs when the network informs your phone of the new channel to which it must switch. The phone then stops receiving and transmitting on the old channel, and it commences transmitting and receiving on the new channel. It goes without saying that this is known as a "Hard Handoff". In CDMA however, every site are on the SAME frequency. In order to begin listening to a new site the phone only needs to change the pseudo-random sequence it uses to decode the desired data from the jumble of bits sent for everyone else. While a call is in progress the network chooses two or more alternate sites that it feels are handoff candidates. It simultaneously broadcasts a copy of your call on each of these sites. Your phone can then pick and choose between the different sources for your call, and move between them whenever it feels like it. It can even combine the data received from two or more different sites to ease the transition from one to the other.

This arrangement therefore puts the phone in almost complete control of the handoff process. Such an arrangement should ensure that there is always a new site primed and ready to take over the call at a moment's notice. In theory, this should put an end to dropped calls and audio interruptions during the handoff process. In practice it works quite well, but dropped calls are still a fact of life in a mobile environment. However, CDMA rarely drops a call due to a failed handoff.A big problem facing CDMA systems is channel pollution.

This occurs when signals from too many base stations are present at the subscriber's phone, but none are dominant. When this situation occurs the audio quality degrades rapidly, even when the signal seem otherwise very strong. Pollution occurs frequently in densely populated urban environments where service providers must build many sites in close proximity. Channel pollution can also result from massive multipath problems caused by many tall buildings. Taming pollution is a tuning and system design issue. It is up to the service provider to reduce this phenomenon as much as possible. In defence of CDMA however, I should point out that the new EVRC CODEC is far more robust than either of the earlier CODECs. Because of its increased robustness it provides much more consistent audio in the face of high frame error rates. EVRC is an 8 kilobit CODEC that provides audio quality that is almost as good to the older 13 kilobit CODEC. Since CDMA consumes only as much of the "ether" as a user talks, switching everyone to an 8 kilobit CODEC was an inevitable move. Don't confuse EVRC with the old (and unlamented) 8 kilobit CODEC implemented in the early days of CDMA deployment. That CODEC was simply awful, and very few good things could be said about it. EVRC is a far more advanced compression algorithm that cleans up many of the stability problems inherent in the two older CODECs. The sound reproduction is slightly muddier than the 13 kilobit CODEC, but the improvement in stability makes up for this.

Supporters often cite capacity as one CDMA's biggest assets. Virtually no one disagrees that CDMA has a very high "spectral efficiency". It can accommodate more users per MHz of bandwidth than any other technology. What experts do not agree upon is by how much. Unlike other technologies, in which the capacity is fixed and easily computed, CDMA has what is known as "Soft Capacity". You can always add just one more caller to a CDMA channel, but once you get past a certain point you begin to pollute the channel such that it becomes difficult to retrieve an error-free data stream for any of the participants The ultimate capacity of a system is therefore dependent upon where you draw the line. How much degradation is a carrier willing to subject their subscribers to before they admit that they have run out of useable capacity? Even if someone does set a standard error rate at which these calculations are made, it does not mean that you personally will find the service particularly acceptable at that error rate.

TDMA

Let's move away from CDMA now and have a look at TDMA. Before we can go any further though, I should note that there are actually three different flavors of TDMA in the PCS market. Each of these technologies implements TDMA in a slightly different way. The most complex implementation is, without a doubt, GSM. It overlays the basic TDMA principles with many innovations that reduce the potential problems inherent in the system.

To reduce the effects of co-channel interference, multipath, and fading, the GSM network can use something known as Frequency Hopping. This means that your call literally jumps from one channel to another at fairly short intervals. By doing this the likelihood of a given RF problem is randomized, and the effects are far less noticeable to the end user. Frequency Hopping is always available, but not mandated. This means that your GSM provider may or may not use it.

iDEN is a proprietary Motorola technology that no other company seems to participate in. Only Motorola makes iDEN phones, and only Motorola makes iDEN infrastructure equipment. Perhaps the company guards its technology on purpose. iDEN was initially deployed as an alternative to standard packet radio systems commonly used by public safety and business users. However, it also provided phone interconnect services that are extinguishable from phone services offered by the other PCS systems, as well as packet data services for web browsing and hooking up your laptop to the Internet.

Finally there is the old IS-136 technology, but this is now an officially dead technology. All of the North American providers who used it (Rogers, Cingular, and AT&T) are abandoning it in favour of GSM. The same is happening in other parts of the world where IS-136 was used. I therefore will not spend much time talking about this variation of TDMA.

Each of these TDMA technologies uses a different CODEC. GSM sports a CODEC called EFR (short for Enhanced Full Rate). This CODEC is arguable the best sounding one available in the PCS world. IS-136 used to sound horrible, but in the fall of 1997 they replaced their old CODEC with a new one. This new CODEC sounds much better than the old, but it doesn't quite match the GSM and CDMA entries. TDMA systems still rely on the switch to determine when to perform a handoff. Unlike the old analog system however, the switch does not do this in a vacuum. The TDMA handset constantly monitors the signals coming from other sites, and it reports this information to the switch without the caller being aware of it. The switch then uses this information to make better handoff choices at more appropriate times.

Perhaps the most annoying aspect of TDMA system to some people is the obviousness of handoffs. Some people don't tend to hear them, and I can only envy those individuals. Those of us who are sensitive to the slight interruptions caused by handoffs will probably find GSM the most frustrating. It's handoffs are by far the most messy. When handoffs occur infrequently (such as when we are stationary or in areas with few sites), they really don't present a problem at all. However, when they occur very frequently (while travelling in an area with a huge number of sites) they can become annoying.

SPECTRAL EFFICIENCY

Channel capacity in a TDMA system is fixed and indisputable. Each channel carries a finite number of "slots", and you can never accommodate a new caller once each of those slots is filled. Spectral efficiency varies from one technology to another, but computing a precise number is still a contentious issue. For example, GSM provides 8 slots in a channel 200 kHz wide, while iDEN provides 3 slots in a channel only 25 kHz wide.

GSM therefore consumes 25 kHz per user, while IS-136 consumes only 8.333 kHz per user. When Direct Connect is used on iDEN, 6 users can be stuffed into a single channel, thus only 4.166 kHz is consumer per user. There is also a new 6:1 interconnect CODEC coming for iDEN which will allow 6 phone users per channel.

One would be sorely tempted to proclaim that iDEN has 3 to 6 times the capacity of GSM. In a one-cell system this is certainly true, but once we start deploying multiple cells and channel reuse the situation becomes more complex. Due to

GSM's better error management and frequency hopping the interference of a co-channel site is greatly reduced. This allows frequencies to be reused more frequently without a degradation in the overall quality of the service.

Capacity is measured in "calls per cell per MHz". An GSM system using N=4 reuse (this means you have 4 different sets of frequencies to spread out around town) the figure is 5.0 We get an efficiency value of 6.6 for N=3. Unfortunately I could not find any figures for iDEN systems, but based on similar figures released for the IS-136 system we can expect efficiency values of 6.0 to 10.0.

Computing this figure for CDMA requires that certain assumptions are made. Formulas have been devised, and using very optimistic assumptions CDMA can provide a whopping 45 users per cell per MHz. However, when using more pessimistic (and perhaps more realistic) assumptions, the value is 12. That still gives CDMA an almost 2:1 advantage over GSM, but questionable advantage over a well-implement iDEN system.

IN-BUILDING COVERAGE

Now let's deal with another issue involving CDMA and TDMA. In-building coverage is something that many people talk about, but few people properly understand. Although CDMA has a slight edge in this department, due to a marginally greater tolerance for weak signals, all the technologies fair about the same. This is because the few dB advantage CDMA has is often "used up" when the provider detunes the sites to take advantage of this process gain.

So, while a CDMA phone might be able to produce a reasonable call with a signal level of -106 dBm, whereas a GSM phone might need -99 dBm to provide the same level of service, does this mean that CDMA networks will always have a 7 dB advantage? If all things were equal, then yes, but they aren't equal.

As I mentioned earlier, channel pollution is a big issue with CDMA networks and to keep channel pollution to a minimum in urban environments a CDMA provider needs to keep site overlap to a minimum. Subsequently, a CDMA network engineer will use that 7 dB advantage to his advantage by de-tuning the network accordingly.

This means that CDMA users will frequently see markedly lower signal levels indoors than a GSM user will, but in the end it all works out about the same. The most important aspect to in-building coverage is the proximity of the nearest site. When a site is located just outside of a building it can penetrate just about any building material. When a site is much further away however, the signals have a much harder time of getting past the walls of a structure.

When it comes to distance, remember that signals are subject to the "distance squared law". This means that signals decrease by the square of the distance. A site at 0.25 kilometers away will have 4 times the signal strength of a site at 0.50 kilometers away, and 16 times that of a site 1.0 kilometers away. Distance squared however is the rate of signal reduction in free space. Recent studies have shown that terrestrial communications are usually subject to rates as high as "Distance cubed", or even "Distance to the 4th". If the latter is true, then a site 1.0 kilometers away will actually be 1/256th as strong than a site 0.25 kilometers away.

In-building penetration is therefore less a technology issue than it is an implementation issue. Service providers who have sites close to the buildings you commonly visit will inevitably look better than those who don't. Never use someone else's in-building experiences unless you expect to go in the same buildings as they do. You cannot make useful generalizations about in-building coverage based upon one person's experience.

CDMA does have one peculiarity concerning in-building penetration that does not affect TDMA. When the number of users on a channel goes up, the general level of signal pollution goes up in tandem. To compensate for this the CDMA system directs each phone to transmit with slightly more power. However, if a phone is already at its limit (such as might be the case inside a building) it cannot do anything to "keep up with the pack". This condition is known as "the shrinking coverage phenomenon" or "site breathing". During slow periods of the day you might find coverage inside a specific building quite good. During rush hour however, you might find it exceedingly poor (or non-existent). Think of this as the difference between one person calling a number and an entire call centre calling the number. The less people using the system, the more likely the call will go through.

SOME FINAL OBSERVATIONS

In the end, can we really proclaim a winner in the CDMA vs TDMA war? For the time being I think not. Perhaps in the future, when newer technologies built around wider bandwidth CDMA technologies come into existence, the issue will warrant another look. By that time, even GSM will have moved to CDMA as its air interface of choice, but don't let that fool you into believing that they think the current TDMA air interface is inadequate for its purpose. Future standards are being built around high speed data.

If you are presently in the market for a new phone my advise to you is to ignore the hype surrounding the technologies and look at service provider instead. Judge each with an eye to price, phone choice, coverage, and reputation. Technology should play a very small roll in your choice (with the exception of IS-136, whose future is extremely limited at this time). If you follow this advice, you'll probably be much happier with the phone and service you inevitably wind up with.

FDMA

DESCRIPTION

Single Carrier Frequency Division Multiple Access (SC-FDMA) is a novel method of radio transmission under consideration for deployment in future cellular systems; specifically, in 3rd Generation Partnership Project Long Term Evolution (3GPP LTE) systems. SC-FDMA has drawn great attention from the communications industry as an attractive alternative to Orthogonal Frequency Division Multiple Access

(OFDMA). Introduction to Single Carrier FDMA places SC-FDMA in the wider context of wireless communications, providing the reader with an in-depth tutorial on SC-FDMA technology.

The book introduces the reader to this new multiple access technique that utilizes single carrier modulation along with orthogonal frequency multiplexing and frequency domain equalization, plus its applications in communications settings. It considers the similarities with and differences from orthogonal frequency division modulation, multiplexing, and multiple access used extensively in cellular, broadcasting, and digital subscriber loop applications. Particular reference is made to the peak power characteristics of an SC-FDMA signal as an added advantage over OFDMA.

This is an essential text for industry engineers who are researching and developing 3GPP LTE systems. It is suitable for engineers designing wireless network equipment, handsets, data cards, modules, chipsets, and test equipment as well as those involved in designing LTE infrastructure. It would also be of interest to academics, graduate students, and industry researchers involved in advanced wireless communications, as well as business analysts who follow the cellular market.

Single Carrier Frequency Division Multiple Access (SC-FDMA) is a novel method of radio transmission under consideration for deployment in future cellular systems; specifically, in 3rd Generation Partnership Project Long Term Evolution (3GPP LTE) systems. SC-FDMA has drawn great attention from the communications industry as an attractive alternative to Orthogonal Frequency Division Multiple Access (OFDMA).

Introduction to Single Carrier FDMA places SC-FDMA in the wider context of wireless communications, providing the reader with an in-depth tutorial on SC-FDMA technology. The book introduces the reader to this new multiple access technique that utilizes single carrier modulation along with orthogonal frequency multiplexing and frequency domain equalization, plus its applications in communications settings. It considers the similarities with and differences from orthogonal frequency division modulation, multiplexing, and multiple access used extensively in cellular, broadcasting, and digital subscriber loop applications. Particular reference is made to the peak power characteristics of an SC-FDMA signal as an added advantage over OFDMA.

- Provides an extensive overview of the principles of SC-FDMA and its relation to other transmission techniques.
- Explains how the details of a specific implementation influence the tradeoffs among various figures of merit.
- Describes in detail the configuration of the SC-FDMA uplink transmission scheme published by 3GPP.
- Features link level simulation of an uplink SC-FDMA system using MATLAB.

This is an essential text for industry engineers who are researching and developing 3GPP LTE systems. It is suitable for engineers designing wireless network equipment, handsets, data cards, modules, chipsets, and test equipment as well as those involved in designing LTE infrastructure.

It would also be of interest to academics, graduate students, and industry researchers involved in advanced wireless communications, as well as business analysts who follow the cellular market.

Analog transmission is considered an "older" cellular phone technology. Analog technology was built in the early 1980's. Analog allows a cellular phone to transmit signals by sending voice, video, and data that are always changing, and so does the network systems. Analog is considered an older method of modulating voice or data information radio signals.

Analog transmissions uses FDMA technology. FDMA stands for "frequency division multiple access". FDMA is used exclusively for analog cellular systems, even though in theory FDMA can also be used with digital. Essentially, FDMA splits the allocated spectrum into many channels. In current analog cell systems, each channel is 30 kHz.

When a FDMA cell phone establishes a call, it reserves the frequency channel for the entire duration of the call. The voice data is modulated into this channel's frequency band (using frequency modulation) and sent over the airwaves. At the receiver, the information is recovered using a band-pass filter. The phone then uses a common digital control channel to acquire channels.

FDMA analog transmissions are the least efficient cellular networks since each analog channel can only be used one user at a time. Analog channels don't take full advantage of bandwidth. Not only are these FDMA channels larger than necessary given modern digital voice compression, but they are also wasted whenever there is silence during a cell phone conversation.

Analog signals are especially susceptible to noise and the extra noise cannot get filtered out. Given the nature of the signal, analog cell phones must use higher power (between 1 and 3 watts) to get acceptable call quality. Given these analog features, it is easy to see why FDMA is being replaced by newer digital networks such as TDMA and CDMA.

ASK, FSK AND PSK FEATURES

DESCRIPTION

In digital communication Data Formatting is very important. The available data stream from PCM transmitter or data from Variable Data Generator ST2111 is converted into different formats best suited to individual transmission system. Various formats are covered in this trainer.

This trainer also covers various carrier modulation techniques required for transmission of digital information. This trainer requires either TDM Pulse Code Modulation Transmitter Trainer (ST2153) or 8 Bit Variable Data Generator (ST2111) for the input of digital data.

FEATURES

On-board Carrier generation circuit (Sine waves synchronized to transmitter data). On-board in phase and quadrate phase carrier for QPSK modulation and DQPSK Different data conditioning formats NRZ (L), NRZ (M), RZ,

Biphase (Manchester), Biphase (Mark), AMI, RB, differentially encoded dibit pair FSK, PSK, ASK ,QPSK & DQPSK carrier modulation.

- Variable carrier and modulation Off-Set
- Variable carrier gain
- On-board Unipolar to Bipolar conversion
- On-board data inverter

EXPERIMENTS THAT CAN BE PERFORMED

Conversion of NRZ data to other data formats NRZ (L), NRZ (M) RZ, AMI, RB, Biphase (Manchester), Biphase (Mark),Differentially encoded dibit pair ASK, FSK, BPSK, DPSK, QPSK & DQPSK Carrier Modulation Techniques & their comparison.

ERROR DETECTING AND CORRECTING CODES

Binary communications opened the road to many innovations in both implementation and theory. One of them was error detection and correction codes. But, what does this really mean to communications? We answer this question with an example.

Consider a channel that requires an expected bit error rate performance of 10-5, or a single error in 100,000 bits received, at a bit rate of 2 Mbit/s and a maximum line length of 2 km. At this rate, 100,000 bits are received within 50 ms, and thus it is expected that there will be on average one error every 50 ms, or 20 errors per second.

Clearly, if we elongate the line length to four kilometers and keep the same rate, then because of attenuation and more noise added to the signal, the BER is expected to increase. For the sake of argument, let us assume that if we double the line length, then BER increases to 10-2, or a single error every 100 bits received.

Then, at 2 Mbit/s, there are expected to be on average one error every 50 ?s, or 20,000 errors per second. The basic problem we have to resolve is that memory and communications technology isn't totally reliable; we have to expect and be ready to deal with errors in the hardware. This document will describe two very different technologies for detecting, and maybe correcting, errors that may occur in data storage and transmission.

The first approach to be described is more appropriate for environments like memory: a relatively small amount of data is fetched in parallel. This approach, called "error detecting and correcting codes," is based on defining a distance between two bit strings in terms of the number of bits that have to change to get from the first string to the second. Extra bits are added to each string, which are set so that some minimum number of bits must change to get from one valid string to another

If the received string isn't valid, it is assumed that the correct string is the one "closest" to the received string. The second approach is more appropriate to environments in which relatively large amounts of data are to be transferred, but they are transferred serially. In this approach a "signature" is appended to the data string; the number of bits in the signature is much less than the number of bits that would be required to do an error correcting code. This approach will lead to adding checksums or cyclic redundancy.checks to the string.

DETECTING AND CORRECTING CODES

R. W. Hamming wrote the paper that both opened and closed this field in 1950. His interest was in providing a means of self-checking in computers, which were just being developed at the time he wrote this.

the paper appeared in the Bell System Technical Journal, April, 1950. Definitely worth tracking down in the library and reading.

Bit Strings as Addresses in Binary Hypercubes

The best starting point for understanding ECC codes is to consider bit strings as addresses in a binary hypercube. A hypercube is a generalization of a cube to various dimensions; we're probably most familiar with the notion of a four-dimensional hypercube. Here's a picture of binary hypercubes for several different dimensionalities:

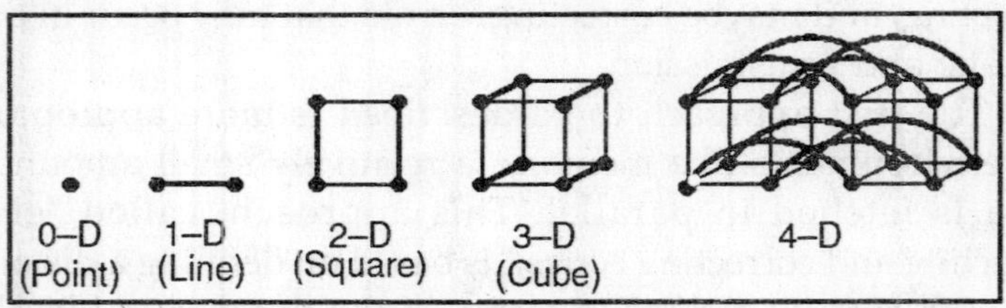

Each of them was created by copying the one to the left twice, and connecting corresponding vertices. We can assign each vertex in a hypercube a location in a coordinate space determined by the dimensionality of the hypercube.

- A zero-dimensional hypercube requires no coordinates to know where you are
- A one-dimensional hypercube can use one bit to tell whether you're at the bottom or the top of the line segment.
- A two-dimensional hypercube can use two bits: first bit is left vs. right, second is inherited from the line.
- A three-dimensional hypercube can use a bit to tell front square from back, and inherit two bits from the square.
- A four-dimensional hypercube can use a bit to tell left cube from right, and inherits three bits from cube.

The Hamming distance between two bit strings is the number of bits you have to change to convert one to the other: this is the same as the number of edges you have to traverse in a binary hypercube to get from one of the vertices to the other. The basic idea of an error correcting code is to use extra bits to increase the dimensionality of the hypercube, and make sure the Hamming distance between any two valid points is greater than one.

- If the Hamming distance between valid strings is only one, a single-bit error results in another valid string. This means we can't detect an error.
- If it's two, then changing one bit results in an invalid string, and can be detected as an error. Unfortunately,

changing just one more bit can result in another valid string, which means we can't know which bit was wrong: so we can detect an error but not correct it.

- If the Hamming distance between valid strings is three, then changing one bit leaves us only one bit away from the original error, but two bits away from any other valid string. This means if we have a one-bit error, we can figure out which bit is the error; but if we have a two-bit error, it looks like one bit from the other direction. So we can have single bit correction, but that's all.
- Finally, if the Hamming distance is four, then we can correct a single-bit error and detect a double-bit error. This is frequently referred to as a SECDED (Single Error Correct, Double Error Detect) scheme.

Parity

The simplest case is by adding a parity bit. Suppose we have a three-bit word (so the bit strings define points in a cube). If we add a fourth bit, we can decree that any time we want to switch a bit in the original three-bit string, we also have to switch the parity bit. If we start with 000 in the left cube, so the full string is 0000, changing any one of the original three bits requires us to change to the other cube: 1001, 1010, and 1100. Now if we change a second bit, we have to move back to the left cube: 0011, 0101, 0110.

And if we change the third bit, we move back to the right cube: 0111. So, there is a Hamming distance of two between any two valid strings. If we get a one-bit error, we know it is an error because it's on one of the invalid vertices. This can be computed by counting the number of 1's, and making sure it's always even (so this is called even parity). We could have selected exactly the opposite set of vertices as the valid ones, which would have given us odd parity. We picked even parity because we'll be using it in the next step.

Error Correction

The weakness of the parity scheme is that we can tell we

had an error, but we can't know which bit is wrong. If we use enough extra bits, we can tell not only that a bit is wrong, but which one it is. Since we need to have enough check bits to spot both an error in the data and in the check bits themselves (after all, they aren't going to be perfect either), we need (log n) + 1 bits (Hamming derives this result much, much more carefully in his paper).

The basic idea in what follows is that we'll divide the data bits into log n subsets where each subset contains roughly half of all the bits, and compute the even parity of each subset. If we have an error, we'll be able to tell which bit has the error because it will be uniquely determined by the set of subsets that turn up with bad parity.

Checksums and Cyclic Redundancy Checks

This technique has seen a lot more development, by a lot more authors, than error correcting codes have. The basic technique as described here appeared in a paper by Peterson and Brown, which appeared in the January, 1961 issue of the Proceedings of the Institute of Radio Engineers (the IRE was, of course, a predecessor organization to the IEEE). Much has been done since on selecting good CRCs.

Checksums

Suppose we have a fairly long message, which can reasonably be divided into shorter words (a 128 byte message, for instance). We can introduce an accumulator with the same width as a word (one byte, for instance), and as each word comes in, add it to the accumulator. When the last word has been added, the contents of the accumulator are appended to the message (as a 129th byte, in this case). The added word is called a checksum.

Now, the receiver performs the same operation, and checks the checksum. If the checksums agree, we assume the message was sent without error. A related approach would be, instead of performing an actual addition, we can just do a bitwise exclusive-or of the new word with the accumulator. If we do this, we calculate a vertical parity on the data. Notice that in the special case of a one-bit word, this is equivalent to calculating the parity of the buffer! Performing a vertical parity has two advantages over a real checksum: it can be performed with less hardware if the data is serial, and it will lead us into performing a CRC.

To see how a vertical parity can be performed with less hardware than a checksum, take a look at the next figure:

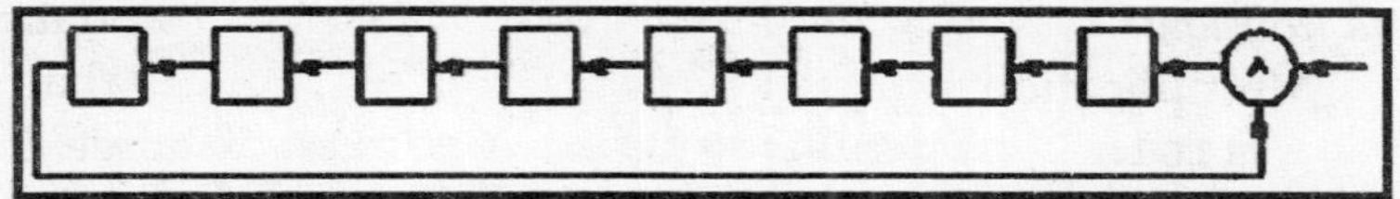

This figure shows an eight bit shift register and an exclusive-or gate. Initially, the shift register is filled with 0's. As each bit is put into it, the new bit is exclusive-ored with the contents of the eighth cell in the register. When the entire message has been passed through the shift register, it contains the vertical parity. Taking a bitwise exclusive-or in place of performing an addition is an example of "Modulo-2 Arithmetic," which is one form of "polynomial arithmetic." I've seen one author call it "CRC arithmetic."

Modulo-2 arithmetic is an arithmetic scheme; like most of the oddities that mathematicians like to study it seems completely useless to a non-mathematician at first glance but turns out to have some very practical applications. In this case, the practical application is in developing CRC checks.

The basic idea of modulo-2 arithmetic is just that we are working in binary, but we don't have a carry in addition or a borrow in subtraction.

This means:

- Addition and subtraction become the same operation: just a bit-wise exclusive-or. Because of this, the total ordering we expect of integers is replaced by a partial ordering: one number is greater than another iff its left-most 1 is farther left than the other's. This will have an impact on division, in a moment.
- Multiplication is just like multiplication in ordinary arithmetic except that the adds are performed using exclusive-ors instead of additions.

- Division is like long division in ordinary arithmetic, except for two differences: the subtractions are replaced by exclusive-ors, and you can subtract any time the leftmost bits line up correctly (since, by the partial ordering described above, they are regarded as equal in this case).

It'll probably help to show examples of modulo-2 multiplication and division:

Multiplication

```
    1101
    0110
    ----
    0000
   11010
  110100
 0000000
 -------
 0101110
```

Division

```
         1101
       --------
 0110)0101110
        0110
        ----
         0111
         0110
          ----
           0011
           0000
           ----
            0110
            0110
            ----
             0000
```

Notice that the first subtraction is possible in modulo-2 arithmetic, while it wouldn't be possible in normal arithmetic. One last thing to say here is that most of the time, when we perform a modulo-2 addition on two numbers we get an answer of 0 or 1. In this case, we're performing the arithmetic on each coefficient of the polynomial modulo-2.

Cyclic Redundancy Checks

Peterson & Brown's Notation

- k is the length of the message we want to send, ie the number of information bits.
- n is the total length of the message we will end up sending: the information bits followed by the check bits. Peterson and Brown call this a code polynomial.
- n-k is the number of check bits. It is also the degree of the generating polynomial. The basic (mathematical) idea is that we're going to pick the n-k check digits in such a way that the code polynomial is divisible by the generating polynomial. Then we send the data, and at the other end we look to see whether it's still divisible by the generating polynomial; if it's not then we know we have a error, if it is we hope there was no error.

The way we calculate a CRC is we establish some predefined n-k+1 bit number P (called the Polynomial, for reasons relating to the fact that modulo-2 arithmetic is a special case of polynomial arithmetic). Now we append n-k 0's to our message, and divide the result by P using modulo-2 arithmetic. The remainder is called the Frame Check Sequence.

Now we ship off the message with the remainder appended in place of the 0's. The receiver can either recompute the FCS and see if it gets the same answer, or it can just divide the whole message (including the FCS) by P and see if it gets a remainder of 0!

As an example, let's set a 5-bit polynomial of 11001, and compute the CRC of a 16 bit message:

```
      ---------------------
11001)10011101010101100000
      11001
      -----
       1010101010101100000
```

```
    11001
     ----
     1100010101011000 0
        11001
        ----
        00011010101100000
           11001
           ----
           0011101100000
             11001
             ----
               100100000
               11001
               -----
                10110000
                11001
                -----
                  1111000
                  11001
                  -----
                    11100
                    11001
                    -----
                     0101
```

CRC's can actually be computed in hardware using a shift register and some number of exclusive-or gates (sounds a bit like the vertical parity calculation, doesn't it?). The key insight is that we can perform a subtraction any time there is a 1 in the bit that lines up with the most significant bit of the polynomial, and we can perform that subtraction by performing an exclusive-or of the bits corresponding to 1's in all the other places of the polynomial. This lets us implement the CRC calculation by using a shift register similar to the one for vertical parity.

You can see how it's done by comparing the division we performed above to the circuit in the next figure. The figure shows a shift register; the string to be checked is inserted from the right. Whenever a "1" exits the left side of the shift register, it means there is a 1 in the most significant bit of the part of the dividend we're working with; since we're working in modulo-2 arithmetic this means we can do a subtraction.

What this works out to is:

- The most significant bit will be xored away, so it falls off to the left.
- For every other bit with a "1" in the divisor, perform an exclusive-or with the corresponding bit in the number being checked.
- For bits with a "0" in the divisor, do nothing.

The figure below attempts to show this for the example CRC polynomial. Each of the square boxes is a position in the shift register, where a value can be stored. Every round box is a position where we may or may not perform an exclusive-or, depending on the polynomial we're using. You can see the value of the CRC polynomial written above the round boxes.

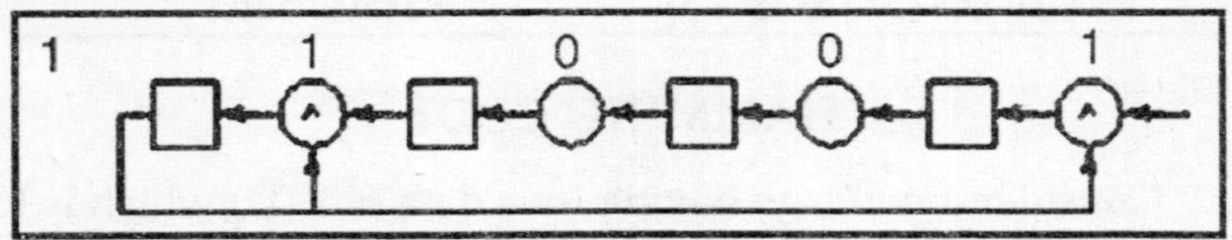

Properties of Cyclic Redundancy

The paper lists a few properties of CRCs, which deserve mention:

- If the rightmost place of the generating polynomial were 0, the generating polynomial would be divisible by X. That being the case, any polynomial divisible by P would also be divisible by X, and so the last bit of the check bits would always be 0. That would be useless, so we always have a 1 in the least significant bit of the generating polynomial

  That's a roundabout way of saying that if you're going to have an n-k bit polynomial, the two outlying bits should be 1's, otherwise you've effectively got a shorter polynomial than that.
- Any error checking code that can always detect a two-bit error can always correct any one-bit error. In the most ridiculous case, we can just check by

flipping every bit of the received message; whenever we flip the wrong bit we get a two-bit error, when we flip the right one we get a 0-bit error. Of course, Hamming's scheme is a lot more clever than this!

- Any cyclic code whose generating polynomial is of length n-k will always detect any burst error of length less than n-k.

There are a few "classic" CRC polynomials of given lengths which are so sell established that they've been given names.

Name	Definition	
	As Polynomial	**As Number**
CRC12	$X^{12} + X^{11} + X^3 + X + 1$	1100000001011
CRC16	$X^{16} + X^{15} + X^2 + 1$	11000000000000101
CRC-CCITT	$X^{16} + X^{12} + X^5 + 1$	10001000000100001
CRC32	$X^{32} + X^{26} + X^{23} + X^{22} + X^{16} + X^{12} + X^{11} + X^{10} + X^8 + X^7 + X^5 + X^4 + X^2 + X + 1$	100000100110000010001 110110110111

HAMMING CODE

Consider a message having four data bits (D) which is to be transmitted as a 7-bit codeword by adding three error control bits. This would be called a (7,4) code. The three bits to be added are three EVEN Parity bits (P), where the parity of each is computed on different subsets of the message bits as shown below.

7	6	5	4	3	2	1	
D	D	D	P	D	P	P	7-BIT CODEWORD
D	-	D	-	D	-	P	(EVEN PARITY)
D	D	-	-	D	P	-	(EVEN PARITY)
D	D	D	P	-	-	-	(EVEN PARITY)

For example, the message 1101 would be sent as 1100110, since:

7	6	5	4	3	2	1	
1	1	0	0	1	1	0	7-BIT CODEWORD
1	-	0	-	1	-	0	(EVEN PARITY)
1	1	-	-	1	1	-	(EVEN PARITY)
1	1	0	0	-	-	-	(EVEN PARITY)

It may now be observed that if an error occurs in any of the seven bits, that error will affect different combinations of the three parity bits depending on the bit position.

For example, suppose the above message 1100110 is sent and a single bit errors such that the codeword 1110110 is received: transmitted message received message

1 1 0 0 1 1 0 → 1 1 1 0 1 1 0

The above error can be corrected by examining which of the three parity bits was affectd by the bad bit:

7	6	5	4	3	2	1		
1	1	1	0	1	1	0	7-BIT CODEWORD	
1	-	1	-	1	-	0	(EVEN PARITY)	NOT!
1	1	-	-	1	1	-	(EVEN PARITY)	OK!
1	1	1	0	-	-	-	(EVEN PARITY)	NOT!

The value of the Hamming code can be summarized:

- Detection of 2 bit errors (assuming no correction is attempted);
- Correction of single bit errors;
- Cost of 3 bits added to a 4-bit message.

The ability to correct single bit errors comes at a cost which is less than sending the entire message twice. (Recall that simply sending a message twice accomplishes no error correction.)

CALCULATING THE HAMMING CODE

The key to the Hamming Code is the use of extra parity bits to allow the identification of a single error.

Create the code word as follows:

- Mark all bit positions that are powers of two as parity bits. (positions 1, 2, 4, 8, 16, 32, 64, etc.)
- All other bit positions are for the data to be encoded. (positions 3, 5, 6, 7, 9, 10, 11, 12, 13, 14, 15, 17, etc.)
- Each parity bit calculates the parity for some of the bits in the code word. The position of the parity bit determines the sequence of bits that it alternately checks and skips.

- *Position* 1: check 1 bit, skip 1 bit, check 1 bit, skip 1 bit, etc. (1,3,5,7,9,11,13,15,...)
- *Position* 2: check 2 bits, skip 2 bits, check 2 bits, skip 2 bits, etc. (2,3,6,7,10,11,14,15,...)
- *Position* 4: check 4 bits, skip 4 bits, check 4 bits, skip 4 bits, etc. (4,5,6,7,12,13,14,15,20,21,22,23,...)
- *Position* 8: check 8 bits, skip 8 bits, check 8 bits, skip 8 bits, etc. (8-15,24-31,40-47,...)
- *Position* 16: check 16 bits, skip 16 bits, check 16 bits, skip 16 bits, etc. (16-31,48-63,80-95,...)
- *Position* 32: check 32 bits, skip 32 bits, check 32 bits, skip 32 bits, etc. (32-63,96-127,160-191,...) etc.

• Set a parity bit to 1 if the total number of ones in the positions it checks is odd. Set a parity bit to 0 if the total number of ones in the positions it checks is even.

Chapter 2

LAN Topologies

LOCAL AREA NETWORK

Local Area Networks (LANs) use one of the following physical layout designs. These designs are referred to as 'topologies'.

Topology	Types
Bus	(Logical Ethernet)
Hub and Spoke (Star)	(Physical Ethernet)
Hybrid (Bus & Star)	Ethernet
Point To Point / Daisy Chaining	Serial
Point to Multipoint	Frame Relay
Ring	FDDI, Token Ring

FOREWORD

Station

A station is a computer workstation or computing device attached to a network.

Segment

A segment is a cable between any two stations or network devices, or between any station and network device.

Network Device

A network device is any device used to interconnect segments of the network. Why do I use these terms? Because the standards documentation uses them and I really should be consistent because the Cisco and Network+ tests use these same terms as the documented standards for most protocols.

BUS TOPOLOGY

Networks employing a bus topology use a common physical connection for communication. That means the physical media is shared between stations. When one station transmits on the bus, all devices hear the transmission. If more than one device transmits at the same time, the two transmissions will collide with each other and both transmissions will destroy each other.

When two or more of these devices attempts to access the network bus at the same time, some method must be used to prevent a collision (CSMA/CD). Historically, bus networks used coaxial cable as their medium of transmission. Bus, Ethernet (Thinnet and Thicknet) are common examples of bus topologies. Although some installations of Ethernet using coaxial cable still exist, all modern installations now use a hub and spoke or star topology.

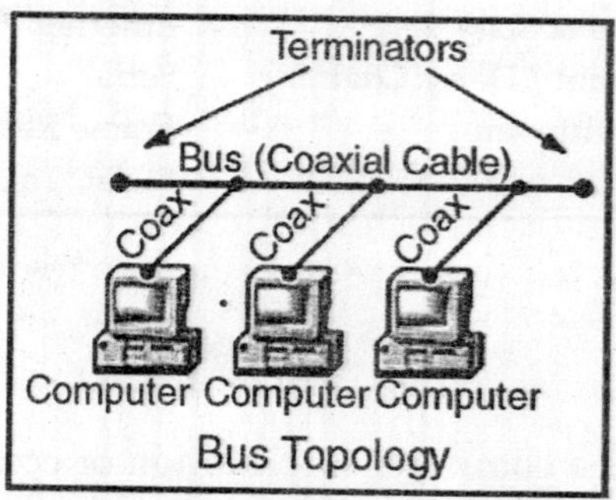

Bus Topology

HUB AND SPOKE (STAR)

Please note that this is not called a hub and spokedesign because there is a network hub in the drawing. This drawing is to show how a star or hub and spoke network resembles the hub and spokes of a wheel.

The Hub and Spoke topology refers to a network topology where there is a central connection point to which multiple devices are connected. A network hub device is not the only device usable in this configuration. A switch may also be used and in some cases, a router. Ethernet utilizing twisted pair still considered a bus architecture from a logical standpoint; however, physically, an Ethernet network can be physically wired as a hub and spoke model.

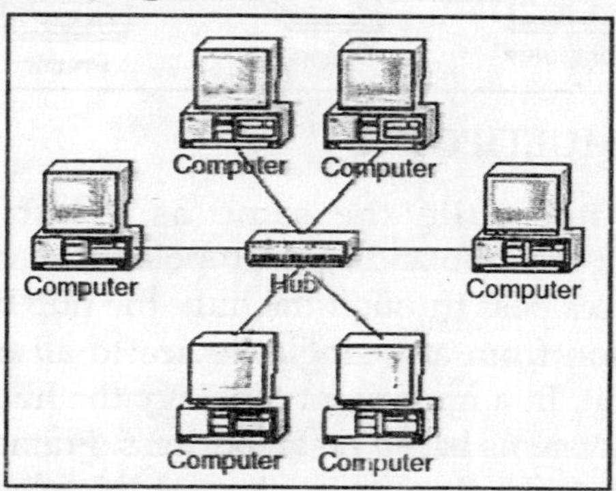

RING

Ring topologies are similar to bus topologies, except they transmit in one direction only from station to station. Typically, a ring architecture will use separate physical ports and wires for transmit and receive. Token Ring is one example of a network technology that uses a ring topology.

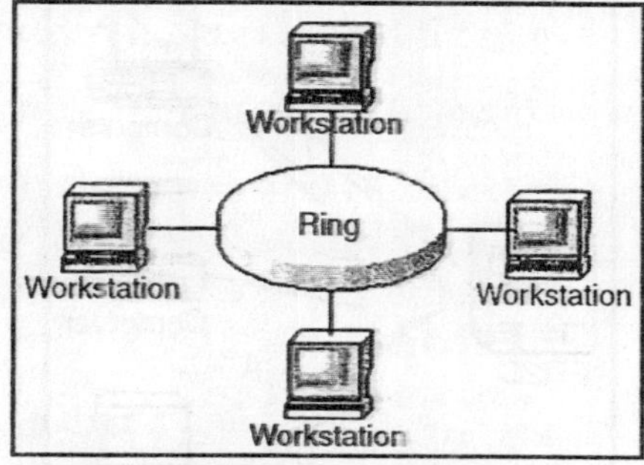

POINT TO POINT (DAISY CHAINING)

Point to Point topologies are simplest and most straightforward. You must picture them as a chain of devices and another name for this type of connectivity is called daisy chaining. Most computers can 'daisy chain' a series of serial devices from one of its serial ports. Networks of routers are often configured as point-to-point topologies.

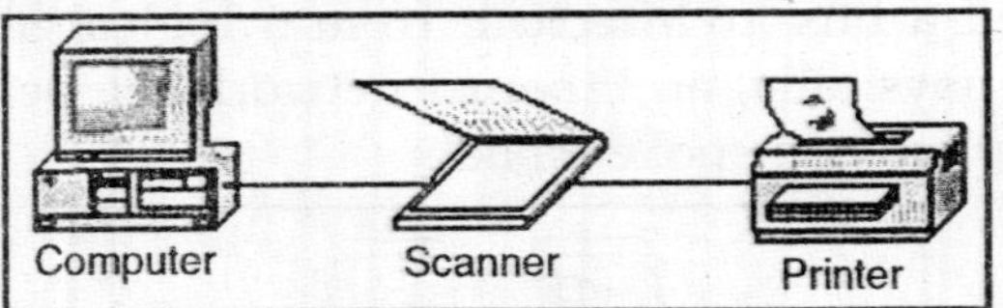

POINT TO MULTIPOINT

This is not quite the same as a hub and spoke configuration. In a hub and spoke topology, all transmissions from all devices pass through the hub--the hub broadcasts all communication from any single device to all other devices connected to it. In a multipoint topology the hub can send to one or more systems based on an address. Frame Relay is the most common technology to implement this scheme, and it is typically used as a WAN technology. All the remote connection points are connected to a single Frame Relayswitch or router port, and communication between sites is managed by that central point. In hub and spoke, all spokes or only one spoke hears a given transmission. In point to multipoint, any number of remote stations can be accessed

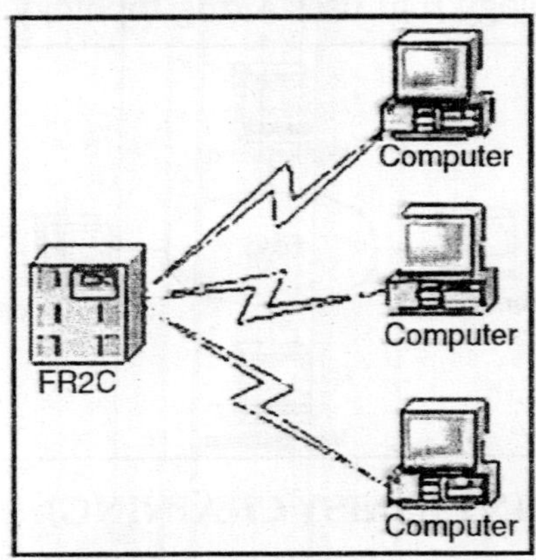

HYBRID TOPOLOGIES

In large network environment, you can attach Switches one to another to create larger LAN to support more devices.

Hybrid topologies combined the above topologies together to form three popular hybrid topologies: tree, hierarcnical star, and star-wireless.

Hierarchical Star Topology

For large network environment you can configure switches in hierarchical star topology.

- Can be used to build large networks.
- Switches can be configured redundantly to avoid single point of uplink failures

Cons:

- Size restrictions due to address space and timing issues without introduction of routing technology. See also Layer 3 Switching

Star Wireless

The most recent hybrid topology has arrived with the advent of wireless technology. Wireless LAN technology in its current implementation requires a user to be in the vicinity of a wireless access point attached to the wired network. See also wireless LAN for more detail.

The star topology is necessary to combine the many access points spread across a building to ensure wireless coverage. All the access points collapse back into the main star hub, where server resources would reside on the network. As wireless technologies continue to evolve, so will the topologies that support them.

TREE TOPOLOGY

The tree topology is a generalization of the bus topology. The transmission medium is a branching cable with no closed loops. The tree layout begins at a point known as the headend, where one or more cables start, and each of these may have branches. The branches in turn may have additional branches to allow quite complex layouts. Again, a transmission from any station propagates throughout the medium and can be received by all other stations. Two problems present themselves in this arrangement. First, because a transmission from any one station can be received by all other stations, there needs to be some way of indicating for whom the transmission is intended. Second, a mechanism is needed to regulate transmission.

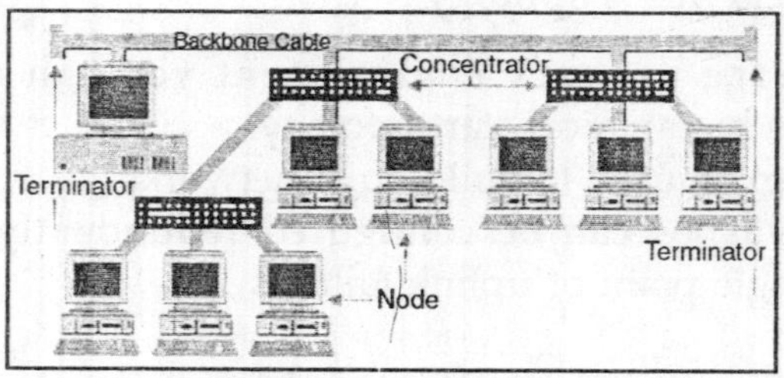

WORKSTATION

DEFINITION

A type of computer used for engineering applications (CAD/CAM), desktop publishing, software development, and other types of applications that require a moderate amount of computing power and relatively high quality graphics capabilities.Workstations generally come with a large, high-resolution graphics screen, at least 64 MB (megabytes) of RAM, built-in network support, and a graphical user interface.

Most workstations also have a mass storage device such as a disk drive, but a special type of workstation, called a diskless workstation, comes without a disk drive. The most common operating systems for workstations are UNIX and Windows NT. In terms of computing power, workstations lie between personal computers and minicomputers, although the line is fuzzy on both ends. High-end personal computers are equivalent to low-end workstations. And high-end workstations are equivalent to minicomputers.

Like personal computers, most workstations are single-user computers. However, workstations are typically linked together to form a local-area network, although they can also be used as stand-alone systems. In networking, workstation refers to any computer connected to a local-area network. It could be a workstation or a personal computer.

SERVER

- In information technology, a server is a computer programme that provides services to other computer programmes (and their users) in the same or other computers.
- The computer that a server programme runs in is also frequently referred to as a server (though it may be used for other purposes as well).
- In the client/server programming model, a server is a programme that awaits and fulfills requests from client programmes in the same or other computers. A given application in a computer may function as a client with requests for services from other programmes and also as a server of requests from other programmes.

Specific to the Web, a Web server is the computer programme (housed in a computer) that serves requested HTML pages or files. A Web client is the requesting programme associated with the user. The Web browser in your computer is a client that requests HTML files from Web servers.

GROWING PAINS

Many office networks grow in an almost organic way. They start life as a single PC, then a second is added and before you know it there are five or ten. Sometimes these are standalone but more often they will be peer-to-peer networked. Eventually this becomes cumbersome and some kind of server solution is desirable. At this point the fledgling IT budget becomes hungrier. Proprietary servers are expensive to buy and licence. Free software has for some time offered a choice of alternatives in this field and this article aims to discuss those options and explain how you might deploy a free software LAN server, which will allow you to start small but which can grow with you with minimal extra outlay.

So, if you are looking to deploy a server but are baulking at the expense and hardware needs of Microsoft Exchange, read on. Figure 1 shows a typical network layout for your server, for the purposes of this article I am talking about five to ten client PCs behind a single ADSL line.If you are looking to deploy a server but are baulking at the expense and hardware needs of Microsoft Exchange, read on.

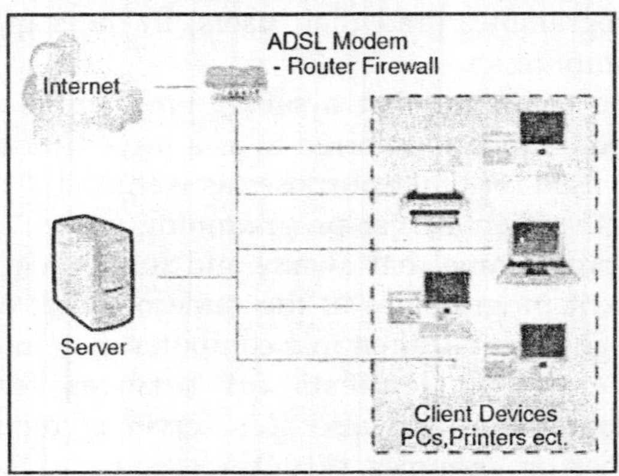

HARDWARE CHOICES

First, I'll look at the hardware choice. Server hardware for this kind of project will not be particularly special. Bear in mind that it won't be running a GUI, so you won't need that 128MB 3D graphics card. Sound is also irrelevant beyond a system beep, so no sub-woofers are required either. CPU, RAM and hard disk will be crucial as will removable storage if you are implementing an on-site backup solution.

The first has a USB DVD writer and the second an AIT-2 tape drive. The first was an old desktop PC which was no longer required and the second was custom-built and rack-mounted. Of course, neither have a (permanent) monitor, keyboard or mouse attached. You can also go, if you like, for hosting dedicated servers, which will give you more choice and bandwidth. But it's totally up to you.

It's unlikely you'll have any hardware issues specific to running free software. Especially considering the advances made by GNU/Linux distributions and the BSD options. If anything, I would be careful of older network cards and devices mounted on motherboards as some of these can use peculiar chipsets If you do have an issue then you can buy fairly cheap GNU/Linux compatible alternatives on-line.

DESIGNED TO SERVE

What might such a server be expected to-er-serve? Here is a suggestion: files (Samba); printers (CUPS); Dynamic Host Configuration Protocol (DHCP); mail (Exim/Procmail/Qmail/Sendmail) and intranet (Apache) internal websites.

The names in parentheses indicate typical free software packages you could use to provide such services. The resources section at the end of this article has links to most of their websites. The mail and intranet services could be provided elsewhere but there may well be situations where a standard ADSL account is used for connectivity and this includes a single catch-all email account. A server like this would give staff individual mail addresses. Similarly, a website may be available, but in a single office environment a local server would provide a more manageable and controllable intranet.

SOFTWARE OPTIONS

Whilst there will be many ways to skin this particular cat, I shall look into two of the most popular ways of deploying a free software LAN server.

- Build it yourself from a typical distribution.
- Download and install a customised made-for-purpose distribution.

So how do you decide? My advice is to work out how much time, budget and skills you have available and go from there. If you have no time at all I would stop now. Installing a server will require some time (even-or especially-a proprietary one). If you have a couple of weeks, know how to use a command line and fancy a challenge then go for the first option. If you have a week and don't know what a command line is then go with the second option. Work out how much time you have available. If you have no time-stop now I'll be looking at one example of each. Of course, your preferences may differ from mine but that's the beauty of free software-choice. Another one is scalability. Both these options will, given adequate hardware, scale to support much larger setups.

DIY SERVERS

Building your own server from a standard distribution will involve more work, particularly in maintaining packages, installing updates, etc., but it will be your server. It will run the software you choose and will be as unique as you want it to be. You are unlikely to get a support contract for it but at this level you are unlikely to need one. This is the "fun" option. That's in the same way that building your own house can be fun. I'm looking at a Debian GNU/Linux-based server.

Base Install

You can download an install CD from the Debian website. I usually go for the NetInst CD. The Debian installer (at time of writing) has a familiar curses-based interface with fairly self-explanatory options. Follow the instructions and then reboot when requested.

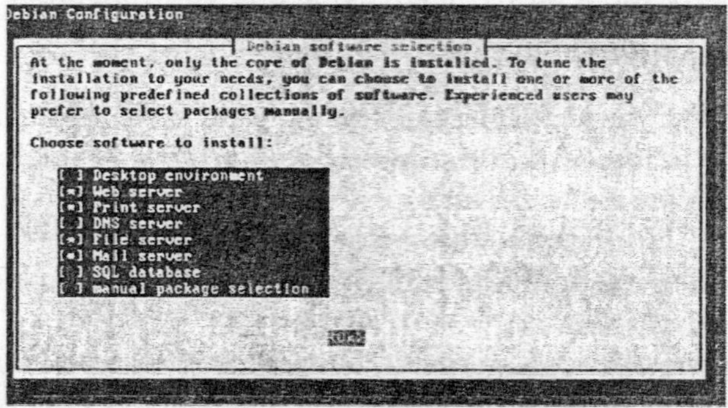

Fig. The Debian Installer Showing Package Collections.

Packages

Once your base system is installed you can install the specific packages you need. The installer has package collections aimed at particular tasks. Figure shows this screen and, as an example, the web server collection will install apache2 and the file server collection will install Samba. Obviously you won't be needing the Desktop Environment collection. This is a server and contrary to what certain software companies believe, running a GUI is a waste of resources.

Any packages not included at this stage, such as dhcp, can be installed using apt-get at the command line. I installed the current stable distribution. You can of course install the testing distribution if you prefer. I would advise against using something like Debian's unstable distribution on a mission centric server like this.

Contrary to what certain software companies believe, running a GUI is a waste of resources for a server Note that you may have particular preferences for some services, Procmail instead of Exim, for example. Debian usually has packages for these but supplies certain ones by default.

This is not the place for a debate on why they have made those choices. Feel free to join the Debian mailing lists if you want to enter that debate. If selected, the installer helps you configure the mail server as shown in figure. It does a good job of helping you setup the basics with well laid out options.

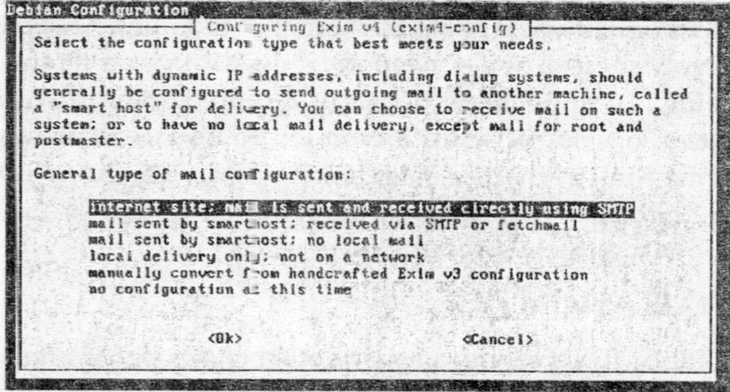

There's no GUI so configuration is with a console based text editor. Debian packages have config files under /etc in fairly obviously named files. What I don't have room for here is detailed instructions for the exact setup for each package, so I'll just layout the options I used for each package where it usually differs from the default installation.

Samba, installed as part of the file server collection, essentially mimics a Windows server with regard to providing shared directories and printers. The Windows clients (and generally their users) remain largely oblivious to the fact that the shared directories are not on a Windows server. Each user's home directory and any CUPS printers are shared by default. In addition to these, I usually add a [public] share (mapped to /home/public) which is browse-able and has no user restrictions. You can setup default and specific permission masks for shares.

Apache is setup with a single site. The ADSL router/ firewall is set to block inbound access to port 80 thus only the clients can access the web server. If you want a public facing website you might be better to host it across something more stable than a domestic ADSL line.

Maintenance

Keeping your server up-to-date is vital if you are to keep on top of security issues and package bugs. Debian provides a simple method for this via apt. It will update installed packages, and the operating system itself, on-the-fly and need a reboot only if you update the kernel or modules. This means that you should never need to reinstall your system and updating an application does not require server downtime. You can, of course, setup a cron job to update your system overnight but perhaps a safer strategy is to use the -d option for apt which will download the required updates ready for you to install them at your convenience.

INSTALLATION

The SME Server installer is another curses-based affair and walks you very easily through each step. Rebooting, as requested, then leads you to package installation and server setup. By the end you are left with a working server ready for you to setup the details, like users and shares. The whole process took around half an hour. Figure shows one of the later options where you choose whether your server is a server only or a gateway as well and whether to enable the firewall.

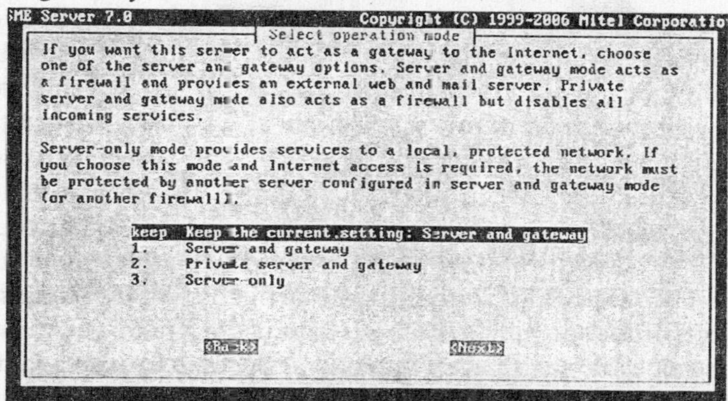

Fig. The SME Server Installer.

Security

SSH access is available within SME Server although enabling remote access to the administration console also enables root logins. This particular hole can be closed but not through administration console so unless you are handy with the command line I would suggest you leave admin logins disabled. If you do make the required changes, then be prepared to keep a note/backup of them because when you upgrade they could well be overwritten.

BACKUPS

For any machine a backup is vital. This is more so for a server where the data is not only more extensive but has more stakeholders in it. Most insurance and business continuity plans require backups be removed from the premises. On-line backup solutions exist which meet this but for a small server like this I would suggest it's more cost-effective to use removable media such as tape or optical discs.

SME Server provides backup facilities to both tape (using flexbackup) and to a desktop client. There is a 2GB maximum limit on backup to desktop and if you are backing up to tape make sure you are using one of the supported tape drives. Flexbackup is also a Debian package so you can install it on the DIY server if you want. There are other solutions, like Amanda. SMEServer does not support optical devices so instead of using the built-in backup solution be prepared to write your own. Personally, I have a set of scripts using tar which I recycle from server to server.

CABLE

NETWORK CABLE

Cable is the medium through which information usually moves from one network device to another. There are several types of cable which are commonly used with LANs. In some cases, a network will utilize only one type of cable, other networks will use a variety of cable types. The type of cable chosen for a network is related to the network's topology, protocol, and size. Understanding the characteristics of different types of cable and how they relate to other aspects of a network is necessary for the development of a successful network.

Network cable is used to connect and transfer data between computers and a network. There are different types of network cable, and the appropriate type to use will depend on the structure and topology of your network. The most commonly used types of network cable are the twisted pair, coaxial, Ethernet cross over, and fiber optic.

The unshielded twisted pair (UTP) cable is used in many Ethernet networks. It has four pairs of wires that are housed inside of the lining of the cable. Each pair is twisted into several additional twists to prevent interference from other devices on the network. The structure of this type of cable increases its reliability and helps minimize network failures.

Coaxial cable, or coax, is another common type of network cable. It has a copper conductor in its centre and a plastic coating serves as an insulator between the centre conductor and a metal shield. The cable is then covered with a coating. The coating may be think or thick - the thicker coating which less pliable provides extra protection. Ethernet crossover cable is used to connect a computer network made up of two or more computers. This type of network cable eliminates the need for network switches or routers. The cable also allows the computers to be connected using their network adaptors, such as the network interface card (NIC).

Fiber optic network cables are used for networks that span large distances. As a result, this type of cabling has several layers of protective coating. It also transmits light as opposed to electrical signals like other cables. This makes it an ideal cable for network environments that are exposed to large amounts of electrical interference. It also transmits information at high speeds and is therefore used in large network environments like those used by big businesses.

As wireless networks become more and more popular, network cable is becoming less necessary. Still, many systems, especially large scale systems, continue to rely on network cables.

UNSHIELDED TWISTED PAIR (UTP) CABLE

Twisted pair cabling comes in two varieties: shielded and unshielded. Unshielded twisted pair (UTP) is the most popular and is generally the best option for school networks.

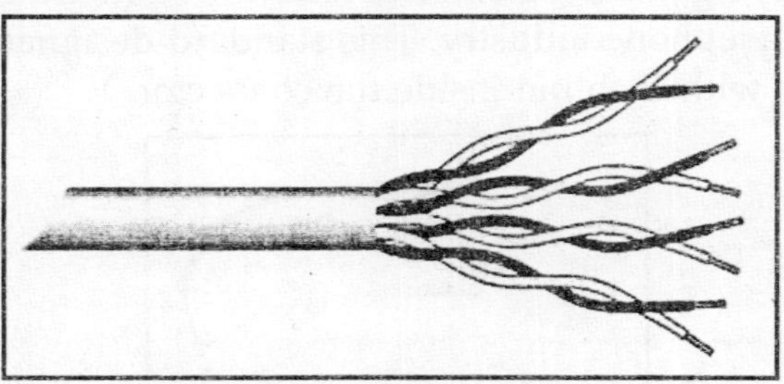

Fig. Unshielded Twisted Pair.

The quality of UTP may vary from telephone-grade wire to extremely high-speed cable. The cable has four pairs of wires inside the jacket. Each pair is twisted with a different number of twists per inch to help eliminate interference from adjacent pairs and other electrical devices. The tighter the twisting, the higher the supported transmission rate and the greater the cost per foot. The EIA/TIA has established standards of UTP and rated six categories of wire.

Table. Categories of Unsthielded Twisted Pair.

Category	Speed	Use
1	1 Mbps	Voice Only (Telephone Wire)
2	4 Mbps (Rarely used)	LocalTalk & Telephone
3	16 Mbps	10BaseT Ethernet
4	20 Mbps	Token Ring (Rarely used)
5	100 Mbps (2 pair)	100BaseT Ethernet
	1000 Mbps (4 pair)	Gigabit Ethernet
5e	1,000 Mbps	Gigabit Ethernet
6	10,000 Mbps	Gigabit Ethernet

Unshielded Twisted Pair Connector

The standard connector for unshielded twisted pair cabling is an RJ-45 connector. This is a plastic connector that looks like a large telephone-style connector. A slot allows the RJ-45 to be inserted only one way. RJ stands for Registered Jack, implying that the connector follows a standard borrowed from the telephone industry. This standard designates which wire goes with each pin inside the connector.

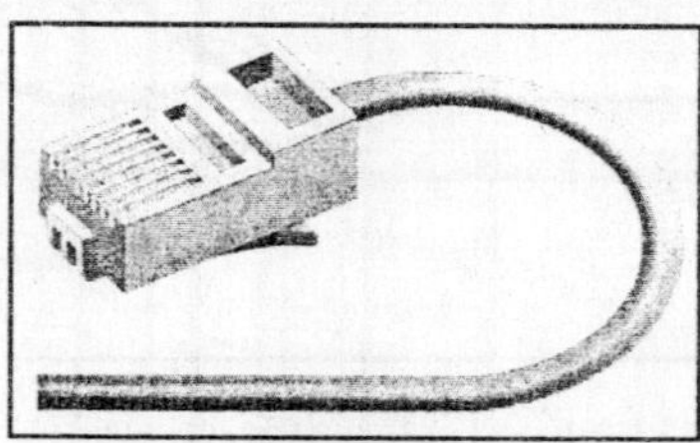

Fig. RJ-45 Connector.

SHIELDED TWISTED PAIR (STP) CABLE

Although UTP cable is the least expensive cable, it may be susceptible to radio and electrical frequency interference (it should not be too close to electric motors, fluorescent lights, etc.). If you must place cable in environments with lots of potential interference, or if you must place cable in extremely sensitive environments that may be susceptible to the electrical current in the UTP, shielded twisted pair may be the solution. Shielded cables can also help to extend the maximum distance of the cables.

Shielded twisted pair cable is available in three different configurations:

- Each pair of wires is individually shielded with foil.
- There is a foil or braid shield inside the jacket covering all wires (as a group).
- There is a shield around each individual pair, as well as around the entire group of wires (referred to as double shield twisted pair).

COAXIAL CABLE

Coaxial cabling has a single copper conductor at its centre. A plastic layer provides insulation between the centre conductor and a braided metal shield. The metal shield helps to block any outside interference from

Fig. Coaxial Cable.

Although coaxial cabling is difficult to install, it is highly resistant to signal interference. In addition, it can support greater cable lengths between network devices than twisted pair cable. The two types of coaxial

Thin coaxial cable is also referred to as thinnet. 10Base2 refers to the specifications for thin coaxial cable carrying Ethernet signals. The 2 refers to the approximate maximum segment length being 200 meters.

In actual fact the maximum segment length is 185 meters. Thin coaxial cable has been popular. Thick coaxial cable is also referred to as thicknet. 10Base5 refers to the specifications for thick coaxial cable carrying Ethernet signals. Thick coaxial cable has an extra protective plastic cover that helps keep moisture away from the centre conductor.

This makes thick coaxial a great choice when running longer lengths in a linear bus network. One disadvantage of thick coaxial is that it does

Coaxial Cable Connectors

The most common type of connector used with coaxial cables is the Bayone-Neill-Concelman (BNC) connector. Different types of adapters are available for BNC connectors, including a T-connector, barrel connector, and terminator. Connectors on the cable are the weakest points in any network. To help avoid problems with your network, always use the BNC connectors that crimp, rather

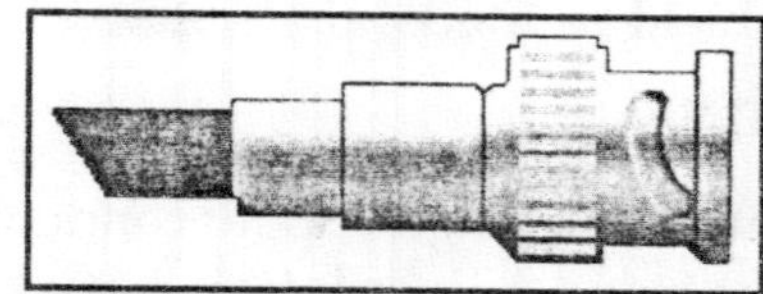

FIBER OPTIC CABLE

Fiber optic cabling consists of a centre glass core surrounded by several layers of protective materials. It transmits light rather than electronic signals eliminating the problem of electrical interference.

This makes it ideal for certain environments that contain a large amount of electrical interference. It has also made it the standard for connecting networks between Fiber optic cabie has the ability to transmit signals over much longer distances than coaxial and twisted pair.

It also has the capability to carry information at vastly greater speeds. This capacity broadens communication possibilities to include services such as video conferencing and interactive services.

The centre core of fiber cables is made from glass or plastic fibers. A plastic coating then cushions the fiber centre, and kevlar fibers help to strengthen the cables and prevent breakage. The outer insulating jacket made of teflon or PVC.

Fig. Fiber Optic Cable

There are two common types of fiber cables -- single mode and multimode. Multimode cable has a larger diameter; however, both cables provide high bandwidth at high speeds. Single mode can provide more distance, but it is more expensive.

Table. Ethernet Cable Summary

Specification	Cable Type
10BaseT	Unshielded Twisted Pair
10Base2	Thin Coaxial
10Base5	Thick Coaxial
100BaseT	Unshielded Twisted Pair
100BaseFX	Fiber Optic
100BaseBX	Single mode Fiber
100BaseSX	Multimode Fiber
1000BaseT	Unshielded Twisted Pair
1000BaseFX	Fiber Optic
1000BaseBX	Single mode Fiber
1000BaseSX	Multimode Fiber

INSTALLING CABLE - SOME GUIDELINES

When running cable, it is best to follow a few simple rules:

- Always use more cable than you need. Leave plenty of slack.
- Test every part of a network as you install it. Even if it is brand new, it may have problems that will be difficult to isolate later.
- Stay at least 3 feet away from fluorescent light boxes and other sources of electrical interference.
- If it is necessary to run cable across the floor, cover the cable with cable protectors.
- Label both ends of each cable.

- Use cable ties (not tape) to keep cables in the same location together.

WIRELESS LANS

More and more networks are operating without cables, in the wireless mode. Wireless LANs use high frequency radio signals, infrared light beams, or lasers to communicate between the workstations and the file server or hubs. Each workstation and file server on a wireless network has some sort of transceiver/antenna to send and receive the data. Information is relayed between transceivers as if they were physically connected. For longer distance, wireless communications can also take place through cellular telephone technology, microwave transmission, or by satellite.

Wireless networks are great for allowing laptop computers or remote computers to connect to the LAN. Wireless networks are also beneficial in older buildings where it may be difficult or impossible to install cables. The two most common types of infrared communications used in schools are line-of-sight and scattered broadcast. Line-of-sight communication means that there must be an unblocked direct line between the workstation and the transceiver. If a person walks within the line-of-sight while there is a transmission, the information would need to be sent again.

This kind of obstruction can slow down the wireless network. Scattered infrared communication is a broadcast of infrared transmissions sent out in multiple directions that bounces off walls and ceilings until it eventually hits the receiver. Networking communications with laser are virtually the same as line-of-sight infrared networks.

Wireless Standards and Speeds

The Wi-Fi Alliance is a global, non-profit organization that helps to ensure standards and interoperability for wireless networks, and wireless networks are often referred to as WiFi (Wireless Fidelity). The original Wi-Fi standard wss adopted in 1997. Since then many variations have emerged (and will continue to emerge). Wi-Fi networks use the Ethernet protocol.

Standard	Max Speed	Typical Range
802.11a	54 Mbps	150 feet
802.11b	11 Mbps	300 feet
802.11g	54 Mbps	300 feet

Advantages of Wireless Networks

- *Mobility*: With a laptop computer or mobile device, access can be available throughout a school, at the mall, on an airplane, etc. More an more businesses are also offering free WiFi access.
- *Fast setup*: If your computer has a wireless adapter, locating a wireless network can be as simple as clicking "Connect to a Network" -- in some cases, you will connect automatically to networks within range.
- *Cost*: Setting up a wireless network can be much more cost effective than buying and installing cables.
- *Expandability*: Adding new computers to a wireless network is as easy as turning the computer on (as long as you do not exceed the maximum number of devices).

Disadvantages of Wireless Networks

- *Security*: Wireless networks are much more susceptible to unauthorized use. If you set up a wireless network, be sure to include maximum security. You should always enable WEP (Wired Equivalent Privacy) or WPA (Wi-Fi Protected Access), which will improve security and help to prevent virtual intruders and freeloaders.
- *Interference*: Because wireless networks use radio signals and similar techniques for transmission, they are susceptible to interference from lights and electronic devices.

- *Inconsistent connections*: How many times have you hears "Wait a minute, I just lost my connection?" Because of the interference caused by electrical devices and/or items blocking the path of transmission, wireless connections are not nearly as stable as those through a dedicated cable.
- *Power consumption:* The wireless transmitter in a laptop requires a significant amount of power; therefore, the battery life of laptops can be adversely impacted. If you are planning a laptop project in your classroom, be sure to have power plugs and/or additional batteries available.
- *Speed*: The transmission speed of wireless networks is improving; however, faster options (such as gigabit Ethernet) are available via cables. In addition, if set up a wireless network at home, and you are connecting to the Internet via a DSL modem (at perhaps 3 Mbps), your wireless access to the Internet will have a maximum of 3 Mbps connection speed.

TYPES OF ETHERNET

Understand the different types of Ethernet frames that can be sent. The Ethernet frame that your server receives and the Ethernet standard that you select in the line description govern the type of frame that your server sends. As noted in the table below, your server will not send a frame in some cases. In the line description, you select the standard through the Ethernet standard (ETHSTD) field. In an SNA environment, if you have the option to use Ethernet standard IEEE 802.3 or Ethernet version 2, use *ALL.

The following table shows what Ethernet frame your server sends according to the frame type the server receives and the value of the ETHSTD field.

Frame Type Received	ETHSTD Value	Frame Type Sent
IEEE 802.3 with SNA or non-SNA data	IEEE80231	IEEE 802.3
	ETHV22	No frame sent
	ALL3	IEEE 802.3

Ethernet version 2 with non-SNA data	IEEE8023	No frame
	ETHV2	Ethernet version 2
	ALL	Ethernet version 2
Ethernet version 2 with SNA data	IEEE8023	IEEE 802.3
	ETHV2	Ethernet version 2, encapsulated SNA4
	ALL	IEEE 802.3

Notes:

- The network uses Ethernet standard IEEE 802.3.
- The network uses Ethernet version 2. In an SNA environment, you use this protocol for only iSeries™-to-iSeries communications.
- The network uses both Ethernet standards (IEEE 802.3 and Ethernet version 2). All TCP/IP multicast packets are sent as 802.3 and Ethernet version 2 frames.
- The type field of the Ethernet version 2 frame to indicate the information field contains the SNA data.
- 10Base5 - Uses Thicknet coaxial cable which requires a transceiver with a vampire tap to connect each computer. There is a drop cable from the transceiver to the Attachment Unit Interface (AIU). The AIU may be a DIX port on the network card. There is a transceiver for each network card on the network. This type of ethernet is subject to the 5-4-3 rule meaning there can be 5 network segments with 4 repeaters, and three of the segments can be connected to computers. It uses bus topology. Maximum segment length is 500 Meters with the maximum overall length at 2500 meters. Minimum length between nodes is 2.5 meters. Maximum nodes per segment is 100.
- *10Base2:* Uses Thinnet coaxial cable. Uses a BNC connector and bus topology requiring a terminator at each end of the cable. The cable used is RG-58A/U or RG-58C/U with an impedance of 50 ohms. RG-58U is not acceptable. Uses the 5-4-3 rule meaning

there can be 5 network segments with 4 repeaters, and three of the segments can be connected to computers.

- *10BaseT*: Uses Unshielded twisted pair (UTP) cable. Uses star topology. Shielded twisted pair (STP) is not part of the 10BaseT specification. Not subject to the 5-4-3 rule. They can use category 3, 4, or 5 cable, but perform best with category 5 cable. Category 3 is the minimum. Require only 2 pairs of wire. Cables in ceilings and walls must be plenum rated. Maximum segment length is 100 meters. Minimum length between nodes is 2.5 meters. Maximum number of connected segments is 1024. Maximum number of nodes per segment is 1 (star topology). Uses RJ-45 connectors.
- *10BaseF*: Uses Fiber Optic cable. Can have up to 1024 network nodes. Maximum segment length is 2000 meters. Uses specialized connectors for fiber optic. Includes three categories.
  - *10BaseFL:* Used to link computers in a LAN environment, which is not commonly done due to high cost.
  - *10BaseFP:* Used to link computers with passive hubs to get cable distances up to 500 meters.
  - *10BaseFB:* Used as a backbone between hubs.
- *100BaseT*: Also known as fast ethernet. Uses RJ-45 connectors. Topology is star. Uses CSMA/CD media access. Minimum length between nodes is 2.5 meters. Maximum number of connected segments is 1024. Maximum number of nodes per segment is 1 (star topology). IEEE802.3 specification.
  - *100BaseTX*: Requires category 5 two pair cable. Maximum distance is 100 meters.
  - *100BaseT4*: Requires category 3 cable with 4 pair. Maximum distance is 100 meters.
  - *100BaseFX*: Can use fiber optic to transmit up to 2000 meters. Requires two strands of fiber optic cable.

100VG-AnyLAN - Requires category 3 cable with 4 pair. Maximum distance is 100 meters with cat 3 or 4 cable. Can reach 150 meters with cat 5 cable. Can use fiber optic to transmit up to 2000 meters. This ethernet type supports transmission of Token-Ring network packets in addition to ethernet packets. IEEE 802.12 specification. Uses demand-priority media access control. The topology is star. It uses a series of interlinked cascading hubs. Uses RJ-45 connectors.

The IEEE naming convention is as follows:

- The transmission speed in Mbps
- Baseband (base) or Broadband data transmission
- The maximum distance a network segment could cover in hundreds of meters.

Table. Comparisons of Some Ethernet Types. Distances are in Meters.

Ethernet Type	Cable	Min length between nodes	Max Segment length	Max overall length
10Base2	Thinnet	0.5	185	925
10Base5	Thicknet	2.5	500	2500
10BaseF	Fiber		2000	
10BaseT	UTP	2.5	100	

TYPES OF ETHERNET FRAMES

- *Ethernet 802.2*: These frames contain fields similar to the ethernet 802.3 frames with the addition of three Logical Link Control (LLC) fields. Novell NetWare 4.x networks use it.
- *Ethernet 802.3*: It is mainly used in Novell NetWare 2.x and 3.x networks. The frame type was developed prior to completion of the IEEE 802.3 specification and may not work in all ethernet environments.
- *Ethernet II:* This frame type combines the 802.3 preamble and SFD fields and include a protocol type field where the 802.3 frame contained a length field. TCP/IP networks and networks that use multiple protocols normally use this type of frames.
- *Ethernet SNAP:* This frame type builds on the 802.2

frame type by adding a type field indicating what network protocol is being used to send data. This frame type is mainly used in AppleTalk networks. The packet size of all the above frame types is between 64 and 1,518 bytes.

ETHERNET MESSAGE FORMATS

The ethernet data format is defined by RFC 894 and 1042. The addresses specified in the ethernet protocol are 48 bit addresses.

Ethernet Data

Destination Address	Source address	Type	Application, Transport,and Network Data	CRC
6bytes	6 bytes	2 bytes	46 to 1500 bytes	4bytes

The types of data passed in the type field are as follows:

- 0800 IP Datagram
- 0806 ARP request/reply
- 8035 RARP request/reply

There is a maximum size of each data packet for the ethernet protocol. This size is called the maximum transmission unit (MTU).

What this means is that sometimes packets may be broken up as they are passed through networks with MTUs of various sizes. SLIP and PPP protocols will normally have a smaller MTU value than ethernet.

This document does not describe serial line interface protocol (SLIP) or point to point protocol (PPP) encapsulation.

TYPES OF ETHERNET CABLES

Even though Ethernet cables all look similar; subtle differences in the construction of the cabling make a difference in how well it will perform.

Ethernet cables use a set of four twisted pair cables and a pair of RJ-45 connectors. The difference between the many types of Ethernet cables is the type of wire used, how it is bundled and the way it is terminated with a connector.

Cat 3 Cable

- Category 3 Cable, or Cat 3, is an older iteration of Ethernet cables that is limited to 10 Mbps (megabits per second). Cat 3 cables are not widely used outside of VOIP (Voice-Over Internet Protocol) and other voice solutions. Cat 3 cables have an issue with cross-talk and interference and were quickly replaced with high quality cables as a standard.

Cat 5 Cable

- Cat 5 was the widely used successor to Cat 3 cable. Cat 5 allows for 10/100 Mbps. Ethernet connections. The way the cable was wrapped changed from Cat 3 to Cat 5 to not allow as many twists per foot. This reduced the amount of interference.

Cat 5e Cable

- Cat 5e is an enhanced version of Cat 5 cabling. Cat 5e will allow for 10/100/1,000 Mbps. Ethernet connections. Gigabit Ethernet (1,000 Mbps.) is widely used in both homes and business applications. Due to its lower price point versus higher end cables, Cat 5e is the most common type of cable sold in stores. Most prebuilt cables will be of Cat 5e design.

Cat 6 Cable

- Cat 6 cable is very similar to Cat 5e; however, it is not as popular. Unless the network is running at close to full speed, a Cat 6 cable will not show much benefit over a Cat 5e cable. Cat 6 cables have thicker wires than Cat 5e, but are made the same way.

Crossover Cables

- Most Ethernet cables you will find are standard, straight-through cables. Each end of the cable will be identical to each other. Crossover cables look almost identical to standard Ethernet cables; however, the order of the wires inside are switched.

The cables are used to bypass a network hub or router and connect one device directly to another. Crossover cables cannot be used in place of standard Ethernet cables.

Normal Ethernet Cables

A normal Ethernet cable is a straight-through cable, where the smaller cables inside the Ethernet cable on both ends will be in the same order of colors, from left to right. There are two standards in which the colors of the cables are arranged, they are; T-568A and T-568B. The variation in their colour order is not an indication of their performance, but just their standard. This type of cable is used to connect the computer to a hub or router to a switch.

Ethernet Cable Categories (Cat)

Cat 3: This category was widely used as a voice cabling format among computer network administrators in the 1990s. It is an unshielded twisted pair (UTP), that can carry up to to 10 Mbit/s with a bandwidth performance of 16 MHz.

Cat 4: Cat 4 was mainly used in token ring networks and the cable consists of four unshielded twisted-pair (UTP) wires, with a data rate of 16 Mbit/s, and performance of up to 20 MHz.

Cat 7: This cable type is a standard for Ethernet and other interconnect technologies, that are backward compatible with traditional Cat 5 and Cat 6 Ethernet cables. As it has more strict specifications for crosstalk and system noise than Cat 6 and Cat 5e, its cables and the wires within are completely shielded. the cable contains four twisted copper wire pairs and supports up to 600Mhz.

Ethernet Crossover Cable

An Ethernet crossover cable is a type of Ethernet cable, that is used to connect computing devices together, without the use of a hub or switch. These cables have different pin points or plugs on each side. The wires within the Ethernet crossover cable can reverse the transmit and receive signals. Starting from the left, the 1st and 3rd wires and the 2nd and

6th wires are crossed, and can be seen through the RJ-45 connectors at each end of the crossover cable.

Ethernet cable types should be determined by your requirement, as there are many types and categories easily available all across the country. Ethernet cables are faster and take less processing from the CPU and other computer networking devices, which can save a lot of time during the transmission of data.

BROADBAND AND BASEBAND

DEFINITION

The two ways to allocate the capacity of transmission media are with baseband and broadband transmissions. Baseband devotes the entire capacity of the medium to one communication channel. Broadband enables two or more communication channels to share the bandwidth of the communications medium. Baseband is the most common mode of operation.

Most LANs function in baseband mode, for example. Baseband signaling can be accomplished with both analog and digital signals. Although you might not realise it, you have a great deal of experience with broadband transmissions. Consider, for example, that the TV cable coming into your house from an antenna or a cable provider is a broadband medium. Many television signals can share the bandwidth of the cable because each signal is modulated using a separately assigned frequency.

You can use the television tuner to choose the channel you want to watch by selecting its frequency. This technique of dividing bandwidth into frequency bands is called 'Frequency-division Multiplexing' (FDM) and works only with analog signals. Another technique, called 'Time-division Multiplexing' (TDM), supports digital signals.

Multiplexing

Multiplexing is a technique that enables broadband media to support multiple data channels. Multiplexing makes sense under a number of circumstances: When media bandwidth is costly. A high-speed leased line, such as a T1 or T3, is expensive to lease.

If the leased line has sufficient bandwidth, multiplexing can enable the same line to carry mainframe, LAN, voice, video conferencing, and various other data types. When bandwidth is idle. Many organizations have installed fiber-optic cable that is used only to partial capacity.

With the proper equipment, a single fiber can support hundreds of megabits -- or even a gigabit or more -- of data. When large amounts of data must be transmitted through low-capacity channels.

Multiplexing techniques can divide the original data stream into several lower-bandwidth channels, each of which can be transmitted through a lower-capacity medium. The signals then can be recombined at the

The copyright of the article What's Baseband & Broadband? (Band Usage) in Local Area Networks is owned by Muhammad Ahsan. Permission to republish What's Baseband & Broadband? (Band Usage) in print or online must be granted by the author in writing. Data signals can be sent over a network cable in one of two ways: broadband or baseband.

One good example of broadband signaling would be how you view different channels through your cable box and a signal coaxial cable carrying multiple signals in cable television. Whereas, baseband signaling only sends a single signal over the cable.

This type of signaling is typically used in Ethernet networks, with the exception of 10Broad3 standard (rarely used). Baseband uses very simple transceiver devices that send and receive signals on a cable.

The simplicity behind baseband signaling is that only three states need to be distinquished: one, zero and idle. Broadband transceivers are much more complex because they must be able to distinquish those same states, but on multiple channels within the same cable. Because of its simplicity, baseband signaling is used on most Ethernet networks.

OPTICAL FIBERS

Optical Fibers are thin rods of glass wrapped in a low density plastic and cabling. In modern days, it is used as an instrument in micro surgery to project images from inside the body and help surgeons see in hard to reach places. It is also used widely in communications, both in computer networks as a fast Internet connection source and in telecommunications both transcontinentally and transoceanically.

REFLECTION AND REFRACTION

The concepts of reflection and refraction are very important in the design of Optical Fibres and has a key part in how Optical fibres work. The law of reflection states that a beam of light striking a flat surface (the incidence ray) would be reflected at the same angle at the normal, the medium dividing the incidence ray and the reflective ray and is perpendicular to the surface of reflection.

That would also mean that the angle of incidence (from the incidence ray to the normal) is also equivalent to the angle of reflection (from the reflective ray to the normal).

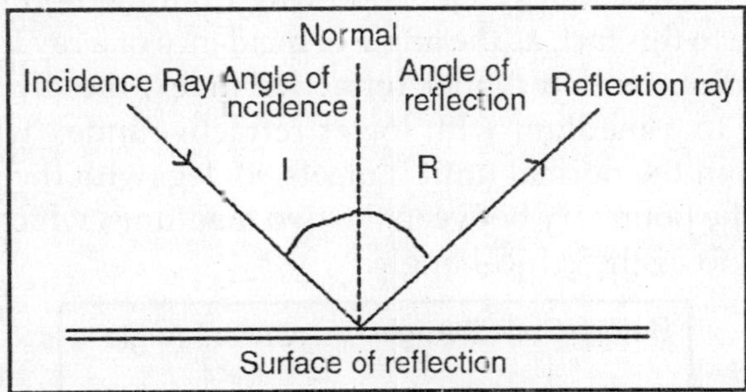

Snell's Law, named after the Dutch mathematician Willebrord van Roijen Snell, states that the product of the refractive index and the sine of the angle of incidence of a ray in one medium is equal to the product of the refractive index and the sine of the angle of refraction in a successive medium. This can be represented algebraically by $n_1 \sin\theta_i = n_2 \sin\theta_r$, where n_1, n_2 are the two values of refractive index and θ_i, θ_r are the angles of the incidence and refraction.

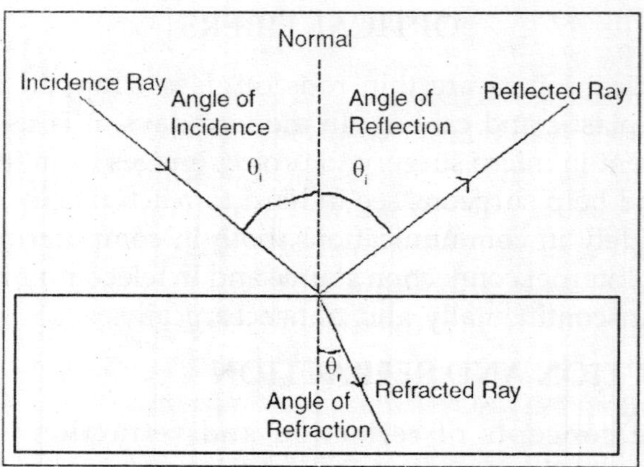

CRITICAL ANGLES

Generally, the refractive index of a denser transparent substance is higher than that of a less dense material, which would mean that light would travel slower in the substance. A general rule is that when a ray travels from a medium to another with a higher refractive index, it'll bend towards the normal. When a ray travels from a medium to another with a lower refractive index, it'll bend away from the normal.

Due to this fact, as the angle of incidence of a ray increases in a medium with a higher refractive index, the ray passing through to a medium with lower refractive index will bend away from the normal until it meets 90 deg. with the normal, and on the boundary between the two mediums, which is then referred to as the critical angle.

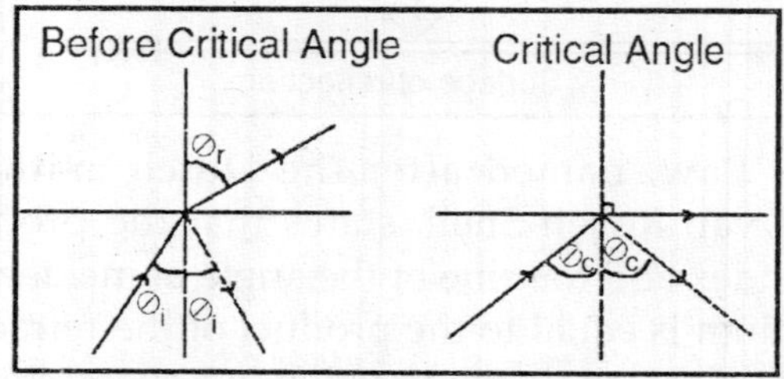

Optical Fibres relies heavily on two concepts of physics, the concepts of refraction, refractive indexes, critical angles and Total Internal Reflection. The concepts of refraction states that a ray of light travelling from a medium with a higher refractive index to a medium with a lower refractive index would bend away from the normal.

With this in mind, it also states that a critical angle would be reached when the ray of light increases to an angle that will bend it 90 deg. away from the normal.

The concept of Total Internal Reflection is apparent when the ray of light travelling from a higher refractive index medium to a lower refractive index medium has an angle so great it is able to refract the light greater than the critical angle, resulting in the ray reflecting back into the first high refractive index medium.

The main function for Optical Fibres is to send information through it by transmitting a beam of light from one end to another, trying to have as little quality loss as possible. The design of modern Optical Fibres reflect this and relies much on the physics involved.

Optical Fibres are more commonly used in surgery as a means of a tiny camera for surgeons in a patient's body and used together in their thousands in Fibre Optic communication cables for telephones and high-speed Internet connections. Each Optical Fibres has a core of thin glass, which is wrapped then by a cladding (usually a plastic with a lower refractive index than glass) and is then finally all wrapped in a harder plastic buffer to prevent damage.

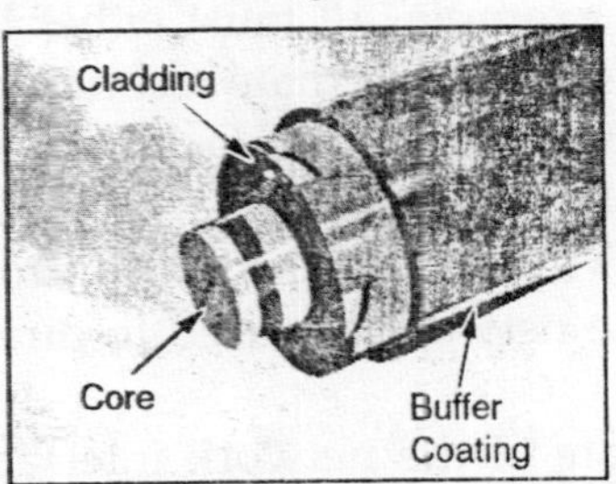

When transmitting a signal, an L.E.D. or laser is used to send a beam of light in on/off pulses (digital) down the Optical Fibre to be received on the other end. It is either transmitted straight down the Optical Fibre, resulting in longer distance travel, or it is transmitted at an angle which is calculated to be greater than critical angle of the glass to the plastic, resulting in Total Internal Reflection and the ability for the beam of light to turn corners.

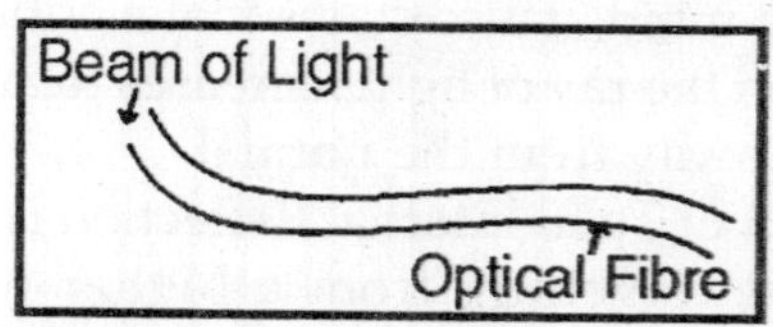

NETWORK INTERFACE CARD

DEFINITION

A network interface card, more commonly referred to as a NIC, is a device that allows computers to be joined together in a LAN, or local area network. Networked computers communicate with each other using a given protocol or agreed-upon language for transmitting data packets between the different machines, known as nodes. The network interface card acts as the liaison for the machine to both send and receive data on the LAN.

The most common language or protocol for LANs is Ethernet, sometimes referred to as IEEE 802.3. A lesser-used protocol is Token Ring. When building a LAN, a network interface card must be installed in each computer on the network and all NICs in the network must be of the same architecture. For example, all must either be Ethernet cards, Token Ring cards, or an alternate technology.

An Ethernet network interface card is installed in an available slot inside the computer. The NIC assigns a unique address called a MAC (media access control) to the machine. The MACs on the network are used to direct traffic between the computers.

The back plate of the network interface card features a port that looks similar to a phone jack, but is slightly larger. This port accommodates an Ethernet cable, which resembles a thicker version of a standard telephone line. Ethernet cable must run from each network interface card to a central hub or switch. The hub or switch acts like a relay, passing information between computers using the MAC addresses and allowing resources like printers and scanners to be shared along with data. A network interface card does not have to be hard wired with physical cable.

Wireless Ethernet cards are installed like their wired counterparts, but rather than a port for an Ethernet cable, the card features a small antenna. The card communi-cates with the central wireless switch or hub via radio waves. Wireless LANs may have some restrictions depending on the material the building is made from. For example, lead in walls can block signals between the network interface card and hub or switch.

When buying components for a LAN, make sure the NICs and hub or switch have the same capabilities. The entire network must be either wired or wireless, so a wireless network interface card cannot talk to a wired switch or hub. In addition, newer versions of hardware will likely support more features and/or greater speeds than older versions. Make sure your central switch or hub can utilize the highest capabilities of the network interface card under consideration.

For those who wish to connect LANs located in different areas of the city, state or country, ATM (asynchronous transfer mode) can create wide area networks or WANs by connecting LANs together. LANs are still built with a network interface card in each networked computer, but ATM uses broadband Internet access to link the LANs to online ATM switches. This type of ATM WAN is referred to as an Internetwork.

ETHERNET SOURCE ADDRESS

Each network interface card is assigned an Ethernet source address by the manufacturer of the network interface card (this is normally stored in a PROM on the network interface card). The addresses are globally unique, and are assigned in blocks of 16 (or 8) million address to the Ethernet interface manufacturers, according to a flat addressing structure. This ensures that no two Ethernet network interface will ever have the same source address.

Chapter 3

Network Accessories

LAN / WAN / MAN

VeriCenter's network services span the gamut, from providing just the physical link to offering full network management. Depending on your requirements and the level of responsibility you want to offload, we can customise a solution for your specific needs.

NETWORK MONITORING

To keep your network at peak availability and performance - and to proactively manage potential issues - you need real-time knowledge, visibility, and control of your IT environment. VeriCenter offers a flexible suite of services that allows you to monitor your IT infrastructure, including routers, switches, and servers.

Our network monitoring services range from simple up/ down status to customized threshold monitoring (such as server CPU and disk utilization) to I/O queue length. VeriCenter provides monitoring and real-time detection of both exception and normal operating conditions for monitored elements. We notify you if pre-defined thresholds are exceeded, allowing you to proactively address potential problems before your customers call you.

Network monitoring is provided through a secure connection to your environment, and reporting information is accessed via our Web-based Customer Portal. This portal not only offers a snapshot of your current system state, but also provides trending analysis to help you manage your environment. VeriCenter's network management services provide comprehensive turnkey support for your local and wide area networks (LANs and WANs). This service is backed by a highly trained team of technicians and engineers with proven expertise in network management and maintenance.

VeriCenter remotely manages your network infrastructure, including routers, hubs, and switches, for the highest reliability and optimized performance. When a problem is detected and isolated, VeriCenter takes the steps necessary to coordinate with hardware vendors and carrier partners for problem resolution. At all times, you're able to access critical information about your network through our secure Web-based Customer Portal. Our services are designed to provide you with complete management of critical network devices within your environment, using the tools and expertise of our Network Operations Centre (NOC).

Every productive data network is made up of two intergral parts - infrastructure (communications environment) and active elements, which utilise the communications environment. The infrastructure can be made up of a structured cabling system based on melicke or optical lines, wireless transfer system etc. The quality and performance of the infrastructure directly affects the resulting attributes and output of the data network.

With the rapid development of Internet applications and technology, more and more emphasis is being put on securing access to data networks and on protection of the actual data with systems against misuse or attack. There is an evident trend of integrating various security functions into basic network elements, such as switches, routers etc.

The convergence trend for data and telephony into one communications infrastructure has brought the need to secure the necessary quality of service (QoS) for operations sensitive to the quality of the data network (IP telephony, video-conferencing). A modern data network is capable of working with several classes of operations and each of these classes is capable of securing the necessary quality of service. Since it was established, GiTy has been oriented to the most up-to-date technologies, which guarantee the maximum possible output for data networks and their long technological lifetime. Key components of data networks developed by us are products from the foremost technological manufacturers, such as Siemon, Cisco Systems, Enterasys Network, 3COM, Allied Telesyn and Crossbeam.

Data networks developed by us provide users with high performance, the maximum level of security and the tools needed for management of the quality of services for individual applications.

WAN/MAN CONNECTIVITY

Once you move your hosted environment to VeriCenter's Tier 1 data centre, how do you access it? Through one of our network solutions. Whether you want secure access for administrative purposes only or gigabit metro area network (MAN) connections to extend the LAN from your site to VeriCenter's, we can accommodate your needs. We can also custom-design a solution to meet specific security or redundancy concerns. VeriCenter's standard offerings include private network access, with speeds from DS1 to DS3. In addition, through our partners, we can offer private Ethernet connections ranging from 10 Mbps to 1,000 Mbps.

LAN

Definition: A local area network (LAN) supplies networking capability to a group of computers in close proximity to each other such as in an office building, a school, or a home. A LAN is useful for sharing resources like files, printers, games or other applications. A LAN in turn often connects to other LANs, and to the Internet or other WAN.

Most local area networks are built with relatively inexpensive hardware such as Ethernetcables, network adapters, and hubs. Wireless LAN and other more advanced LAN hardware options also exist.

Specialized operating system software may be used to configure a local area network. For example, most flavors of Microsoft Windows provide a software package called Internet

Connection Sharing (ICS) that supports controlled access to LAN resources. The term LAN party refers to a multiplayer gaming event where participants bring their own computers and build a temporary LAN.

WAN

Definition: A WAN spans a large geographic area, such as a state, province or country. WANs often connect multiple smaller networks such as local area networks (LANs) or metro area networks (MANs). The world's most popular WAN is the Internet. Some segments of the Internet, like VPN-based extranets, are also WANs in themselves.

Finally, many WANs are corporate or research networks that utilize leased lines. WANs generally utilize different and much more expensive networking equipment than do LANs. Key technologies often found in WANs include SONET, Frame Relay, and ATM.

HUB

DEFINITION

One of the most commonly used networking hardware devices are hubs. However, the inexpensive switch is rapidly replacing the hub. Anyway, hubs serve as central connection points for local area networks (LANs) that typically embrace the star topology. The basic hub contains no active electronics and cannot be used to extend a LAN past its cabling distance specifications. Yet, hubs organize your cables and relay data signals to all computers that exist on your LAN.

Hubs are used on networks where twisted-pair cabling is used. The ports, which are available on the hub, provide connection points for the devices on the network. Computers and devices are connected to the hub via network cables to individual ports.

In cases where a LAN outgrows the size of its hub, a new hub can be attached by daisy-chaining them together using a short connection cable, which is often referred to as a rattail. The FS100 series Fast Ethernet switches brings the 100 Mbps switching technology and simplifies it for the small office marketplace. These products provide a cost effective way to instantaneously boost network performance while preserving your network infrastructure, including installed cabling and desktop software and hardware. Since each port is auto-speed-sensing, installation is plug and play and each connection can easily be upgraded from 10 to 100 Mbps. Manufacturer Part No. FS108NA. SKU# 070423.

Features: 5 or 8 switched 10/100 Mbps ports Each port provides dedicated 10 or 100 Mbps bandwidth for connecting one or multiple PCs, servers, and hubs. In full-duplex mode, each port supports up to 200 Mbps of throughput. Automatic speed and full/half-duplex sensing The switch supports n-way auto negotiation, and each port automatically senses and operates at the proper speed and duplex mode, taking the burden of configuration off the user.

Vistajacks with built-in LEDs clearly indicate port status, simplifying installation and troubleshooting. The switch is plug and play with no software to configure. Versatile and compatible The switch is protocol independent and is compatible with all popular networks such as the Internet or TCP/IP, NetWare, Microsoft Windows, or LANTASTIC

BRIDGE

DEFINITION

The bridges used in computer networking are not like your typical bridge. This type of bridge is a internetworking device used to help conserve the bandwidth on the network. When LANs are really starting to grow, network data traffic begins to become a little overwhelming to the available bandwidth on the network media.

One way of conserving this network traffic is to slice the network up into smaller segments. These segments are connected to a bridge. Bridges are smarter than hubs and repeaters. They also use software to help get the job done. Bridges are able to read MAC addresses, which are also known as hardware addresses that are burned onto the NIC inside every computer on the network, of each data packet the is circulated on the network segments connected on the bridge. It is by learning which MAC addresses are live on the network that the bridge is able to control traffic that is local to a particular segment and keep it from spreading to other network segments that are being serviced by another bridge.

A bridge device filters data traffic at a network boundary. Bridges reduce the amount of traffic on a LAN by dividing it into two segments. Bridges operate at the data link layer (Layer 2) of the OSI model. Bridges inspect incoming traffic and decide whether to forward or discard it. An Ethernet bridge, for example, inspects each incoming Ethernet frame - including the source and destination MAC addresses, and sometimes the frame size - in making individual forwarding decisions.

Bridges serve a similar function as switches, that also operate at Layer 2. Traditional bridges, though, support one network boundary, whereas switches usually offer four or more hardware ports. Switches are sometimes called "multi-port bridges" for this reason.

Computer networks serve the purpose of connecting many different computers or terminals to each other, host computers, printers, file servers etc. so that expensive computing assets, programmes, files and other data may be shared among many users. A large network may typically contain one or more gateways, routers and bridges operating in conjunction with one or more network segments.

A segment is section of a network connected to a group of machines which may communicate with each other via repeater operations without having to traverse a bridge or router. Bridges and routers are useful in that they allow connections of multiple segments such that more computers may communicate with each other than would otherwise be possible given the limited bandwidth of the media.

A network bridge is a transmission device for carrying out bidirectional data transmission across a plurality of networks connected via ports. The function of the bridge is to monitor frames transferred over the LAN and to transfer them from one network to another on the basis of the physical address of the data packets. Only frames having a destination address indicating transmission to the side of the other network are able to cross the bridge. The bridge thus acts as an insulator which reduces the load in other network portions. A LAN bridge interconnects a LAN with one or more other LANs, through an interconnecting link or links, to form a larger network in which messages can be sent from a device on one LAN to one or more devices on another LAN.

Each network bridge and router requires certain other peripheral circuitry to support it such as LAN controllers, a CPU, a power supply, a network management process, memory to store bridge source and destination address tables and various other things like status registers etc. Typically, a network bridge is connected to a hub by a separate local area network segment which itself requires two port interface circuits such as LAN controllers and AUI's (generic network interfaces) with appropriate port drivers adapted for the specific media used for the bridge-hub LAN segment.

SWITCH

DEFINITION

A network switch is a small hardware device that joins multiple computers together within one local area network (LAN). Technically, network switches operate at layer two (Data Link Layer) of the OSI model.

Network switches appear nearly identical to network hubs, but a switch generally contains more intelligence (and a slightly higher price tag) than a hub. Unlike hubs, network switches are capable of inspecting data packets as they are received, determining the source and destination device of each packet, and forwarding them appropriately. By delivering messages only to the connected device intended, a network switch conservesnetwork bandwidth and offers generally better performance than a hub.

As with hubs, Ethernet implementations of network switches are the most common. Mainstream Ethernet network switches support either 10/100 Mbps Fast Ethernet or Gigabit

Ethernet (10/100/1000) standards. Different models of network switches support differing numbers of connected devices. Most consumer-grade network switches provide either four or eight connections for Ethernet devices. Switches can be connected to each other, a so-called daisy chaining method to add progressively larger number of devices to a LAN.

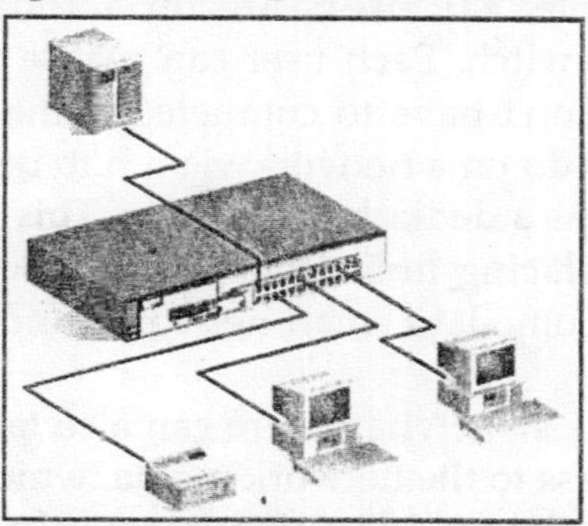

A switch is another internetworking device used to manage bandwidth on a large network. Switches are rapidly becoming one of the most used internetworking devices from connecting even smaller networks because they allow you to have some control over the use of the bandwidth on the network.

A switch, which is referred to as a "bridge on steroids" controls how data flows by using the MAC addresses that are placed on each data packet. Remember that this MAC address on the data packet is the same MAC address on the network card of that particular computer.

Switches divide networks into what is known as a Virtual LAN or VLAN. The best thing about a VLAN, which is also a logical grouping of computers on a network into what is described as some sort of communication group, is that the computers really do not have to be in close proximity or even on the same floor. This is because it allows the computers to be grouped by the similarities in the types of users in the VLAN.

Switches use a combination of software and hardware to switch packets between computers and other devices on the network. This software is the switches operating system. And, because switches offer a higher density of connection ports, they can easily replace hubs on the network. This means that each computer on the network can be connected to its own port on the switch. When the computers are directly connected to the switch, the switch can supply each of the computers with a dedicated amount of bandwidth.

For example, say users are on a 100Mbps Ethernet network via a switch. Each user can realise a bandwidth of 100Mbps and don't have to compete for the bandwidth the way computers do on a network via a hub because each port on the switch has a dedicated 100Mbps. This is why switches are rapidly replacing hubs. Inexpensive switches are even available to accomodate small networks and home network markets.

Some of the switch hardware can also take advantage of full-duplex access to the network media, which allows for the sending and receiving of data simultaneously. Essentially, this provides access to an Ethernet network that is collision free, when an Ethernet network is pretty much known to have data collisions. A computer existing on a Fast Ethernet network, typically running at 100Mbps, would see a 200Mbps throughput because sending and receiving would occur simultaneously on a full-duplex media.

Since switches are becoming very popular on both the small and large networks, they have all but replaced bridges as the internetworking devices for conserving network bandwidth and expanding LANs into larger corporate internetworks. But, they are also making hubs a device of the past for smaller networks. A network switch is a device that provides a switching function in a data communications network. Data communication in a computer network involves the exchange of data between two or more entities interconnected by communication links and subnetworks.

A network switch is an intermediate station which interconnects the communication links and subnetworks to enable transmission of data between the end stations. Switching involves transferring information, such as digital data packets or frames, among entities of the network. A switch functions as an interchange and provides path switching for data being transported over a network. Typically, a switch supports one network protocol (e.g. Ethernet), meaning that the switch manages data in a particular format. Switched local area networks use a network switch for supplying data frames between network stations or other network nodes (such as routers or gateways), where each network node is connected to the network switch by a media.

A network switch for routing packets between network buses includes a set of input switch ports for receiving packets arriving on the network buses, a set of output switch ports for forwarding packets outward on the network buses, and a switch fabric for routing packets between the input and output switch ports. Each input switch port includes a memory for storing packets arriving on a network until the switch fabric can forward them to an output switch port.

The input port may convert each packet arriving on a network bus to a sequence of cells of uniform size which can be efficiently stored in uniformly-sized buffer memory storage locations until the input port can forward them in proper sequential order through the switch fabric to one of the switch's output ports. Each output switch port may also include a memory for storing packets it receives via the switch fabric until the port can forward them outward on a network bus.

Each output switch port stores each cell sequence arriving from an input port in its own buffer memory. The output port later reassembles them into the packet from which they were derived, then forwards the packet outward on an another network bus.

ROUTER

DEFINITION

Routers are physical devices that join multiple wired or wireless networks together. Technically, a wired or wireless router is a Layer 3 gateway, meaning that the wired/wireless router connects networks (as gateways do), and that the router operates at the network layer of the OSI model.

Home networkers often use an Internet Protocol (IP) wired or wireless router, IP being the most common OSI network layer protocol. An IP router such as a DSL or cable modembroadband router joins the home's local area network (LAN) to the wide-area network (WAN) of the Internet.

By maintaining configuration information in a piece of storage called the routing table, wired or wireless routers also have the ability to filter traffic, either incoming or outgoing, based on the IP addresses of senders and receivers. Some routers allow the home networker to update the routing table from a Web browser interface. Broadband routers combine the functions of a router with those of a network switch and a firewall in a single unit.

A hardware device designed to take incoming packets, analyzing the packets and then directing them to the appropriate locations, moving the packets to another network, converting the packets to be moved across a different type of network interface, dropping the packets, or performing any other number of other types of actions. To the right is a picture of the Linksys BEFSR11 router and is similar to what most home users would use for their home network.

A router has a lot more capabilities than other network devices such as a hub or a switch that are only able to perform basic network functions. For example, a hub is often used to transfer data between computers or network devices, but does not analyse or do anything with the data it is transferring.

Routers however can analyse the data being sent over a network, change how it is packaged and send it to another network or over a different type of network. For example, routers are commonly used in home networks to share a single Internet connection with multiple computers.

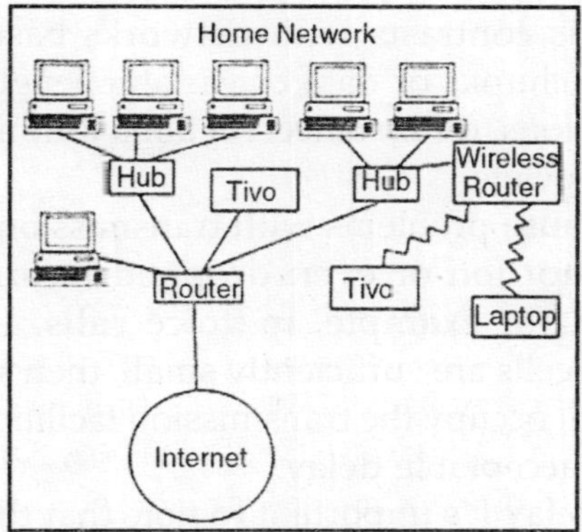

In the above example of a home network there are two different examples of a router, the router and the wireless router. As can be seen in the example the router is what allows all the computers and other network devices access the Internet. Below are some additional examples of different types of routers used in a large network.

Brouter

Short for Bridge Router, a "brouter" is a networking device that serves as both abridge and a router.

Core Router

A core router is a router in a computer network that routes data within a network but not between networks.

Edge Router

An edge Router is a router in a computer network that routes data between one or more networks.

Virtual Router

A Virtual Router is a backup router used in a VRRP setup:

- Document CH001200 for additional information about adjusting the settings on your home router.

GETAWAYS CELL RELAY

CELL RELAY

A concept in which data is sent over a network in relatively small, fixed-size packets, or cells (ATM is based on cell relay). This contrasts with networks based on frames, which may be chunks of data of variable lengths. The frame relay specifications, for instance, set a maximum frame length of about 4,000 octets.

This can cause problems with transmissions where delay ight cause distortion or even dropped information at the receiving end, for example, in voice calls. In a cell relay network, if the cells are sufficiently small, then so are the odds that one cell will occupy the transmission facilities long enough to cause an unacceptable delay.

With cell relay it's important to note that the cells may be of any size as long as all of the cells within that closed system are the same size. And the slower the transmission speed, the smaller the optimal cell size.

Using relatively short cells makes it easier to mix data, which is not sensitive to minor delays, with highly delay-sensitive voice. A statistically multiplexed interface protocol for packet switched data communications that uses fixed-length packets, i.e., cells, to transport data. Note 1: Cell relay transmission rates usually are between 56 kb/s and 1.544 Mb/s, i.e.,the data rate of a DS1 signal.

Note 2: Cell relay protocols (a) have neither flow control nor error correction capability, (b) are information-content independent, and (c) correspond only to layers one and two of the ISO Open Systems Interconnection--Reference Model. Note 3: Cell relay systems enclose variable-length user packets in fixed-length packets, i.e., cells, that add addressing and verification information.

Frame length is fixed in hardware, based on time delay and user packet-length considerations. One user data message may be segmented over many cells.

FRAME RELAY

OVERVIEW

Frame relay is a synchronous HDLC protocol based network. Data is sent in HDLC packets, referred to as "frames". The diagram below of an HDLC frame may be familiar, since without adding specific definitions of how the Address, Control and CRC is used, the diagram is applicable to IBM's SDLC, to X.25, to HDLC, to Frame Relay, as well as other protocols.

The protocol is similar to that of an X.25 network, except all circuits are permanently assigned. What is a circuit? A circuit is a link between user end points. In frame relay and X.25 networks, circuits are known as "permanent virtual circuits", or PVC's.

The circuits are known as virtual because they are not electrical ciruits where there is a direct electrical connection from end to end. Rather, there is a "logical" connection, or virtual connection, where the user data moves from end to end, but without a direct electrical circuit.

X.25 circuits can be initiated and ended from the users terminals. Frame relay circuits are set up at the time of installation and are maintained 24 hours per day, 7 days per week. Frame relay circuits are not created and ended by user at their terminals or PC's.

However, the user may have an application running over a frame relay circuit where computer to terminal sessions are initiated and ended by the user. These sessions are related to the application, not to the underlying frame relay network. Frame relay relies on the customer equipment to perform end to end error correction.

Each switch inside a frame relay network just relays the data (frame) to the next switch. X.25, in contrast, performs error correction from switch to switch. The networks of today are sufficiently error free to move the burden of error correction to the end points. Most modern protocols do error correction anyway, protocols such as SDLC, HDLC, TCP/IP, stat mux protocols, etc.

Because frame relay passes blocks of data from switch to switch without error correction, propagation from customer end to customer end through the network is very fast. Propagation time in a DCB mux test at Wiltel (LDDS Worldcom) indicated a 70 millisecond round trip delay from Tulsa, Oklahoma to New York City and back.

Network Characteristic	Frame Relay	X.25
Propagation Delay	Low	High
Error Correction	None, done by the terminal equipment at each end of the link	Node to Node
Protocol family	HDLC	HDLC
Good for interactive use?	Yes	Barely acceptable. Rather slow with one second or more round trip delay.
Good for polling protocols?	OK, sometimes, requires "spoofing"	Slow, even with spoofing
Good for LAN file transfer	Yes	Slow
Good for voice?	Good, standards developing	No
Ease of implementation	Easy	Difficult

This is equal to or less than the propagation time through 9600 bps modems over the same distance. Similar propagation times have been measured by DCB over Sprint, AT&T and MCI frame relay networks. An X.25 network would experience a delay of a least one half second, and probably a second or more for the same distance.

Topology

Topology is the map, or visual layout of the frame relay network. Frame relay network topology must be viewed from several perspectives to fully understand the network and the equipment used to construct the network. Topological views include an overview map, a logical connection map, perhaps a functional map, a map showing the detail equipment and channel links, an address map.

The map below is an overview where the frame relay switching is in the cloud in the centre. The lines going out from the cloud represent the connections from the frame relay provider (phone company) to the customer premises. These are typically lines ranging in speed from 56000 bps to T-1 (1.544 Mbps) and faster. One or more DLCI numbers is assigned to each line end point.

DLCI is discussed in more detail below. Over 900 DLCI's can be assigned, but frame relay networks rarely have that many, because a user does not need that many in most cases. There may also be limits due to constraints in the frame relay switching equipment. Also, a single network that is too large will be difficult to maintain.

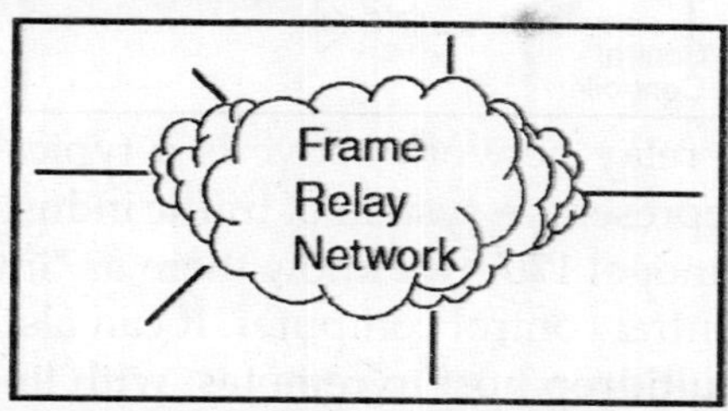

The frame relay network shown above as a cloud can also be shown as a connection of end points tied to a central site, or a number of end points that are all meshed together. End points tied to a central site is the traditional host to terminal model. The map below has 6 end points, just as in the previous map. Below, the end points are given meaning by defining one end as the host, the other 5 as the remotes.

DLCI addressing could be assigned as follows:

Location	DLCI #
Host end	16,17,18,19,20
Remote 1	16
Remote 2	16
Remote 3	16
Remote 4	16
Remote 5	16

At the frame relay switch, all remotes are mapped back to the host. At the host, Host 16 is mapped to Remote 1, Host 17 to Remote 2, Host 18 to Remote 3, Host 19 to Remote 4, and Host 20 to Remote 5. In practice, data from the host for Remote 5 arrives at the frame relay switch, from the customer equipment, with the destination address of 20. The frame relay switch, using its internal lookup table, finds that the data is for Remote 5, a physical port on the frame relay switch, that has a local address of 16. In the frame relay switch, address 20 is replaced with address 16 and the data is then delivered to Remote.

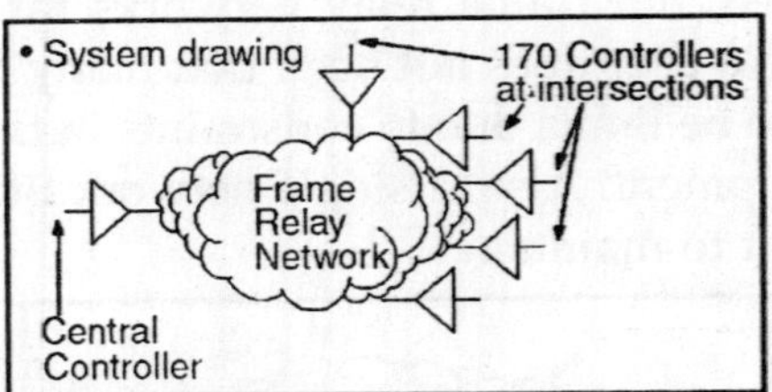

The frame relay network above is a typical installation. This drawing represents a system of traffic industry controllers known as "the model 170" (we know them as "intersection red lights" and a central control computer. It can also be shown as a traditional multidrop host to remotes, with lines bridged in the middle, as shown below:

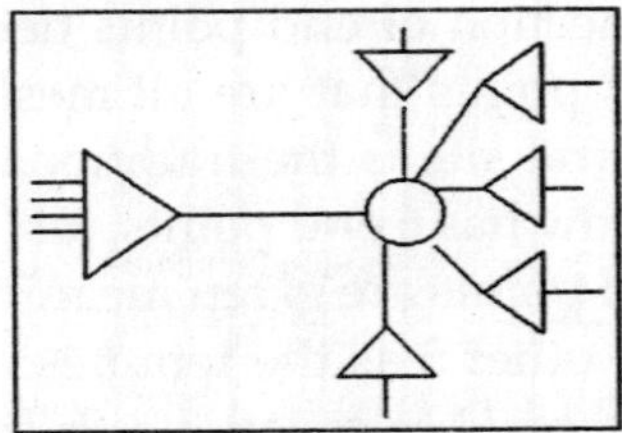

Frame relay also allows meshed networks. Since each endpoint can have one or more DLCI addresses, each user location can be connected to one other location, several locations, or all locations. If every location were connected to every other location, the network would be said to be "fully meshed". An illustration with all locations interconnected is below, next page.

Meshed Network

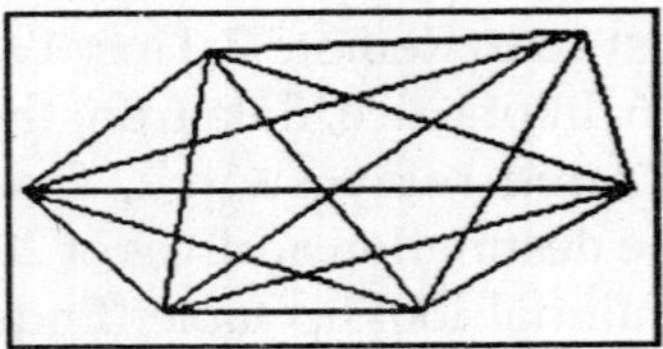

The fully meshed network mapping of DLCI's looks like this:

```
Location      DLCI #
Location 1    16,17,18,19,20
Location 2    16,17,18,19,20
Location 3    16,17,18,19,20
Location 4    16,17,18,19,20
Location 5    16,17,18,19,20
Location 6    16,17,18,19,20
```

This addressing can also be shown as a mapping table showing the addresses from the perspective of each one of the 6 locations. A frame relay switch requires this type of cross reference map.

The switch uses the map to route the frame relay packets from one internal port of the switch to another port. The following table shows the local port number and the DLCI destination mapping that would be typical for a meshed network.

FRAD

Frame Relay Assembler/Disassembler. A FRAD is a piece of networking equipment that assembles and disassembles data frames. For example, the DCB SR and SRX series of multiplexers assemble asynchronous data into frame relay frames. Hence, the SR is a FRAD for async data. Async data packaged by DCB multiplexers onto frame relay networks includes "dumb" terminal data. It includes PC data for remote control software of programmes like PC Anywhere, Reachout, Carbon Copy and CoSession.

DCB multiplexers are used to encapsulate in frame relay PPP protocol between host systems and PC's, between routers that use async PPP. There are many examples of devices that encapsulate other protocols into frame relay protocol, and hence are know as FRADs. Frads are used to encapsulate ethernet MAC layer protocol, TCP/IP protocol, IPX protocol, IBM SDLC protocol, bisync protocol, Poll/Select polling protocols. Voice is being encoded for transmission over frame relay, especially voice that has been compressed via CELP, VSELP and similar methods.

PVC

Permanent Virtual Circuits. PVC's contrast with Switched Virtual Circuits (SVC). A connection to a network that allows connection and disconnection to various points is a switched virtual circuit. Circuits that are routed through software switching devices like X.25 pads and frame relay networks are virtual. A hard wired connected in a plain old circuit, not a virtual circuit.

DLC

Data Link Connections

DLCI

Data Link Connection Identifier. This number identifies a virtual circuit. For a stat mux applications, a head end DCB SRX multiplexer might have 4 DLCI,s associated with it, while each of 4 remotes would have just a single DLCI. The example illustrates that DCLI numbers have significance at the user's end point only. Chicago has 4 addresses, 16, 17, 18 and 19.

At each remote, each location has the same number 16. The telephone company providing the frame relay service has a frame relay switch that translates the addresses. When these permanent virtual circuits are established, the relationship of the physical ports is mapped and then assigned DLCI numbers.

DCB Frame Relay Multiplexers

Vendors of frame relay services focus almost exclusively on LANs when explaining and selling frame relay. They also expect that a typical application with a single host site has a single line coming into the site, often at a high speed that is many times that of the remote locations. For example, the host may have a 256 Kbps router, and remotes (5, 10, 15 or more) at 56 Kbps each. DCB frame relay multiplexers, such as the SRX-32, have a limited number of ports. Therefore, DCB may have the customer put in several 56 or 64 Kbps lines at the host, each serving a limited number of remote sites, typically between 2 and 8 (4 to 16 ports per remote site).

Special DLCI Numbers

DLCI 0 (zero) and 1023 are reserved for management

DLCI 1 to 15 and 1008 to 1022 have been reserved for future use.

DLCI 992 to 1007 are reserved for layer 2 management of frame relay bearer service.

DLCI numbers 16 to 991 are available for subscribers for each user frame relay network

Management Protocols

Protocols for exchanging information between a user FRAD and the frame relay network equipment. The protocols are:

LMI - The original interim management protocol, uses DLCI 1023. LMI was specified by the Frame Relay Forum.

Annex D - An ANSI T1.617 management protocol standard, uses DLCI 1. Annex D was specified by the ANSI T1.617 specification.

Annex A - Nearly identical to Annex D, used in Europe.

Status Inquiry

The is an inquiry from the frame relay user to the network every x seconds. The time value can be 5 to 30 seconds. The default value is 10 seconds for LMI and for Annex D. If the user does not make this inquiry every 10 seconds, the carrier network equipment will generate an alarm. The network equipment default value is 15 seconds. That is, the user should make an inquiry every 10 seconds, and the network expects the request every 15 seconds. The 5 second difference is a buffer time that allows for a small delay.

The status inquiry returns status about the network. Sending the inquiry tells the network that the user FRAD is in service. When a status inquiry is not sent, the network will generate an alarm. An alarm may result in a "pro active" call to the customer from the service vendor. Status information is often collected by a FRAD and formatted into a MIB (management information base) for reporting via SNMP (simple network management protocol). Agents interface to the devices to collect the MIB's to deliver them to a manager.

Full Status Inquiry

This inquiry gets more information returned by network than is obtained in the Status Inquiry. Full status responses to the user from the network also returns all of the active DLCI numbers. The value can range from 1 to 255. The default value is 6, which means the user equipment sends 5 regular status inquiries, then the full status inquiry.

Link Integrity Verification Timer

Indicates how frequently the FRAD should initiate a Status Inquiry Message. This is the 10 second timer referred to under the term "Status Inquiry".

MIB

Management Information Base, a piece of information collected for an SNMP manager.

Agent

A device that collects MIB's to report them to SNMP managers. HP's Open View is an example of a manager. The DCB product PA2000 is an agent, specifically a proxy agent that collects data from non-SNMP devices and reports the data to an SNMP manager like HP Open View, reporting the data in SNMP fomat.

SNMP

NETWORK MANAGEMENT PROTOCOL

Frame Relay and DCB Products

DCB is the leading manufacturer of "Async Framds", multiplexers for encapsulating async data over frame relay. The SR, SRX and Unimux series of multiplexers range in size from 4 to 32 ports. The multiplexers directly encapsulate async data without the need for external frads. A DCB frame relay multiplexer supports from 1 to 16 DLCI's, or locations, per host unit. With various digital sharing devices available from DCB, the frame relay multiplexers can be expanded to virtually any number of ports supported over a single frame relay link.

DCB frame relay multiplexers, since they directly encapsulate async data in frame relay protocol, eliminating the need for external frads, are very cost effective. DCB multiplexers can be directly cabled into your DSU, even a router.

DCB supplies other frame relay products to the market, including 56/64 Kbps DSU's, T1 and fractional T1 multiplexers, multi-protocol frads, frame relay routers. DCB sales and technical support personnel assist customers in evaluating the cost effectiveness of frame relay solutions. They also assist in selecting the optimum solutions among the many alternatives available.

Further, frame relay links can be very cost effective for delivering data from a central site to remote locations. Frame relay is very cost effective at distances of several hundred miles or more.

In some areas of the U.S., frame relay is also very cost effective on a short distance basis. A short distance is the same LATA (local access and transport area). A LATA is the area served by your local phone company. As of this writing, frame relay is usually not cost effective on a local basis in the midwest.

Consider frame relay for your network. It is no longer an experimental new service. Frame relay is tried and true, cost effective and reliable. Frame relay should be considered just one of many alternate ways of providing network services. Evaluate frame relay on an equal basis along side dial up, private line, DDS, T1, ISDN and similar services.

Frame Relay is a protocol standard for LAN internet working which provides a fast and efficient method of transmitting information from a user device to LAN bridges and routers.

The Frame Relay protocol uses a frame structured similar to that of LAPD, except that the frame header is replaced by a

2-byte Frame Relay header field. The Frame Relay header contains the user-specified DLCI field, which is the destination address of the frame. It also contains congestion and status signals which the network sends to the user.

VIRTUAL CIRCUITS

The Frame Relay frame is transmitted to its destination by way of virtual circuits (logical paths from an originating point in the network) to a destination point. Virtual circuits may be permanent (PVCs) or switched (SVCs). PVCs are set up administratively by the network manager for a dedicated point-to-point connection; SVCs are set up on a call-by-call basis.

ADVANTAGES OF FRAME RELAY

Frame Relay offers an attractive alternative to both dedicated lines and X.25 networks for connecting LANs to bridges and routers. The success of the Frame Relay protocol is based on the following two underlying factors:

- Because virtual circuits consume bandwidth only when they transport data, many virtual circuits can exist simultaneously across a given transmission line. In addition, each device can use more of the bandwidth as necessary, and thus operate at higher speeds.
- The improved reliability of communication lines and increased error-handling sophistication at end stations allows the Frame Relay protocol to discard erroneous frames and thus eliminate time-consuming error-handling processing.

These two factors make Frame Relay a desirable choice for data transmission; however, they also necessitate testing to determine that the system works properly and that data is not lost.

FRAME RELAY STRUCTURE

Standards for the Frame Relay protocol have been developed by ANSI and CCITT simultaneously. The separate LMI specification has basically been incorporated into the

ANSI specification. The following discussion of the protocol structure includes the major points from these specifications. The Frame Relay frame structure is based on the LAPD protocol. In the Frame Relay structure, the frame header is altered slightly to contain the Data Link Connection Identifier (DLCI) and congestion bits, in place of the normal address and control fields. This new Frame Relay header is 2 bytes in length and has the following format:

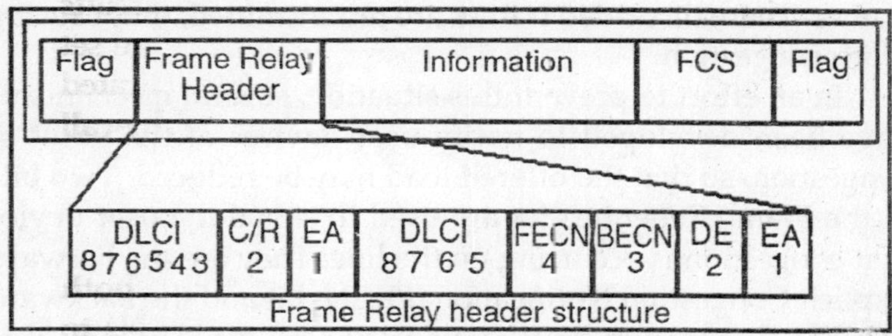

Frame Relay header structure

DLCI

10-bit DLCI field represents the address of the frame and corresponds to a PVC.

C/R

Designates whether the frame is a command or response.

EA

Extended Address field signifies up to two additional bytes in the Frame Relay header, thus greatly expanding the number of possible addresses.

FECN

Forward Explicit Congestion Notification.

BECN

Backward Explicit Congestion Notification.

DE

Discard Eligibility.

Information

The Information field may include other protocols within it, such as an X.25, IP or SDLC (SNA) packet.

EXPLICIT CONGESTION NOTIFICATION (ECN) BITS

When the network becomes congested to the point that it cannot process new data transmissions, it begins to discard frames. These discarded frames are retransmitted, thus causing more congestion.

In an effort to prevent this situation, several mechanisms have been developed to notify user devices at the onset of congestion, so that the offered load may be reduced. Two bits in the Frame Relay header are used to signal the user device that congestion is occurring on the line: They are the Forward Explicit Congestion Notification (FECN) bit and the Backward Explicit Congestion Notification (BECN) bit. The FECN is changed to 1 as a frame is sent downstream toward the destination location when congestion occurs during data transmission.

In this way, all downstream nodes and the attached user device learn about congestion on the line. The BECN is changed to 1 in a frame traveling back toward the source of data transmission on a path where congestion is occurring. Thus the source node is notified to slow down transmission until congestion subsides.

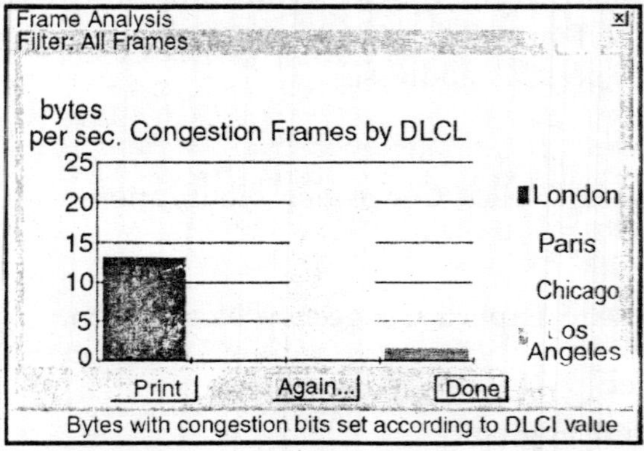

CONSOLIDATED LINK LAYER MANAGEMENT

It may occur that there are no frames traveling back to the source node which is causing the congestion. In this case, the network will want to send its own message to the problematic source node. The standard, however, does not allow the network to send its own frames with the DLCI of the desired virtual circuit. To address this problem, ANSI defined the Consolidated Link Layer Management (CLLM). With CLLM, a separate DLCI (number 1023) is reserved for sending link layer control messages from the network to the user device. The ANSI standard (T1.618) defines the format of the CLLM message. It contains a code for the cause of the congestion and a listing of all DLCIs that should act to reduce their data transmission to lower congestion.

STATUS OF CONNECTIONS (LMI)

Each DLCI corresponds to a PVC (Permanent Virtual Circuit). It is sometimes necessary to transmit information about this connection (e.g., whether the interface is still active) the valid DLCIs for the interface and the status of each PVC. This information is transmitted using the reserved DLCI 1023 or DLCI 0, depending on the standard used.

A multicast status may also be sent with the LMI. Multicasting is where a router sends a frame on a reserved DLCI known as a multicast group. The network then replicates the frame and delivers it to a predefined list of DLCIs, thus broadcasting a single frame to a collection of destinations.

DISCARD ELIGIBILITY (DE)

When there is congestion on the line, the network must decide which frames to discard in order to free the line. Discard Eligibility provides the network with a signal to determine which frames to discard. The network will discard frames with a DE value of 1 before discarding other frames. The DE bit may be set by the user on some of its lower-priority frames. Alternatively, the network may set the DE bit to indicate to other nodes that a frame should be preferentially selected for discard, if necessary.

FRAME RELAY STANDARDS

ANSI T1.618

T1.618 describes the protocol supporting the data transfer phase of the Frame Relay bearer service, as defined in ANSI T1.606. T1.618 is based on a subset of ANSI T1.602 (LAPD) called the "Core Aspects" and is used by both switched and permanent virtual calls.

T1.618 also includes the Consolidated Link Layer Mechanism (CLLM). The generation and transport of CLLM is optional. With CLLM, DLCI 1023 is reserved for sending link layer control messages.

T1.618 issues implicit congestion notification from the network to the user device. The congestion notification contains a code indicating the cause of the congestion and lists all DLCIs that have to reduce their traffic in order to lower congestion.

ANSI T1.617

To establish a Switched Virtual Circuit (SVC) connection, Frame Relay users must establish a dialog with the network using the signalling specification in T1.617. The procedure results in the assignment of a DLCI.

Once the dialog is established, the T1.618 procedures apply. To establish a Permanent Virtual Circuit (PVC), a setup protocol is used which is identical to the ISDN D-channel protocol and defined in T1.617. With ISDN, users can use the D-channel for setup. For non-ISDN callers, there is no D-channel, so the dialog between the user and the network must be separated from the ordinary data transfer procedures. In T1.617, DLCI 0 is reserved. T1.617 also contains specifications on how Frame Relay service parameters are negotiated.

ANSI LMI

ANSI LMI is a Permanent Virtual Circuit (PVC) management system defined in Annex D of T1.617. ANSI LMI is virtually identical to the Manufacturers' LMI, without the optional extensions. ANSI LMI uses DLCI 0.

Manufacturers' LMI

Manufacturers' LMI is a Frame Relay specification with extension-document number 001-208966, September 18, 1990.

Manufacturers' LMI defines a generic Frame Relay service based on PVCs for interconnecting DTE devices with Frame Relay network equipment. In addition to the ANSI standard, Manufacturers' LMI includes extensions and LMI functions and procedures. Manufacturers' LMI uses DLCI 1023.

ISDN

DEFINITION

ISDN, which stands for Integrated Services Digital Network, is a system of digital phone connections which has been available for over a decade. This system allows voice and data to be transmitted simultaneously across the world using end-to-end digital connectivity.

With ISDN, voice and data are carried by bearer channels (B channels) occupying a bandwidth of 64 kb/s (bits per second). Some switches limit B channels to a capacity of 56 kb/s. A data channel (D channel) handles signaling at 16 kb/s or 64 kb/s, depending on the service type. Note that, in ISDN terminology, "k" means 1000 (10^3), not 1024 (2^{10}) as in many computer applications (the designator "K" is sometimes used to represent this value); therefore, a 64 kb/s channel carries data at a rate of 64000 b/s.

A new set of standard prefixes has recently been created to handle this. Under this scheme, "k" (kilo-) means 1000 (10^3), "M" (mega-) means 1000000 (10^6), and so on, and "Ki" (kibi-) means 1024 (2^{10}), "Mi" (mebi-) means 1048576 (2^{20}), and so on.

(An alert reader pointed out some inconsistencies in my use of unit terminology throughout this Tutorial. He also referred me to a definitive web site. As a result, I have made every effort to both conform to standard terminology, and to use it consistently. I appreciate helpful user input like this!)

There are two basic types of ISDN service: Basic Rate Interface (BRI) and Primary Rate Interface (PRI). BRI consists of two 64 kb/s B channels and one 16 kb/s D channel for a total of 144 kb/s. This basic service is intended to meet the needs of most individual users. PRI is intended for users with greater capacity requirements. Typically the channel structure is 23 B channels plus one 64 kb/s D channel for a total of 1536 kb/s. In Europe, PRI consists of 30 B channels plus one 64 kb/s D channel for a total of 1984 kb/s. It is also possible to support multiple PRI lines with one 64 kb/s D channel using Non-Facility Associated Signaling (NFAS).

H channels provide a way to aggregate B channels. They are implemented as:

- H0=384 kb/s (6 B channels)
- H10=1472 kb/s (23 B channels)
- H11=1536 kb/s (24 B channels)
- H12=1920 kb/s (30 B channels) - International (E1) only

To access BRI service, it is necessary to subscribe to an ISDN phone line. Customer must be within 18000 feet (about 3.4 miles or 5.5 km) of the telephone company central office for BRI service; beyond that, expensive repeater devices are required, or ISDN service may not be available at all. Customers will also need special equipment to communicate with the phone company switch and with other ISDN devices. These devices include ISDN Terminal Adapters (sometimes called, incorrectly, "ISDN Modems") and ISDN Routers.

ISDN (Integrated Services Digital Network) is a set of CCITT/ITUstandards for digital transmission over ordinary telephone copper wire as well as over other media. Home and business users who install an ISDNadapter (in place of a telephone modem) receive Web pages at up to 128Kbps compared with the maximum 56 Kbps rate of a modem connection.

ISDN requires adapters at both ends of the transmission so your access provider also needs an ISDN adapter. ISDN is generally available from your phone company in most urban areas in the United States and Europe. In many areas where DSL and cable modem service are now offered, ISDN is no longer as popular an option as it was formerly. There are two levels of service: the Basic Rate Interface (BRI), intended for the home and small enterprise, and the Primary Rate Interface (PRI), for larger users. Both rates include a number of B-channels and a D-channels. Each B-channel carries data, voice, and other services. Each D-channelcarries control and signaling information.

The Basic Rate Interface consists of two 64 Kbps B-channels and one 16 Kbps D- channel. Thus, a Basic Rate user can have up to 128 Kbps service. The Primary Rate consists of 23 B-channels and one 64 Kpbs D-channel in the United States or 30 B-channels and 1 D-channel in Europe.

ISDN in concept is the integration of both analog or voice data together with digital data over the same network. Although the ISDN you can install is integrating these on a medium designed for analog transmission, broadbandISDN (BISDN) is intended to extend the integration of both services throughout the rest of the end-to-end path using fiber optic and radio media. Broadband ISDN encompasses frame relay service for high-speed data that can be sent in large bursts, the Fiber Distributed-Data Interface (FDDI), and the Synchronous Opical Network (SONET). BISDN is intended to support transmission from 2 Mbps up to much higher, but as yet unspecified, rates.

BENEFITS OF ISDN

- Single connection can support both voice and data.
- High quality services being digital right from subs, premises (End to End).
- Eight terminals can be connected on a single line.
- High speed data transfer from PC to PC is possible - 64 Kbps against existing 9.6 Kbps (6 times faster).
- Two calls can be established simultaneously on a single pair of wires.
- The call set time is very short (1-2 seconds).
- A number of supplementary services are supported like in pots.

Calling Line Identification , Call Forwarding , Call Forwarding on busy signal , Call Forwarding on no reply ,

Call Forwarding unconditional , Advice of Charge , Terminal Portability , Multiple Subscriber Number , Closed User Group.

BENEFITS OF ISDN FOR NETWORK OPERATORS

- Avoidance of separate networks for different services.
- Economical use of the equipment of the digitalised telephone network, especially the copper pair of the subscriber line.
- Reduction in costs due to simplified operation and maintenance procedures.

ISDN LINE SUPERIOR TO THE PHONE LINE

- The signal on the ISDN line - voice or data, is sent in digital mode.
- The signal level at subscriber's terminal equipment is independent on line length.
- An ISDN subscriber can establish two simultaneous independent calls which could be voice, data, image or combination of any two whereas only one call is possible on ordinary telephone lines.
- The call set-up time between two ISDN subscribers is extremely short.

Access to Internet

ISDN subscribers can have access to Internet with a higher bandwidth of 64/128 Kbps.

SERVICES OFFERED BY ISDN

The following services are offered on a dial-up basis between any two ISDN subscribers:

- Photo-Telephone-Calling where called party can see each other's pictures on screen.
- Desk Top Video Conferencing on dial-up basis using a single ISDN line at 128 Kbps.
- High Quality Video Conferencing on dial-up basis

between any two ISDN subscribers by using three ISDN lines at 384 Kbps.

- Teleconferencing which facilitates the transmission of pictures, documents and drawings etc., apart from voice & video images of the participants, white board sharing & document sharing is also possible.
- High speed data transmission at 128 Kbps. Very high quality in digital mode on account of very high immunity from the noise. High speed facsimile. Time taken to send FAX messages reduced to 1/4th. All other services which a conventional old telephone line provides. Subscriber can see his metering pulses at his premises.

ISDN supports all Phone-Plus services available to conventional old telephone line. In addition the following additional facilities are available.

B-ISDN

DEFINITION

There may be many popular meanings for BISDN with the most popular definition being that of Broadband Integrated Services Digital Network. We searched our database and could not find a definition other than Broadband Integrated Services Digital Network for BISDN

If you have more information or know of another definition for BISDN, please let us know so that we can review it and add that information to our database. Every attempt has been made to provide you with the correct acronym for BISDN. If we missed the mark, we would greatly appreciate your help by entering the correct or alternate meaning in the box. Definitions have been compiled from popular search engines and multiple results provided for your review.

A standard for transmitting voice, video and data at the same time over fiber telephone lines. Broadband ISDN can support data rates of 1.5 million bits per second (bps), but it has not been widely implemented. ISDN (Integrated Services Digital Network) development began in the 1980s as part of a plan by the carriers to develop a single integrated network transmitting voice, video, and data communications. B-ISDN development began in 1988 as developers saw a need for bandwidth above 155 Mbits/sec in anticipation of future video and multimedia services. ATM was developed from this work as the underlying transport, with B-ISDN being the overlying technology for controlling the network. Figure B-10 illustrates the B-ISDN architecture. ATM cells are delivered across a physical SONET network.

In general, ISDN is based on 64-Kbit/sec channels. These channels are just wide enough to handle a digitized voice call. All other ISDN implementations are some multiple of this basic service. A typical user signs up for basic rate ISDN, which consists of two 64-Kbit/sec channels (called the B channels) and one 16-Kbit/sec D channel used for signaling. The B channels can be used individually for separate voice calls or combined to create a 128-Kbit/sec data channel. Primary rate ISDN consists of 23 B channels and one 64-Kbit/sec signaling channel. ISDN is useful for networking because the customer can add bandwidth in increments of 64 Kbits/sec as needed.

ISDN is a switched service and is designed around intelligent switching components in the carrier network. It allows users to dial any other ISDN point on the network and create a high-speed digital link that can mimic point-to-point T1 lines. However, T1 lines are usually permanently established between two points, while ISDN allows the switching of the line between many different points by the customer. This is due to the intelligent network components. The intelligent network also supports a variety of other services, including call forwarding, caller ID, and channel bonding.

B-ISDN provides the intelligent telecommunications services above ATM. It manages the establishment of point-to-point and point-to-multipoint connections through the switched network. It supports on-demand, reserved, and permanent services, as well as connection-oriented and connectionless services. The carriers had big plans to use B-ISDN for services like videotelephony, videoconferencing, electronic newspapers, and TV distribution. Now, B-ISDN is rarely discussed. All you hear about is ATM. SONET is the physical transport backbone of B-ISDN.

It is a fiber-optic-based networking standard that defines a hierarchy of transmission rates and data-framing formats. It is used as a transmission medium to interconnect carrier-switching offices worldwide, and so forms the structure of the communications network. SONET is now used as the medium between carrier-switching offices and customers. SONET transmission rates start at 51.4 Mbits/sec and increase in 52-Mbit/sec building blocks.

ATM is the switching technology for B-ISDN and provides B-ISDN users access to the SONET fiber-optic network. Information received at the ATM layer is placed in fixed-length cells, addressed, and transmitted over the SONET network. ATM provides very high-speed switching of these packets between the links attached to the SONET network. ATM takes full advantage of the transmission speeds available on fiber-optic cable.

Note that neither ISDN nor B-ISDN has gained the popularity envisioned by the carriers. IP networking has gained in popularity and the latest trend is to build converged networks where voice travels in packets. See "NPN (New Public Network)," "Voice/Data Networks," and "Voice over IP (VoIP)."

Chapter 4

OSI Model

NETWORK DEVICES

Compatible interconnection of network devices is fundamental to reliable network communications. Developing a set of standards that equipment manufacturers could adhere to went a long way towards providing an open environment for network communications.

In the late 1970s the International Organization for Standardization (ISO) worked on a seven layer model for LAN architectures by defining the Open Systems Interconnection Basic Reference Model (OSI). Alongside this The ISO developed a set of protocols that fit within this model. Since then, other models such as the 5 layer TCP/IP model were developed, however the OSI model is still used to map and categorise protocols because of its concise and clear way of representing network functions.

The IEEE formed the 802 committee in February 1980 with the aim of standardising LAN protocols. This resulted in the IEEE 802 series of committees that sit to develop worldwide standards for communications.

Within the OSI model, the Data Link layer was split into two, the Media Access Control (MAC) sub-layer and the 802.2 Logical Link Control (LLC) sub-layer. You can make up expressions to remember the order of the 7 layers, for example, 'Angus Prefers Sausages To Nibbling Dried Pork' or 'A Pretty Silly Trick Never Does Please'. I remember it best using the natty expression 'Application, Presentation, Session, Transport, Network, Datalink, Physical'. It just rolls off the tongue!

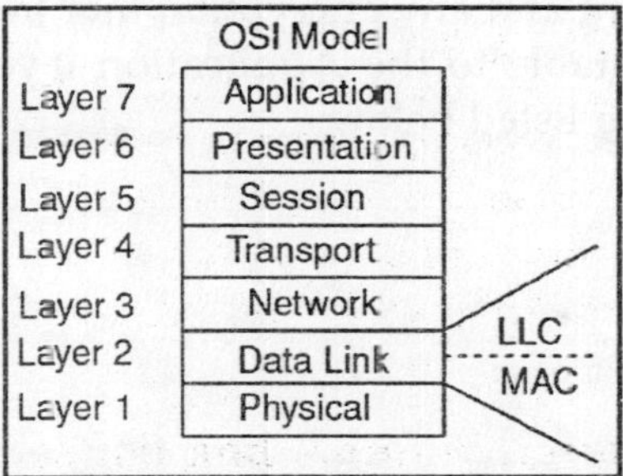

The OSI protocol set is rarely used today, however the model that was developed serves as a useful guide when referencing other protocol stacks such as ATM, TCP/IP and SPX/IPX.

LAYERS

APPLICATION LAYER 7

It is employed in software packages which implement client-server software. When an application on one computer starts communicating with another computer, then the Application layer is used. The header contains parameters that are agreed between applications. This header is often only sent at the beginning of an application operation. Examples of services within the application layer include:

- FTP
- DNS
- SNMP
- SMTP gateways
- Web browser
- Network File System (NFS)
- Telnet and Remote Login (rlogin)
- X.400
- FTAM
- Database software
- Print Server Software

PRESENTATION LAYER 6

This provides function call exchange between host operating systems and software layers. It defines the format of data being sent and any encryption that may be used, and makes it presentable to the Application layer. Examples of services used are listed below:

- MIDI
- HTML
- GIF
- TIFF
- JPEG
- ASCII
- EBCDIC

SESSION LAYER 5

The Session layer defines how data conversations are started, controlled and finished. The Session layer manages the transaction sequencing and in some cases authorisation. The messages may be bidirectional and there may be many of them, the session layer manages these conversations and creates notifications if some messages fail. Indications show whether a packet is in the middle of a conversation flow or at the end. Only after a completed conversation will the data be passed up to layer 6.

Examples of Session layer protocols are listed below:

- RPC
- SQL
- NetBIOS names
- Appletalk ASP
- DECnet SCP

TRANSPORT LAYER 4

This layer is resonsible for the ordering and reassembly of packets that may have been broken up to travel across certain media. Some protocols in this layer also perform error recovery. After error recovery and reordering the data part is passed up to layer 5.

Examples are:

- TCP
- UDP
- SPX

NETWORK LAYER 3

This layer is responsible for the delivery of packets end to end and implements a logical addressing scheme to help accomplish this. This can be connectionless or connection-oriented and is independent of the topology or path that the data packets travel. Routing packets through a network is also defined at this layer plus a method to fragment large packets into smaller ones depending on MTUs for different media (Packet Switching). Once the data from layer 2 has been received, layer 3 examines the destination address and if it is the address of its own end station, it passes the data after the layer 3 header to layer 4.

Examples of Layer 3 protocols include:

- Appletalk DDP
- IP
- IPX
- DECnet

DATA LINK LAYER 2

This layer deals with getting data across a specific medium and individual links by providing one or more data link connections between two network entities. End points are specifically identified, if required by the Network layer Sequencing. The frames are maintained in the correct sequence and there are facilities for Flow control and Quality of Service parameters such as Throughput, Service Availability and Transit Delay.

Examples include:

- IEEE 802.2
- IEEE 802.3
- 802.5 - Token Ring
- HDLC
- Frame Relay
- FDDI
- ATM
- PPP

The Data link layer performs the error check using the Frame Check Sequence (FCS) in the trailer and discards the frame if an error is detected. It then looks at the addresses to see if it needs to process the rest of the frame itself or whether to pass it on to another host. The data between the header and the trailer is passed to layer 3. The MAC layer concerns itself with the access control method and determines how use of the physical transmission is controlled and provides the token ring protocols that define how a token ring operates. The LLC shields the higher level layers from concerns with the specific LAN implementation.

PHYSICAL LAYER 1

This layer deals with the physical aspects of the media being used to transmit the data. The electrical, mechanical, procedural and functional means This defines things like pinouts, electrical characteristics, modulation and encoding of data bits on carrier signals. It ensures bit synchronisation and places the binary pattern that it receives into a receive buffer. Once it decodes the bit stream, the physical layer notifies the data link layer that a frame has been received and passes it up.

Examples of specifications include:

- V.24
- V.35
- EIA/TIA-232
- EIA/TIA-449
- FDDI
- 802.3
- 802.5
- Ethernet
- RJ45
- NRZ
- NRZI

You will notice that some protocols span a number of layers (e.g. NFS, 802.3 etc.). A benefit of the seven layer model is that software can be written in a modular way to deal specifically with one or two layers only, this is often called Modular Engineering. Each layer has its own header containing information relevant to its role. This header is passed down to the layer below which in turn adds its own header (encapsulates) until eventually the Physical layer adds the layer 2 information for passage to the next device which understands the layer 2 information and can then strip each of the layers' headers in turn to get at the data in the right location.

OSI MODEL CONCEPTS

The standard model for networking protocols and distributed applications is the International Standard Organization's Open System Interconnect (ISO/OSI) model. It defines seven network layers. Short for Open System Interconnection, an ISO standard for worldwide communications that defines a networking framework for implementing protocols in seven layers. Control is passed from one layer to the next, starting at the application layer in one station, proceeding to the bottom layer, over the channel to the next station and back up the hierarchy.

At one time, most vendors agreed to support OSI in one form or another, but OSI was too loosely defined and proprietary standards were too entrenched. Except for the OSI-compliant X.400 and X.500 e-mail and directory standards, which are widely used, what was once thought to become the universal communications standard now serves as the teaching model for all other protocols. Understanding how the OSI Model works is not only useful for taking certification exams, but also for real life scenarios. Read How to use the OSI Model to Troubleshoot Networks for more info.

LAYER 1 - PHYSICAL

Physical layer defines the cable or physical medium itself, e.g., thinnet, thicknet, unshielded twisted pairs (UTP). All media are functionally equivalent. The main difference is in convenience and cost of installation and maintenance. Converters from one media to another operate at this level.

LAYER 2 - DATA LINK

Data Link layer defines the format of data on the network. A network data frame, aka packet, includes checksum, source and destination address, and data. The largest packet that can be sent through a data link layer defines the Maximum Transmission Unit (MTU). The data link layer handles the physical and logical connections to the packet's destination, using a network interface. A host connected to an Ethernet would have an Ethernet interface to handle connections to the outside world, and a loopback interface to send packets to itself. Ethernet addresses a host using a unique, 48-bit address called its Ethernet address or Media Access Control (MAC) address. MAC addresses are usually represented as six colon-separated pairs of hex digits, e.g., 8:0:20:11:ac:85. This number is unique and is associated with a particular Ethernet device. Hosts with multiple network interfaces should use the same MAC address on each. The data link layer's protocol-specific header specifies the MAC address of the packet's source and destination.

LAYER 3 - NETWORK

NFS uses Internetwork Protocol (IP) as its network layer interface. IP is responsible for routing, directing datagrams from one network to another. The network layer may have to break large datagrams, larger than MTU, into smaller packets and host receiving the packet will have to reassemble the fragmented datagram. The Internetwork Protocol identifies each host with a 32-bit IP address. IP addresses are written as four dot-separated decimal numbers between 0 and 255, e.g., 129.79.16.40. The leading 1-3 bytes of the IP identify the network and the remaining bytes identifies the host on that network. The network portion of the IP is assigned by InterNIC Registration Services, under the contract to the National Science Foundation, and the host portion of the IP is assigned by the local network administrators. For large sites, the first two bytes represents the network portion of the IP, and the third and fourth bytes identify the subnet and host respectively.

LAYER 4 - TRANSPORT

Transport layer subdivides user-buffer into network-buffer sized datagrams and enforces desired transmission control. Two transport protocols, Transmission Control Protocol (TCP) and User Datagram Protocol (UDP), sits at the transport layer. Reliability and speed are the primary difference between these two protocols. TCP establishes connections between two hosts on the network through 'sockets' which are determined by the IP address and port number. TCP keeps track of the packet delivery order and the packets that must be resent. Maintaining this information for each connection makes TCP a stateful protocol. UDP on the other hand provides a low overhead transmission service, but with less error checking. NFS is built on top of UDP because of its speed and statelessness. Statelessness simplifies the crash recovery.

LAYER 5 - SESSION

The session protocol defines the format of the data sent over the connections. The NFS uses the Remote Procedure Call (RPC) for its session protocol. RPC may be built on either TCP or UDP. Login sessions uses TCP whereas NFS and broadcast use UDP.

LAYER 6 - PRESENTATION

External Data Representation (XDR) sits at the presentation level. It converts local representation of data to its canonical form and vice versa. The canonical uses a standard byte ordering and structure packing convention, independent of the host.

LAYER 7 - APPLICATION

The OSI Reference Model is founded on a suggestion developed by the International Organization for Standardization (ISO). The model is known as ISO OSI (Open Systems Interconnection) Reference Model because it relates with connecting open systems - that is, systems that are open for communication with other systems.

OSI Model is a set of protocols that try to identify and homogenize the data communication practices. The OSI Model has the support of most computer and network vendors, many big customers, and most governments, including the United States.

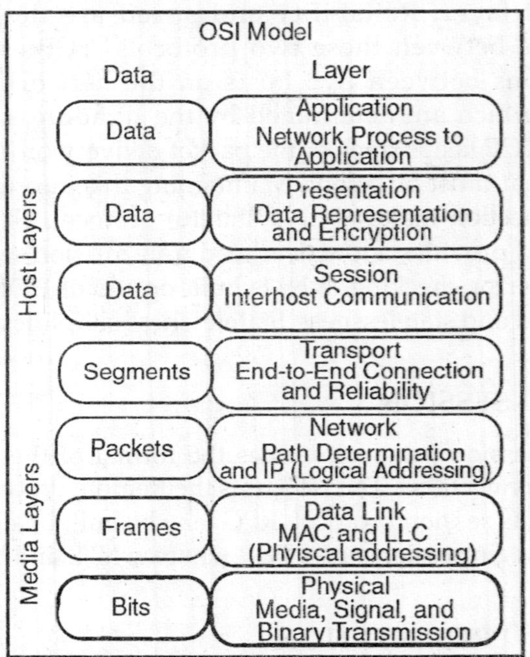

The OSI Model is a model that illustrates how data communications should take place. It segregates the process into seven groups, called layers. Into these layers are integrated the protocol standards developed by the ISO and other standards organization, including the Institute of Electrical and Electronic Engineers (IEEE), American National Standards Institute (ANSI), and the International Telecommunications Union (ITU), formerly known as the CCITT (Comite Consultatif Internationale de Telegraphique et Telephone). The OSI Model affirms what protocols and standards should be used at each layer. It is modular, each layer of the OSI Model functions with the one above and below it.

The short form used to memorize the layer names of the OSI Model is "All People SeemTo Need Data Processing". The lower two layers are normally put into practice with hardware and software. The remaining five layers are only implemented with software.

The layered approach to network communications gives the subsequent advantages: Reduced intricacy, enhanced teaching/learning, modular engineering, accelerated advancement, interoperable technology, and standard interfaces.

TCP / IP MODEL

TCP/IP Model:

- Application Layer
- Transport Layer
- Internet Layer
- Network Interface Layer

The most significant downside with the TCP/IP model is that if you reference it, fewer people will know what you are talking about! For a better description of why the OSI model should go the way of the dodo, disco, and DivX, read Kill the Beast: Why the Seven-Layer Model Must Die.

OSI 7 LAYERS REFERENCE MODEL

Open Systems Interconnection (OSI) model is a reference model developed by ISO (International Organization for Standardization) in 1984, as a conceptual framework of standards for communication in the network across different equipment and applications by different vendors. It is now considered the primary architectural model for inter-computing and internetworking communications. Most of the network communication protocols used today have a structure based on the OSI model.

The OSI model defines the communications process into 7 layers, which divides the tasks involved with moving information between networked computers into seven smaller, more manageable task groups. A task or group of tasks is then assigned to each of the seven OSI layers. Each layer is reasonably self-contained so that the tasks assigned to each layer can be implemented independently. This enables the solutions offered by one layer to be updated without adversely affecting the other layers. The OSI 7 layers model has clear characteristics.

Layers 7 through 4 deal with end to end communications between data source and destinations. Layers 3 to 1 deal with communications between network devices. On the other hand, the seven layers of the OSI model can be divided into two groups: upper layers (layers 7, 6 & 5) and lower layers (layers 4, 3, 2, 1).

The upper layers of the OSI model deal with application issues and generally are implemented only in software. The highest layer, the application layer, is closest to the end user. The lower layers of the OSI model handle data transport issues. The physical layer and the data link layer are implemented in hardware and software.

The lowest layer, the physical layer, is closest to the physical network medium (the wires, for example) and is responsible for placing data on the medium.

BROADCASTING

NATURE OF THE INDUSTRY

Goods and Services

The broadcasting industry consists of radio and television stations and networks that create content or acquire the right to broadcast prerecorded television and radio programmes. Networks transmit their signals from broadcasting studios via satellite signals to local stations or cable distributors.

Broadcast signals then travel over cable television lines, satellite distribution systems, or the airwaves from a station's transmission tower to the antennas of televisions and radios. Anyone in the signal area with a radio or television can receive the programming. Cable and other pay television distributors provide television broadcasts to most Americans. Although cable television stations and networks are included in this statement, cable and other pay television distributors are classified in the telecommunications industry.

Industry Organization

Radio and television stations and networks broadcast a variety of programmes, such as national and local news, talk shows, music programmes, movies, other entertainment, and advertisements. Stations produce some of these programmes, most notably news programmes, in their own studios; however, much of the programming is produced outside the broadcasting industry. Revenue for commercial radio and television stations and networks comes from the sale of advertising time. The rates paid by advertisers depend on the size and characteristics (age, gender, and median income, among others) of a program's audience. Educational and noncommercial stations generate revenue primarily from donations by individuals, foundations, government, and corporations.

These stations generally are owned and managed by public broadcasting organizations, religious institutions, or school systems. Establishments that produce filmed or taped programming for radio and television stations and networks-but that do not broadcast the programming-are in the motion picture industry. Many television networks own production companies that produce their many shows.

Within the broadcasting industry, 73 per cent of workers were employed in television and radio broadcasting, with the remaining 27 per cent in cable broadcasting. Cabie and other programme distributors compensate local television stations and cable networks for rebroadcast rights. For popular cable networks and local television stations, distributors pay a fee per subscriber and/or agree to broadcast a less popular channel owned by the same network.

Recent Developments

The U.S. Federal Communications Commission (FCC) is a proponent of digital television (DTV), a technology that uses digital signals to transmit television programmes. Digital signals consist of pieces of simple electronic code that can carry more information than conventional analog signals. This code allows for the transmission of better quality sound and higher resolution pictures, often referred to as high-definition television (HDTV). Beginning in 2009, FCC regulations required all stations to turn off their analog signals and broadcast only in digital. The transition to HDTV broadcasting has accelerated the conversion of other aspects of television production from analog to digital. Many stations have replaced specialized hardware with less specialized computers equipped with software that performs the same functions. Stations are beginning to switch away from tapes and instead use digital recording devices. This way footage can be more easily transferred to a computer for editing and storage. Many major network shows now use HDTV cameras and editing equipment as well.

The transition to digital broadcasting also is occurring in radio. Most stations already store music, edit clips, and broadcast their analog signals with digital equipment. Satellite radio services, which offer more than 100 channels of digital sound, operate on a subscription basis, like pay television services. To compete, some radio stations are embedding a digital signal into their analog signals. With a specially equipped radio, these digital services offer better quality sound and display some limited text, such as the title of the song and the artist.

WORKING CONDITIONS

Hours

Many broadcast employees have erratic work schedules, sometimes having to work early in the morning or late at night. In 2008, workers in broadcasting averaged 35.8 hours a week, compated with 33.6 for workers in all private industry. Workers in television worked longer hours than those in radio broadcasting. Only 7 per cent of employees work part time, compared with 16 per cent for all industries.

Work Environment

Most employees in this industry work in clean, comfortable surroundings in broadcast stations and studios. Some employees work in the production of shows and broadcasting, while other employees work in advertising, sales, promotions, and marketing. Television news teams made up of reporters, camera operators, and technicians travel in electronic news-gathering vehicles to various locations to cover news stories. Although such location work is exciting, some assignments, such as reporting on military conflicts or natural disasters, may be dangerous. These assignments also may require outdoor work under adverse weather conditions. Camera operators working on such news teams must have the physical stamina to carry and set up their equipment. Broadcast technicians on electronic news-gathering trucks must ensure that the mobile unit's antenna is correctly positioned for optimal transmission quality and to prevent electrocution from power lines.

Field service engineers work on outdoor transmitting equipment and may have to climb poles or antenna towers; their work can take place under a variety of weather conditions. Broadcast technicians who maintain and set up equipment may have to do heavy lifting. Technological changes have enabled camera operators also to fulfill the tasks of broadcast technicians, operating the transmission and editing equipment on a remote broadcasting truck. News operations, programming, and engineering employees work under a great deal of pressure in order to meet deadlines. As a result, these workers are likely to experience varied or erratic work schedules, often working on early morning or late evening news programmes. Sales workers may face stress meeting sales goals. Aside from sometimes erratic work schedules, management and administrative workers typically find themselves in an environment similar to that of any other office. For many people, the excitement of working in broadcasting compensaies for the demanding nature of the work. Although the industry is noted for its high pressure and long hours, the work generally is not hazardous.

EMPLOYMENT

Broadcasting provided about 316,000 wage and salary jobs in 2008. Although 38 per cent of all establishments employed fewer than 5 people, most jobs were in large establishments; 74 per cent of all jobs were in establishments with at least 50 employees. Broadcasting establishments are found throughout the country, but jobs in larger stations are concentrated in large cities.

OCCUPATIONS IN THE INDUSTRY

Occupations at large broadcast stations and networks fall into five general categories: Programme production, news related, and technical, all of which in turn fall under professional and related, sales, and management occupations. At small stations, jobs are less specialized and employees often perform several functions. Although on-camera or on-air positions are the most familiar occupations in broadcasting, the majority of employment opportunities are behind the scenes.

Programme Production Occupations

Most television programmes are produced by the motion picture and video industry; actors, directors, and producers working on these prerecorded programmes are not employed by the broadcasting industry. Employees in programme production occupations at television and radio stations create programmes such as news, talk, and music shows.

Assistant producers provide clerical support and background research; assist with the preparation of musical, written, and visual materials; and time productions to make sure that they do not run over schedule. Assistant producers also may operate cameras and other audio and video equipment.

Video editors select and assemble prerecorded video to create a finished programme, applying sound and special effects as necessary. Conventional editing requires assembling pieces of videotape in a linear fashion to create a finished product. The editor first assembles the beginning of the programme and then works sequentially towards the end. Newer computerized editing allows an editor to electronically cut and paste video segments. This electronic technique is known as nonlinear editing, because the editor is no longer restricted to working sequentially. A segment may be moved at any time to any location in the programme.

Producers plan and develop live or taped productions, determining how the show will look and sound. They select the script, talent, sets, props, lighting, and other production elements. Producers also coordinate the activities of on-air personalities, production staff, and other personnel. Web site or Internet producers, a relatively new occupation in the broadcasting industry, plan and develop Internet sites that provide news updates, programme schedules, and information about popular shows. These producers decide what will appear on the Internet sites and design and maintain them.

Announcers read news items and provide other information, such as programme schedules and station breaks for commercials or public-service information. Many radio announcers, referred to as disc jockeys, play recorded music on radio stations. Disc jockeys may take requests from listeners; interview guests; and comment on the music, weather, or traffic. Most stations now have placed all of their advertisements, sound bites, and music on a computer, which is used to select and play or edit the items. Technological advances have simplified the monitoring and adjusting of the transmitter, leaving disc jockeys responsible for most of the tasks associated with keeping a station on the air. Traditional tapes and CDs are used only as backups in case of a computer failure. Announcers and disc jockeys need a good speaking voice. Disc jockeys also need a significant knowledge of music.

Programme directors are in charge of on-air programming in radio stations. They decide what type of music will be played, supervise on-air personnel, and often select the specific songs and the order in which they will be played. Considerable experience, usually as a disc jockey, is required, as is a thorough knowledge of music.

News-related Occupations

News, weather, and sports reports are important to many television stations because these reports attract a large audience and account for a large proportion of revenue. Many radio stations depend on up-to-the-minute news for a major share of their programming.

Programme production staffs, such as producers and announcers, also work on the production of news programmes. Reporters gather information from various sources, analyse and prepare news stories, and present information on the air. Correspondents report on news occurring in U.S. and foreign cities in which they are stationed.

Newswriters write and edit news stories from information collected by reporters and correspondents. Newswriters may advance to positions as reporters or correspondents. Broadcast news analysts, also known as news anchors and newscasters, analyse, interpret, and broadcast news received from various sources.

News anchors present news stories and introduce videotaped news or live transmissions from on-the-scene reporters. Newscasters at large stations may specialize in a particular field.

Weathercasters, also called weather reporters, report current and forecasted weather conditions. They gather information from national satellite weather services, wire services, and local and regional weather bureaus.

Some weathercasters are trained atmospheric scientists and can develop their own weather forecasts. Sportscasters, who are responsible for reporting sporting events, usually select, write, and deliver the sports news for each newscast. Assistant news directors supervise the newsroom.

They coordinate wire service reports, tape or film inserts, and stories from individual newswriters and reporters. Assignment editors assign stories to news teams, sending the teams on location if necessary.

News directors have overall responsibility for the news team, made up of reporters, writers, editors, and newscasters, as well as responsibility for studio and mobile unit production crews. This senior administrative position carries with it duties that include determining what events to cover and how and when they will be presented in a news broadcast.

Technical Occupations

Employees in these occupations operate and maintain the electronic equipment that records and transmits radio or television programmes. The titles of some of these occupations use the terms "engineer," "technician," and "operator" interchangeably.

Radio operators manage equipment that regulates the strength and clarity of signals and the range of sounds of broadcasts. They also monitor and log the outgoing signals and operate transmitters. Audio and video equipment technicians operate equipment that regulates the volume, sound quality, brightness, contrast, and visual quality of a broadcast. Broadcast technicians set up and maintain electronic broadcasting equipment. Their work can extend outside the studio, as when they set up portable transmitting equipment or maintain stationary towers.

Television and video camera operators set up and operate studio cameras, which are used in the television studio, and electronic news-gathering cameras, which are mobile and used outside the studio when a news team is pursuing a story at another location. In both cases, cameras are evolving from tape to disc-based formats. Camera operators need training in video production, as well as some experience in television production.

Master control engineers ensure that all of the radio or television station's scheduled programme elements, such as on-location feeds, prerecorded segments, and commercials, are transmitted smoothly. They also are responsible for ensuring that transmissions meet FCC requirements.

Management Occupations

General managers, or station managers, coordinate all radio and television station activities. In very small stations, the manager and a bookkeeper may handle all of the accounting, purchasing, hiring, and other routine office work. In larger stations, the general administrative staff includes business managers, accountants, lawyers, personnel workers, public relations workers, and others. These professionals are assisted by office and administrative support workers, such as secretaries, word processors, typists, and financial clerks.

TRAINING AND ADVANCEMENT

Professional, management, and sales occupations generally require a college degree; technical occupations often do not. It is easier to obtain employment and gain promotions with a degree, especially in larger, more competitive markets. Advanced schooling usually is required for supervisory positions-including technical occupations-having greater responsibility and higher salaries.

Employees in the radio and television broadcasting industry often find their first job in broadcast stations that serve smaller markets. Competition for positions in large metropolitan areas is stronger, and stations in these areas usually seek highly experienced personnel. Because many radio and television stations are small, workers in this industry often must change employers to advance. Relocation to other parts of the country frequently is necessary for advancement.

Programme Production Pccupations

Entry-level jobs in news or programme production increasingly are requiring a college degree and some broadcast experience. About 1,300 institutions offer programmes in communication, journalism, and related occupations.

As of 2008, more than 100 schools were accredited by the Accrediting Council on Education in Journalism and Mass Communications. Some community colleges offer 2-year programmes in broadcasting. Broadcast trade schools offer courses that last 6 months to a year and teach radio and television announcing, writing, and production.Individuals pursuing a career in broadcasting often gain their initial experience through work at college radio and television stations or through internships at professional stations. Although these positions usually are unpaid, they sometimes provide college credit or tuition.

More importantly, they provide hands-on experience and a competitive edge for a candidate who is applying for a job.

In this highly competitive industry, broadcasters are less willing to provide on-the-job training and instead seek candidates who can perform the job immediately.

Technical Occupations

Some technical positions require only a high school diploma or brief postsecondary training. However, many broadcast stations seek individuals with training in broadcast technology, electronics, or engineering from a 4-year college. Because of the increase in the use of digital technology, an understanding of computer networks and software is especially important for potential employees. Supervisory technical positions and jobs in large stations generally require a college degree.

The Society of Broadcast Engineers (SBE) issues certification to technicians who pass a written examination. Several classes of certification are available, requiring increasing levels of experience and knowledge for eligibility.

Sales and Related Occupations

These positions generally require a 4-year degree. As with the rest of the industry, it is easier to begin work in a small station or market and move on to a larger one as experience is acquired.

Management Occupations

Station managers should have a 4-year degree and significant experience working at a television or radio station. The administrative staff is extremely varied and will require different amounts of education and training, depending on the job.

OUTLOOK

Keen competition is expected for many jobs, particularly in large metropolitan areas, because of the large number of jobseekers attracted by the glamour of this industry. Job prospects will be best for applicants with a college degree in broadcasting, journalism, or a related field, as well as relevant work experience, such as work at college radio and television stations or internships at professional stations.

Employment Change

Employment in broadcasting is expected to increase by 7 per cent over the 2008-18 period, less than the 11 per cent increase projected for all industries combined. Factors contributing to the relatively slow rate of growth include industry consolidation, the introduction of new technologies, and competition from other media outlets. The slow growth will be tempered, however, by growth in the cable and subscription division of broadcasting.

The consolidation of individual broadcast stations into large networks, especially in radio, continues. This trend will limit employment growth as networks use workers more efficiently. For example, a network can run eight radio stations from one office, producing news programming at one station and then using that programming for broadcast from other stations, thus eliminating the need for multiple news staffs.

Similarly, technical workers, upper-level management, and marketing and advertising sales workers are pooled to work for several stations simultaneously. In the radio industry, several major companies own numerous stations nationwide. These companies achieve cost savings through consolidation and economies of scale, limiting employment growth.

The introduction of new technology also is slowing employment growth. Conventional broadcast equipment used to be relatively specialized; each piece of equipment served a separate function and required an operator with specialized knowledge. Newer computerized equipment often combines the functions of several older pieces of equipment and does not require specialized knowledge for its operation. This reduces the need for certain types of workers, including those responsible for editing, recording, and creating graphics.

Job growth in television also is being constrained by the increased competition created by services outside the broadcasting industry. Portable music players, cable TV, and especially the Internet have created new challenges that the industry must adapt to in order to continue to be successful. Employment in radio broadcasting is expected to decline. In addition to consolidation and new technology, the major threats to the radio industry, especially to smaller, marginal stations, are from MP3 players and from satellite radio, which functions like cable television, with subscribers paying a monthly fee. Radio broadcasters are building their own HD radio stations. If successful, these could result in more technical and production job growth.

Job Prospects

Keen competition is expected for many jobs, particularly in large metropolitan areas, because of the large number of jobseekers attracted by the glamour of this industry. Job prospects will be best for applicants with a college degree in broadcasting, journalism, or a related field, as well as relevant work experience, such as work at college radio and television stations or internships at professional stations.

Technology in the broadcasting industry is rapidly changing and forcing workers to continually update their skills. Those who receive continued technical training will increasingly have an advantage over others in the production and news-related occupations, as well as in technical occupations. Workers with little job experience will find it easier to gain employment in smaller markets or at small stations in large markets. Large stations usually hire only people with more experience.

MULTICASTING

DEFINITION

To transmit a single message to a select group of recipients. A simple example of multicasting is sending an e-mail message to a mailing list. Teleconferencing and videoconferencing also use multicasting, but require more robust protocols and networks. Standards are being developed to support multicasting over a TCP/IPnetwork such as the Internet. These standards, IP Multicast and Mbone, will allow users to easily join multicast groups. Note that multicasting refers to sending a message to a select group whereas broadcasting refers to sending a message to everyone connected to a network. The terms multicast and narrowcast are often used interchangeably, although narrowcast usually refers to the business model whereas multicast refers to the actual technology used to transmit the data.

Multicast is communication between a single sender and multiple receivers on a network. Typical uses include the updating of mobile personnel from a home office and the periodic issuance of online newsletters. Together with any cast and unicast, multicast is one of the packet types in the Internet Protocol Version 6 (IPv6). Multicast is supported through wireless data networks as part of the Cellular Digital Packet Data (CDPD) technology. Multicast is also used for programming on the MBone, a system that allows users at high-bandwidth points on the Internet to receive live video and sound programming. In addition to using a specific high-bandwidth subset of the Internet, Mbone multicast also uses a protocol that allows signals to be encapsulated as TCP/IP packet when passing through parts of the Internet that can not handle the multicast protocol directly.

Consumers also benefit from the DTV Transition because digital broadcasting allows stations to offer improved picture and sound quality, and digital is much more efficient than analog. For example, rather than being limited to providing one analog programme, a broadcaster is able to offer a super sharp "high definition" (HD) digital programme or multiple "standard definition" (SD) digital programmes simultaneously through a process called "multicasting." Multicasting allows broadcast stations to offer several channels of digital programming at the same time, using the same amount of spectrum required for one analog programme. Multicasting helps you conserve bandwidth by reducing the number of live streams in use. It requires a specially configured network. You can multicast RealMedía, Windows Media, MPEG, and a number of RTP-based formats. Multicasting to the QuickTime Player is not available.

OVERVIEW

Multicasting is a way of sending a single live stream to multiple clients, rather than sending a stream to every single client. The players establish a data connection to the stream, rather than to the Helix Universal Proxy and to Helix Universal Server, as shown in the following illustration.

Description

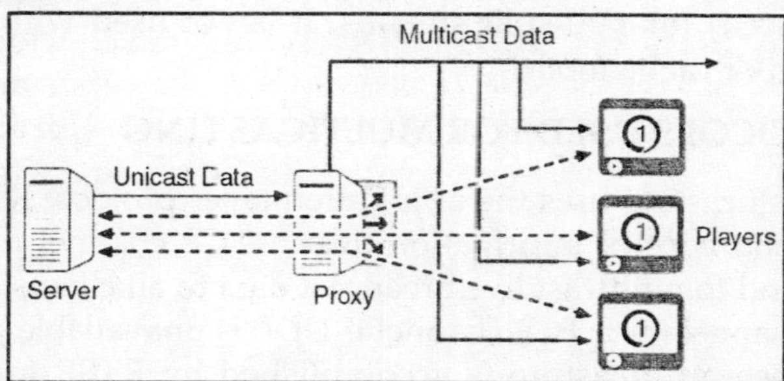

Helix Universal Proxy supports a form of multicasting called back-channel multicasting. In this method of multicasting, each media player maintains a control channel to Helix Universal Proxy and to Helix Universal Server. A media player uses its channel to send commands such as Stop. The channel lets Helix Universal Proxy and Helix Universal Server receive a user name and password if authentication is used in either product. It also enables the Proxy Monitor described in to track how many players are viewing the proxied multicast. Back-channel multicasting works with all RealNetworks media players, including older players that use only the PNA protocol.

Unicasting

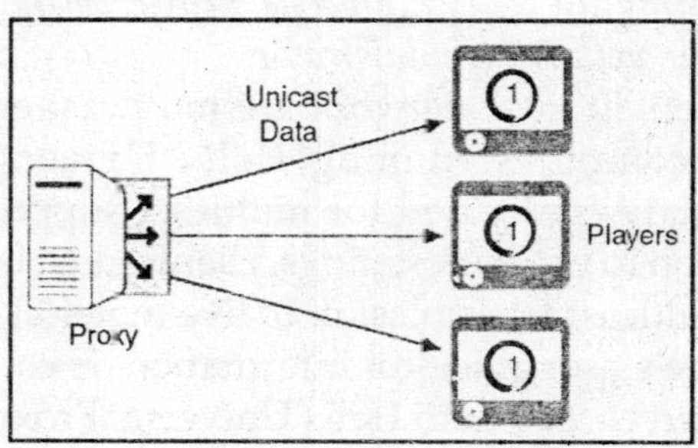

To take advantage of multicasting, both Helix Universal Proxy and clients, as well as the routers between them, must be multicast-enabled. For this reason, multicasting is mostly used with intranets where routers can be configured for multicasts.

Multicast delivery can be performed over the Internet only where intermediary network devices have been multicast-enabled. Multicast is automatically used (when available and configured) for pull-split streams. It is not used with pass-through or cache mode.

PROTOCOLS USED FOR MULTICASTING

Multicasting uses the application-layer protocol RTSP to both send control information over a TCP channel to each client and to multicast live broadcast data to all clients over a UDP channel (or a TCP channel if UDP is unavailable.)

Since multicasting is accomplished by RTSP for both control information and live data, it offers the following features:

- Connection statistics-Helix Universal Proxy can receive client connection information.
- SureStream-these multiply-encoded files are supported.

DEFINING MULTICASTING

Before you set up multicasting, you need to do two things:

- Configure the network for multicasting.
- Select the addresses you'll use for your multicasts.

Setting Up the Network for Multicasting

Before setting up Helix Universal Proxy, verify the following items with your network administrator:

- Routers in your network are multicast-enabled.
- The computer running Helix Universal Proxy is correctly configured for multicast support.

In addition to network settings, clients must be configured to request multicast transmission of live material. Consult the client software's user guide for information on configuring the client. As noted earlier, both Helix Universal Proxy and clients, as well as the routers between them, must be multicast-enabled in order for you to distribute presentations using the multicast features.

Helix Universal Proxy

There are two factors to take into account when establishing the addresses and port numbers that Helix Universal Proxy will use for multicasting:

- Select addresses from a legal range of available addresses. Valid ranges are between 224.0.0.0 and 239.255.255.255. The network administrator should know which multicast addresses are available on your intranet. On the Internet, certain ranges such as the addresses between 224.0.0.0 and 224.0.0.255 are reserved for other uses; see RFC 1700, "Assigned Numbers" for a complete list of restricted addresses.
- You must select enough addresses for the type of file you are multicasting. "Determining Required Addresses and Port Numbers" for information on selecting the appropriate number. You'll need to know how many bit rates are included in each file that you are multicasting, and set aside the appropriate number.

Although the information in this document will help you calculate the number of addresses and port numbers you'll need for multicasting, you'll still need to consult with your network administrator regarding the actual addresses you'll use.

Required Addresses and Port Numbers

For each file that you are transmitting using multicast, you must calculate the number of addresses you'll need. The number of addresses is based on the number of bit rates in the file. For simple RealVideo files, figuring the number of addresses and port numbers is relatively simple. SureStream files are more complex, as they can contain several bit rates, each with its own number of streams.

Configuring Back-Channel Multicasting

Follow the instructions below to set up Helix Universal Proxy for back-channel multicasting.

- In Helix Administrator, click Proxy Setup. Click Multicasting.
- In the RTSP Port box, type the port number to which Helix Universal Proxy will direct its RTSP multicast streams. The value in this box refers to the client's port number. A typical value is 554.
- Specify the range of addresses to which you want to multicast streams by filling in the IP Address Range box. Helix Universal Proxy uses the first available address in this range. If your multicast streams are referenced in SMIL files, you will need one address for each stream. Refer to "Determining Required Addresses and Port Numbers" to calculate the exact number of addresses you'll need.
- Indicate how far multicast packets can travel over a network by typing a value in the Time to Live box. Each time a multicast data packet passes through a multicast-enabled router, its Time to Live is decreased by 1. When the value is decremented to 0, the router discards the data packet.

  The value for Time to Live can range from 0 to 255. The larger the Time to Live, the greater the distance a data packet will travel.

Table. Time to Live (TTL) Values.

TTL Value	Packet Range
0	Local host
1	Local network (subnet)
32	Site
64	Region
128	Continent
255	World

- To allow missing packets to be resent to clients that request them, select Yes from the Resend list. This setting is optional. It adds some overhead to the traffic on your network; however, clients receive better quality multicasts.
- Indicate which clients will be able to view your

multicast presentations by configuring the user list. To require that clients with IP addresses in the user list must connect in multicast mode, set Multicast Delivery Only to Yes. When this is selected, those clients not configured for multicast will not be able to receive the multicast, and will receive an error message instead. Use this feature when you want to restrict the multicast to a limited number of clients, or if you are multicasting a high-bandwidth presentation and do not want unicast to be an option.

- Select Yes from the Multicast Delivery Only list.
- Click the "+" icon, and then in the Edit Client Access Rule Number box, type a rule number. The rule number is used by Helix Universal Proxy for sorting the address rules.
- Click Edit. The rule number is added to the Client Access Rules box.
- Type the IP Address of the client allowed to receive the multicast in the Client IP Address box. To allow any client to access the multicast, type Any.
- In Client Netmask, specify the range of client IP addresses around the one you entered in the preceding step by selecting a bit mask. If Client IP Address is set to Any, though, leave Client Netmask set to None. for details about assigning a range of IP addresses using a bit mask.

Multicasting is a way of efficiently transmitting text, audio, and video on the Internet or an internal network to a select group of people, much like a conference call includes a select group of people. Instead of sending information in individual packets to each recipient, a single message is sent to a multicast group, which includes all the people that want to participate in the multicast session.

While multicasting is possible on a variety of networks, this topic concentrates on Internet multicasting. Multicasting is a one-to-many transmission. In contrast, the traditional method of sending messages on the Internet, called unicasting, is a one-to-one transmission. If multicasting is comparable to a conference call, then unicasting is like a private call between two people. Broadcasting is a one-to-all technique in which messages are sent to everybody.

Internet routers block broadcasts from propagating everywhere. Multicasting provides a way for one host to send packets to a selective group of hosts. The key word is "selective." Users choose to be part of a specific multicast. Multicast packets then travel to the user from the multicast source.

An important point is that multicast packets only travel across routes where there is an end user that has requested to be part of the multicast. This keeps multicast packets from crossing parts of the network that do not have multicast participants. Still, on the Internet, a multicast group is potentially huge, with members located around the world.

The trick to multicasting is that users indicate to their local router that they want to be part of a particular multicast group. That router then indicates to the next router closest to the source of the multicast that it wants to receive the multicast. This process continues until a path is established between the multicast source and the person who wants to join the multicast. The result is that only routers that need multicast packets for end systems actually receive those packets. Nonparticipating routers do not receive the packets, making the process more efficient.

Most multicasts are multimedia related, although a multicast host may simply broadcast a message or an occasional news item to participants. This sounds similar to electronic mailing lists, but IP Multicast uses special addressing and special protocols to achieve high- performance and efficiency. "Web casting" for an example of how multicasting is used.

RTP (Real-time Transport Protocol) is a protocol that works in conjunction with multicasting to transport real-time audio, video, simulation data, and other information over multicast networks. While IP Multicast defines how to set up multicast groups, RTP defines how to transport real-time information to the members of the groups and monitor the quality of the information that is delivered.

IP MULTICAST PROTOCOLS

IP Multicast is an open IETF (Internet Engineering Task Force) standard for distributing data to multiple recipients. The multicast recipient group can change dynamically. A host may decide to join or leave a group at any time, and a host may be a member of more than one multicast group. In addition, any host can be a multicast source by simply sending packets addressed to a particular multicast group.

Routers in this scheme must be "multicast enabled." When a multicast source transmits a multicast datagram, the local router forwards the packet to other routers with attached networks that include members of the multicast group.

IP Multicast uses class D addressing, which is a special form of the IP address designed for multicasting. The class scheme for IP addresses is discussed under "IP (Internet Protocol)." The first four bits of a class D address identify it as a class D address. The remaining 28 bits identify a particular multicast group. A class D address can be compared to the channel number of a TV station. When you tune in to a particular class D address, you receive packets that are being multicast by other systems that multicast on the address.

Internet Group Management Protocol

Multicast receivers must indicate their desire to be included in a multicast session. This is done with IGMP, a protocol that runs between hosts and their immediately neighboring multicast routers. In addition, a multicast router can use IGMP to occasionally broadcast a query on a network to determine if any hosts still want to receive broadcasts from the multicast transmitters from which it is accepting packets.

Distance Vector Multicast Routing Protocol

DVMRP is a distance vector routing protocol for multicast. DVMRP is used when a router receives a multicast packet and it wants to find out if other multicast routers it has connections to need to receive the packet (that is, they have attached hosts that are members of the group). DVMRP sends the packet to all attached routers and waits for a reply. Routers with no group members return a "prune" message, which essentially prevents further multicast messages for that group from reaching the router.

Multicast Open Shortest Path First

As the name implies, MOSPF is an Open Shortest Path First routing protocol. MOSPF routers build maps of the network topology, including the location of islands and tunnels, and then determine the best path through the network to a particular multicast router. Note that MOSPF is designed for use within autonomous systems.

Protocol-Independent Multicast

PIM is a new concept for multicast routing and is an alternative to DVMRP and MOSPF. It uses two modes: PIM-dense and PIM-sparse. Dense mode operates like DVMRP. It floods the network with traffic-a bad thing unless the group has enough participants to warrant such an action. PIM-sparse avoids flooding (and wasted bandwidth) in cases where a group is small. Instead, a rendezvous point is established and all members send packets to it.

Multicast Transport Protocol

MTP defines a flow-controlled multicasting transport protocol that operates on top of any network protocol as long as the data link layer includes multicast. MTP ensures that all messages are delivered reliably, in order, and at the same time. MTP can retransmit packets to a specific branch of a multicast group, thus reducing excess traffic in branches that don't need the retransmission.

For more information, refer to the IETF Working Groups page listed on the related entries page. A number of working groups are defining various aspects of multicasting, and their Web sites provide links to drafts and related RFCs. See "Webcasting" for related information.

An industry consortium called the IPMI (IP Multicast Initiative) is dedicated to advancing IP Multicasting and making information about it available.

Multicasting (and broadcasting which is also discussed in this article) provides a means to direct a single packet to more than one host. Special addresses are defined for this purpose and are handled specially by network adapters, networking hardware, and IP stacks. IPv4 specifications provide broadcasting and multicasting; IPv6 provides multicasting but replaces broadcasting by special multicast modes.

UNIX domain sockets do not know broadcasting or multicasting. The following examples use UDP/IPv4 only. However, they can easily be adapted for raw IPv4 sockets. IPv6 multicasting has not yet been successfully used with socat; please contact the author if you have positive experiences or ideas that go beyond IPV6_ADD_MEMBERSHIP. All multicast examples presented in this document use multicast address 224.1.0.1; it can be replaced by any valid IPv4 multicast address (except all-systems).

We assume a local network with address 192.168.10.0 and mask 255.255.255.0; an eventual "client" has 192.168.10.1, example "server" and example peer have 192.168.10.2 in all examples. Change these addresses and mask to your own requirements.

All the following examples work bidirectionally except when otherwise noticed. For "clients" we just use STDIO, and for "servers" we use EXEC:hostname which ingores its input but shows us which host the reply comes from. Replace these socat addresses with what is appropriate for your needs (e.g. shell script invocations). Port 6666 can be replaced with any other port (but for ports < 1024 root privilege might be required).

Different kinds of broadcast addresses exist: 255.255.255.255 is local network only; for the IPv4 network 192.168.10.0/24 the "official" broadcast address is 192.168.10.255; the network address 192.168.10.0 is also interpreted as broadcast by some hosts. The two latter forms are routed by gateways. In the following examples we only use broadcast address 192.168.10.255.

Example

Multicast Client and Servers:

This example builds something like a "supervisor" or "client" that communicates with a set of "servers". The supervisor may send packets to the multicast address, and the servers may send response packets. Note that the servers would also respond to other clients' requests.

Multicast Server:

```
socat UDP4-RECVFROM:6666,ip-add-membe
rship=224. 1.0.1: 192.168.10.2,fork
EXEC:hostname
```

This command receives multicast packets addressed to 224.1.0.1 and forks a child process for each. The child processes may each send one or more reply packets back to the particular sender.

192.168.10.2 means the address of the interface where multicasts should be received. Run this command on a number of hosts, and they will all respond in parallel.

Multicast Client:

```
socat STDIO UDP4-
DATAGRAM:224.1.0.1:6666,range=192.168.10.0/24
```

This process transfers data from stdin to the multicast address, and transfers packets received from the local network to stdout. It does not matter in which direction the first data is passed.

A packet from the network is accepted by the IP stack for our socket if:

- It is an incoming UDP/IPv4 packet
- Its target port matches the local port assigned to the socket (random)
- Its target address matches one of the hosts local addresses or the any-host multicast address

Of these packets, socat handles only those matching the following criteria:

- The source address is within the given range
- The source port is 6666

Broadcast Server:

```
socat UDP4-RECVFROM:6666,broadcast,fork EXEC:
hostname
```

This command receives packets addressed to a local broadcast address and forks a child process for each. The child processes may each send one or more reply packets back to the particular sender. Run this command on a number of hosts, and they will all respond in parallel.

Broadcast client

```
socat STDIO UDP4-
DATAGRAM :192.168.10.255:666 6,broadcast,range=
192.168.10.0/24
```

This process transfers data from stdin to the broadcast address, and transfers packets received from the local network to stdout. It does not matter in which direction the first data is passed. A packet from the network is accepted by the IP stack for our socket if:

- It is an incoming UDP/IPv4 packet
- Its target port matches the local port assigned to the socket (6666)
- Its target address matches one of the hosts local addresses or the any-host multicast address, or a local broadcast address

Of these packets, socat handles only those matching the following criteria:

- The source address is within the given range
- The source port is 6666

The broadcast option is only required for sending or receiving local broadcasts.

Example 3: Multicast peers

It is possible to combine multicast sender and receiver in one socat address. This allows to start processes on different hosts on the local network that will communicate symmetrically, so each process can send messages that are received by all the other ones.

```
socat STDIO UDP4-
DATAGRAM:224.1.0.1:6666,bind=:6666,range=
192.168.10.0/24,ip-add-
membership=224.1.0.1:192.168.10.2
```

This command is valid for host 192.168.10.2; adapt this address to the particular interface addresses of the hosts.

Starting this process opens a socket on port 6666 that will receive packets directed to multicast address 224.1.0.1. Only packets with matching source address and source port 6666 will be handled though.

When this process sends data to the network the packets will be addressed to 224.1.0.1:6666 and have a source address of 192.168.10.2:6666, matching the accept criteria of the peers on the local network.

Just as with multicast, it is possible to combine broadcast sender and receiver in one socat address.

```
socat STDIO UDP4-
DATAGRAM:255.255.255.255:6666,bind=:6666,
range=192.168.10.0/24,broadcast
```

Starting this process opens a socket on port 6666 that will receive packets directed to a local broadcast addresses. Only packets with matching source address and source port 6666 will be handled though.

When this process sends data to the network the packets will be addressed to 255.255.255.255:6666 and have a source address of 192.168.10.2:6666, matching the accept criteria of the peers on the local network.

TROUBLESHOOTING

If you do not get an error message during operation, but the packets do not reach the target processes, use tcpdump to see if the packets have the correct source and destination addresses and ports, and if they leave and enter the hosts as expected. The following subsections discuss some typical sources of trouble.

IP Filters

If you do not succeed in receiving multicast or broadcast packets, check if iptables are activated on the receiving or sending host. They might be configured to disallow this traffic.

Do Not Bind()

When using multicast communications, you should not bind the sockets to a specific IP address. It seems that the (Linux) IP stack compares the destination address with the bind address, not taking care of the multicast property of the incoming packet.

Routing

When you receive an error like E sendto(3, 0x80c2e44, 4, 0, AF=2 224.1.0. 1:6666, 16): Network is unreachable you have a routing problem. The (Linux) IP stack seems to handle multicast addresses just like unicast addresses when determining their route (interface and gateway), i.e. the routing table needs an entry that somehow matches the target address.

For the same reason, multicast packets will probably leave your host on the interface with the default route if it is specified. *Set a multicast/broadcast route with the following command (Linux)*: route add -net 224.0.0.0/3 gw 192.168.10.2

ALL-SYSTEMS Multicast Address

224.0.0.1 is the all-systems multicast address: all datagram sockets appear to be automatically member of this group on all interfaces. This membership cannot be dropped on Linux (you need iptables to filter packets).

(IN)SECURITY

When you use the above examples you should understand that all datagram sockets without exception accept all packets that are directly addressed to them; the multi- and broadcast receiving features are just extensions to this functionality. socat currently has no means to handle incoming packets differently whether they are addressed to unicast, multicast, or broadcast addresses. However, for EXEC'd scripts socat can provide this info in environment variables. It is very easy to fake the source address of UDP (or raw IP) packets. You should understand whether your network is protected from address spoofing attacks. Broadcast and multicast traffic can trivially be received by any host on the local network.

HISTORY

Starting with version 1.5.0, socat provides a set of address types that allow various operations on datagram oriented sockets:

- SENDTO: send packets to a remote socket and receive packet from this remote socket only
- RECV: receive all packets that arrive on the local socket, but do not reply
- RECVFROM: receive all packets that arrive on the local socket, and reply using child processes

These modes already enable several different client/server oriented operations. Moreover, the SENDTO addresses can send to multicast and broadcast addresses (the latter requires the broadcast option though). RECV and RECVFROM also would accept packets addressed to a local broadcast address (with optionbroadcast) or the all-systems multicast address.

These address types had, however, two major caveats:

- Missing control of multicast group membership in the RECV and RECVFROM addresses
- The SENDTO address would never accept a reply to a broadcast or multicast addressed packet because the source address of incoming replies would not match the target address of the sent packet.

New Features in Socat 1.6.0

Socat version 1.6.0 addresses these problems and provides a new more generic datagram address type (*-DATAGRAM) and the new address option IP-ADD-MEMBERSHIP. Please note that the new features could not be successfully tested on IPv6; these sections thus apply to IPv4 only.

New Features in Socat 1.7.0

Socat version 1.7.0 helps to find more information about

incoming packets in environment variables that can be used in scripts or programmes invoked by socat. The option ip-pktinfo (on non-BSD systems) or ip-recvdstaddr (on BSD systems) is required to get basic information about incoming packets.

Example:

Start a receiver of the following form (tried on Linux):

```
soca  -u UDP-RECVFROM:8888,reuseaddr,ip-add-
membership=224.1.0.1:192.168.10.2,
ip-pktinfo,fork SYSTEM:export
```

Then send a multicast packet from the client:

```
echo |socat -u STDIO UDP-DATAGRAM:224.1.0.1:8888
```

On the server the following text should appear:

```
export SOCAT_IP_DSTADDR="224.1.0.1"
export SOCAT_IP_IF="eth0"
export SOCAT_IP_LOCADDR="192.168.10.2"
export SOCAT_PEERADDR="192.168.10.1"
export SOCAT_PEERPORT="41159"
```

SOCAT_IP_IF shows the interface where the packet entered the server; SOCAT_IP_LOCADDR shows the IP address of this interface; SOCAT_IP_DSTADDR shows the target address of the packet; SOCAT_PEERADDR and SOCAT_PEERPORT are the client socket values.

SENDING MULTICAST PACKETS

The IP addresses 224.0.0.0 through 239.255.255.255 are reserved for multicast messages. Simply sending a UDP messsage to an address in that range is sufficient. One minor refinement is to set the TTL (Time To Live) option on the socket. My understanding is that this controls how far the packet is propagated. As polite net-citizens, we don't want our multicast packets travelling too far abroad, so we set the TTL value to 1 (we need the ugly packing stuff because the value is passed directly to the C level setsockopt() function with no interpretation by Ruby).

So the Ruby code to send a multicast message is:

```
require 'socket'
MULTICAST_ADDR = "225.4.5.6"
```

```
PORT= 5000
begin
socket = UDPSocket.open
socket.setsockopt(Socket::IPPROTO_IP,
Socket::IP_TTL, [1].pack('i'))
socket.send(ARGV.join(' '), 0, MULTICAST_ADDR,
PORT)
ensure
socket.close
end
```

RECEIVING MULTICAST MESSAGES

Receiving a multicast message is a bit tricker. Since multicast messages are generally ignored unless someone has explicitly registered an interest in a particular address, there is a bit of setup that needs to be done.

Here's the code for receiving multicast messages:

```
require 'socket'
require 'ipaddr'
MULTICAST_ADDR = "225.4.5.6"
PORT = 5000
ip = IPAddr.new(MULTICAST_ADDR).hton +
IPAddr.new("0.0.0.0").hton
sock = UDPSocket.new
sock.setsockopt(Socket::IPPROTO_IP,
Socket::IP_ADD_MEMBERSHIP, ip)
sock.bind(Socket::INADDR_ANY, PORT)
loop do
msg, info = sock.recvfrom(1024)
puts "MSG: #{msg} from #{info[2]} (#{info[3]})/
#{info[1]} len #{msg.size}"
end
```

The tricky part was figuring out the right setsockopt options and values needed to register interest in our multicast address. I had to do a little reading in the Unix man pages on the C level setsockopt() function call. The third option to the C function is a structure that contains two 4-byte IP addresses. The first IP address is the multicast address, and the second

IP address is the address of the local host adapter that we wish to use to listen for the multicast. The 0.0.0.0 address means use any of the local network adapters. IPAddr handles parsing the human readable form of the IP address and returns a string of 4 bytes in the order needed by the C level setsockopt() function.

USAGE

Save the above code in files named send.rb and rcv.rb. In one console window, type:

```
ruby rcv.rb
```

In another console window on the same or different machine (on the same local network), type:

```
ruby send.rb This is a test.
```

UPDATE

I added the Time To Live option on send.

POINT-TO-POINT COMMUNICATIONS

A point-to-point connection is a dedicated communication link between two systems or processes. Think of a wire that directly connects two systems. The systems use that wire exclusively to communicate. The opposite of point-to-point communications is broadcasting, where one system transmits to many. A telephone call is a circuit-oriented, point-to-point link between two phones. However, calls are usually multiplexed across telephone company trunks; so, while the circuit itself may be virtual, the users are engaging in a point-to-point communication session.

An end-to-end connection refers to a connection between two systems across a switched network. For example, the Internet is made up of a mesh of routers. Packets follow a hop-by-hop path from one router to the next to reach their destinations. Each hop consists of a physical point-to-point link between routers. Therefore, a routed path consists of multiple point-to-point links. In the ATM and frame relay environment, the end-to-end path is called a virtual circuit that crosses a predefined set of point-to-point links.

A shared LAN such as Ethernet provides a form of point-to-point communications. Keep in mind that on shared LANs, all nodes listen to signals on the cable, so broadcasting is supported. However, when one node addresses frames to another node and only that node receives the frames, one could say that the two nodes are engaged in point-to-point communications across a shared medium.

Point-to-multipoint connections are possible over multidrop links. A mainframe and its terminals is an example. The device that provides the multipoint connection is usually an intelligent controller that manages the flow of information from the multiple devices attached to it. Point-to-point communications is defined in the physical and data link layers of the OSI protocol stack.

Process one (myrank = 1) receives this message with the receive operation MPI_RECV. The message to be received is selected according to the value of its envelope, and the message data is stored into the receive buffer. In the example above, the receive buffer consists of the storage containing the string message in the memory of process one.

The first three parameters of the receive operation specify the location, size and type of the receive buffer. The next three parameters are used for selecting the incoming message. The last parameter is used to return information on the message just received.

The next sections describe the blocking send and receive operations. We discuss send, receive, blocking communication semantics, type matching requirements, type conversion in heterogeneous environments, and more general communication modes. Nonblocking communication is addressed next, followed by channel-like constructs and send-receive operations.

We then consider general datatypes that allow one to transfer efficiently heterogeneous and noncontiguous data. We conclude with the description of calls for explicit packing and unpacking of messages. The basic communication mechanism of MPI is the transmittal of data between a pair of processes, one side sending, the other, receiving. We call this ``point to point communication." Almost all the constructs of MPI are built around the point to point operations and so this chapter is fundamental. It is also quite a long chapter since: there are many variants to the point to point operations; there is much to say in terms of the semantics of the operations; and related topics, such as probing for messages, are explained here because they are used in conjunction with the point to point operations.

MPI provides a set of send and receive functions that allow the communication of typedtyped data data with an associated tag.tagmessage tag Typing of the message contents is necessary for heterogeneous support - the type information is needed so that correct data representation conversions can be performed as data is sent from one architecture to another. The tag allows selectivity of messages at the receiving end: one can receive on a particular tag, or one can wild-card this quantity, allowing reception of messages with any tag. Message selectivity on the source process of the message is also provided.

A fragment of C code appears in Example for the example of process 0 sending a message to process 1. The code executes on both process 0 and process 1. Process 0 sends a character string using MPI_Send(). The first three parameters of the send call specify the data to be sent: the outgoing data is to be taken frommsg; it consists of strlen(msg)+1 entries, each of type MPI_CHAR (The string "Hello there" contains strlen(msg)=11 significant characters. In addition, we are also sending the tex2html_html_special_mark_quot''" string terminator character). The fourth parameter specifies the message destination, which is process 1. The fifth parameter specifies the message tag. Finally, the last parameter is a communicator that specifies a communication domaincommunication domain for this communication.

Among other things, a communicator serves to define a set of processes that can be contacted. Each such process is labeled by a process rank.rank Process ranks are integers and are discovered by inquiry to a communicator (see the call to MPI_Comm_rank()).MPI_COMM_WORLDMPI_COMM_WORLD is a default communicator provided upon start-up that defines an initial communication domain for all the processes that participate in the computation. Much more will be said about communicators in Chapter .

We have already said rather a lot about a simple transmittal of data from one process to another, but there is even more. To understand why, we examine two aspects of the communication: the semantics semantics of the communication primitives, and the underlying protocols that protocols implement them. Consider the previous example, on process 0, after the blocking send has completed. The question arises: if the send has completed, does this tell us anything about the receiving process? Can we know that the receive has finished, or even, that it has begun?

Such questions of semantics are related to the nature of the underlying protocol implementing the operations. If one wishes to implement a protocol minimizing the copying and buffering of data, the most natural semantics might be the ``rendezvous''rendezvous version, where completion of the send implies the receive has been initiated (at least). On the other hand, a protocol that attempts to block processes for the minimal amount of time will necessarily end up doing more buffering and copying of data and will have ``buffering'' semantics.buffering

The trouble is, one choice of semantics is not best for all applications, nor is it best for all architectures. Because the primary goal of MPI is to standardize the operations, yet not sacrifice performance, the decision was made to include all the major choices for point to point semantics in the standard.

The above complexities are manifested in MPI by the existence of modesmodes for point to point communication. Both blocking and nonblocking communications have modes. The mode allows one to choose the semantics of the send operation and, in effect, to influence the underlying protocol of the transfer of data.

In standard modestandard mode the completion of the send does not necessarily mean that the matching receive has started, and no assumption should be made in the application programme about whether the out-going data is buffered by MPI. In buffered mode buffered mode the user can guarantee that a certain amount of buffering space is available. The catch is that the space must be explicitly provided by the application programme. In synchronous mode synchronous mode a rendezvous semantics between sender and receiver is used. Finally, there is ready mode. ready mode This allows the user to exploit extra knowledge to simplify the protocol and potentially achieve higher performance. In a ready-mode send, the user asserts that the matching receive already has been posted. Modes are covered in Section .

IP ADDRESSING

An IP (Internet Protocol) address is a unique identifier for a node or host connection on an IP network. An IP address is a 32 bit binary number usually represented as 4 decimal values, each representing 8 bits, in the range 0 to 255 (known as octets) separated by decimal points. This is known as "dotted decimal" notation.

Every IP address consists of two parts, one identifying the network and one identifying the node. The Class of the address and the subnet mask determine which part belongs to the network address and which part belongs to the node address.

There are 5 different address classes. You can determine which class any IP address is in by examining the first 4 bits of the IP address.

- Class A addresses begin with 0xxx, or 1 to 126 decimal.
- Class B addresses begin with 10xx, or 128 to 191 decimal.
- Class C addresses begin with 110x, or 192 to 223 decimal.
- Class D addresses begin with 1110, or 224 to 239 decimal.
- Class E addresses begin with 1111, or 240 to 254 decimal.

Addresses beginning with 01111111, or 127 decimal, are reserved for loopback and for internal testing on a local machine; Class D addresses are reserved for multicasting; Class E addresses are reserved for future use. They should not be used for host addresses.

PRIVATE SUBNETS

There are three IP network addresses reserved for private networks. The addresses are 10.0.0.0, Subnet Mask 255.0.0.0, 172.16.0.0, Subnet Mask 255.240.0.0, and 192.168.0.0, Subnet Mask 255.255.0.0. These addresses are also notated 10.0.0.0/8, 172.16.0.0/12, and 192.168.0.0/16; this notation will be explained later in this tutorial. They can be used by anyone setting up internal IP networks, such as a lab or home LAN behind a NAT or proxy server or a router. It is always safe to use these because routers on the Internet by default will never forward packets coming from these addresses. These addresses are defined in RFC 1918.

IP ADDRESSING AND SUBNETTING

This document gives you basic information needed to configure your router for routing IP, such as how addresses are broken down and how subnetting works. You learn how to assign each interface on the router an IP address with a unique subnet. There are many examples to help tie everything together.

Prerequisites

Requirements: There are no specific prerequisites for this document.

Additional Information

If definitions are helpful to you, use these vocabulary terms to get you started:

- Address-The unique number ID assigned to one host or interface in a network.
- Subnet-A portion of a network sharing a particular subnet address.
- Subnet mask-A 32-bit combination used to describe

which portion of an address refers to the subnet and which part refers to the host.

- Interface-A network connection.

If you have already received your legitimate address(es) from the Internet Network Information Centre (InterNIC), you are ready to begin. If you do not plan to connect to the Internet, Cisco strongly suggests that you use reserved addresses from RFC 1918 .

Network Masks

A network mask helps you know which portion of the address identifies the network and which portion of the address identifies the node. Class A, B, and C networks have default masks, also known as natural masks, as shown here:

```
Class A: 255.0.0.0
Class B: 255.255.0.0
Class C: 255.255.255.0
```

An IP address on a Class A network that has not been subnetted would have an address/mask pair similar to: 8.20.15.1 255.0.0.0. To see how the mask helps you identify the network and node parts of the address, convert the address and mask to binary numbers.

```
8.20.15.1 = 00001000.00010100.00001111.00000001
255.0.0.0 = 11111111.00000000.00000000.00000000
```

Once you have the address and the mask represented in binary, then identifying the network and host ID is easier. Any address bits which have corresponding mask bits set to 1 represent the network ID. Any address bits that have corresponding mask bits set to 0 represent the node ID.

```
8.20.15.1 = 00001000.00010100.00001111.00000001
255.0.0.0 = 11111111.00000000.00000000.00000000
net id | host id
netid = 00001000 = 8
hostid = 00010100.00001111.00000001 = 20.15.1
```

ATM

The next generation of computer and telecommunication networks will use the asynchronous transfer mode (ATM).

ATM networks use small fixed size cells to transmit information. This allows them to share the same network for voice, video, and data at a wide range of distances. Most computer and telecommunication companies are working on ATM products and services.

In this tutorial seminar, we will give a brief history and overview of the ATM technology. The key features that allow this technology to work better than the current packet networks will be presented including why this technology allows wider ranges of distance and number of nodes. Various networking interfaces that are being standardized will be explained.

ATM, or Asynchronous Transfer Mode is a solid option for high-bandwidth network deployments that require guaranteed service levels and robust reliability. Backed by years of technology maturity, ATM now offers a widely supported platform for building global networks as well as high bandwidth, inter-regional trunks.

Pacnet ATM Service is a high speed, scalable networking service that enables service providers or enterprise customers to transport multiple network applications (voice, data and video). ATM offers quality of service (QoS) over a single connection between geographically distant locations via a public network of shared circuits, that is scalable from 2Mbps to 155Mbps.

With Pacnet's ATM service, you get access to a state-of-the-art ATM network that spans all key business centers in more than 25 countries.

FEATURES

- Wide range of ATM port speed, including nxT1/E1, DS3 and STM1.
- Any-to-any end-point connectivity through PVC implementation.
- Full internetworking support between ATM and Frame Relay to support smaller branch connections.
- Supports different application mixes through multiple Classes-of-Service, including CBR for real-

time applications, VBR-rt for time-sensitive applications, VBR-nrt for non-real time applications with bursty traffic characteristics and UBR, best effort service for non-critical applications.

- Upgrade and downgrade options to match market requirements.
- Fully managed services portfolio and industry-leading SLAs with the following components.
- Network Availability
- Network Transit Delay
- Cell Delivery
- Mean Time-To-Repair
- Installation
- Expert support by network design and provisioning professionals focused on
  both PoP-to-PoP and last mile access.

TUNNELING

DEFINITION

Tunneling, also known as "port forwarding," is the transmission of data intended for use only within a private, usually corporate network through a public network in such a way that the routing nodes in the public network are unaware that the transmission is part of a private network. Tunneling is generally done by encapsulating the private network data and protocol information within the public network transmission units so that the private network protocol information appears to the public network as data. Tunneling allows the use of the Internet, which is a public network, to convey data on behalf of a private network.

One approach to tunneling is the Point-to-Point Tunneling Protocol (PPTP) developed by Microsoft and several other companies. The PPTP keeps proprietary data reasonably secure, even though part of the path(s) between or among end users exists in public communication channels. The PPTP makes it possible for authorized users to gain access to a private network - called a virtual private network (VPN) -

through an Internet service provider (ISP) or online service. Another commonly used tunneling protocol is generic routing encapsulation (GRE), developed by Cisco Systems. There are numerous, less common tunneling protocols.

Tunneling, and the use of a VPN, is not intended as a substitute for encryption/decryption. In cases where a high level of security is necessary, the strongest possible encryption should be used within the VPN itself, and tunneling should serve only as a convenience.

EXPLANATION

Tunneling, or port forwarding, is a way to forward otherwise insecure TCP traffic through SSH Secure Shell for Workstations. You can secure for example POP3, SMTP and HTTP connections that would otherwise be insecure.

Fig. Encrypted SSH2 Tunnel.

The tunneling capability of SSH Secure Shell for Workstations is a feature that allows, for example, company employees to access their email, company intraweb pages and shared files securely by even when working from home or on the road.

Tunneling makes it possible to access email from any type of Internet service (whether accessed via modem, a DSL line or a cable connection, or a hotel Internet service). As long as the user has an IP connection to the Internet she can get her mail and access other resources from anywhere in the world securely.

This often is not the case with more traditional IPSec based VPN technologies because of issues with traversing networks that are implementing Network Address Translation (NAT) - this is especially the case in hotels. NAT breaks an IPSec connection unless special protocols such as NAT-Traversal are implemented on the client and gateway.

The client-server applications using the tunnel will carry out their own authentication procedures, if any, the same way they would without the encrypted tunnel. The protocol/ application might only be able to connect to a fixed port number (e.g. IMAP 143). Otherwise any available port can be chosen for port forwarding.

HTTP-TUNNELING

If you answer yes to any of these, HTTP-Tunnel is the answer:

- Need to bypass any firewall
- Need secure internet browsing
- Need to use favorite programmes with out being monitored by work, school, ISP or gov.
- Extra security for online transactions
- Encrypt all your Internet traffic.
- Need play online games
- Visit sites that you are previously blocked
- Prevent 3rd party monitoring or regulation of your Internet browsing and downloads
- Use your favorite applications previously blocked
- Hide your IP address
- Make it next to impossible for you to identify online.
- Free unlimited data transfer
- Compatible with most major Internet applications
- Secure and virus-free servers
- 99% uptime
- No spam, pop-ups, or banners

Applications

A list of some of the more popular supported applications can be found here. Also, user guides to help you configure your HTTP-Tunnel Client can be found.

Low Bandwidth Service Features

- Free option for moderate users
- Sufficient for Instant Messaging programmes

- Good for users who only need to access blocked web sites
- No spam, pop-ups, or banners

High Bandwidth Service Features

- High speed option for power users
- No bandwidth limitation
- Ideal for users behind a high speed internet connection (Cable/DSL modem, T1, etc.)
- Good for applications which are transfer-intensive (peer-to-peer programmes, FTP, etc.)
- No spam, pop-ups, or banners

If any technical problems are encoutered, it is recommended to visit the support page for assistance prior to asking for a refund.

OS Requirements

HTTP-Tunnel runs on a variety of Windows operating systems (Windows 98, ME, NT 4.X, 2000, XP and Vista). There are currently no releases available for Unix or MacIntosh platforms.

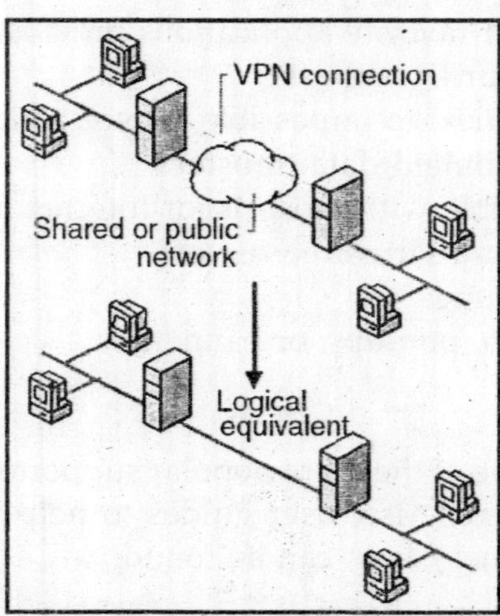

Tunneling is a way in which data is transferred between two networks securely. All the data that is being transferred are fragmented into smaller packets or frames and then passed through the tunnel. This process is different from a normal data transfer between nodes. Every frame passing through the tunnel will be encrypted with an additional layer of tunneling encryption and encapsulation which is also used for routing the packets to the right direction.

This encapsulation would then be reverted at the destination with decryption of data which is later sent to the desired destined node. A tunnel is a logical path between the source and the destination endpoints between two networks. Every packet is encapsulated at the source will be de-capsulated at the destination. This process will keep happening as long as the logical tunnel is persistent between the two endpoints.

TUNNELING PROTOCOLS

The Windows Server 2003 family supports the following tunneling protocols for secure communication:

- Point-to-Point Tunneling Protocol (PPTP)
  - PPTP employs user-level PPP authentication methods and Microsoft Point-to-Point Encryption (MPPE) for data encryption.
  - PPTP uses TCP1723 and Protocol 47 (GRE).
  - PPTP uses only NTLM authentication.
  - PPTP provides 56 bit or 128 bit Microsoft Point-to-Point Encryption (MPPE).
- Layer Two Tunneling Protocol (L2TP)
  - L2TP is an industry-standard Internet tunneling protocol with roughly the same functionality as the Point-to-Point Tunneling Protocol (PPTP). Based on the Layer Two Forwarding (L2F) and Point-to-Point Tunneling Protocol (PPTP) specifications, you can use L2TP to set up tunnels across intervening networks. Like PPTP, L2TP encapsulates Point-to-Point Protocol (PPP) frames, which then encapsulate IP or IPX protocols, allowing users to remotely run programmes that are dependent on specific network protocols.

  - L2TP uses the UDP 1701.
  - L2TP does not provide any encryption by itself.
- L2TP with Internet Protocol security (L2TP/IPSec)
  - L2TP/IPSec employs user-level PPP authentication methods over a connection that is encrypted with IPSec. IPSec requires host authentication using either the Kerberos protocol, shared secret or computer-level certificates.
  - L2TP with IPSec uses UDP 500 = ISAKMP, Protocol 50 = Encapsulated Security Payload (ESP) and possibly Protocol 51 = Authentication Header (AH).
  - L2TP/IPSec uses both Mutual authentication and NTLM authentication.
  - IPSec provides DES (56 bit) and 3DES (168 bit) encryption.

WORKING OF TUNNELING

As we know VPN connection are of two type, PPTP (Point-to-Point tunneling protocol) and L2TP (Layer 2 tunneling protocol). Both PPTP and L2TP tunnels are nothing but local sessions between two different endpoints. Incase they have to communicate then the tunneling type must be negotiated between the endpoint, either PPTP or L2TP and then more configurable parameters like encryption, address assignment, compression etc must be configured in order to get the best possible security over the internet based private logical tunnel communication.

This communication is created, maintained and terminated using a tunnel management protocol. Data can be sent once the tunnel is in place and clients or server can use the same tunnel to send and receive data across the internetwork. The data transfer depends upon the tunneling protocols being used for the transfer.

For example, whenever the client wants to send data or payload (the packets containing data) to the tunneling server, the tunnel server adds a header to each packet. This header packet contains the routing information which informs the packet about the destination across the internetwork communication. Once the payload is received at the destination, the header information is verified. After which destination tunnel server sends the packet to the destined node or client or server.

Point-to-Point Protocol (PPP)

It is very obvious that the PPTP and L2TP protocoasl arefully dependent upon PPP connection and it is very much important to understand and examine PPP a little more closely. Initially PPP was designed to work with only dial-up connections or dedicated connections.

If the data transfer is happening over PPP connection, then the packets going over PPP are encapsulated within PPP frames and then send across or transmitted over to the destination dial-up or PPP, server. There are four distinct phases of negotiation in a PPP connection. Each of these four phases must complete successfully before the PPP connection is ready to transfer user data.

Phase 1: PPP Link Establishment First step is where PPP uses the LCP or Link Control Protocol to connect to the destination network. Apart from establishing the connection, LCP is also responsible for maintaining and terminating the connection too. Take for example, during this phase 1, LCP connects to the destination and prepares the authentication protocol which will be used in phase 2. Next step would be to negotiate and find out if these two nodes in a PPP connection would agree on any compression or encryption algorithm. If the answer is yes then the same is be implemented in Phase 4.

Phase 2: A User Authentication Second step is where the user credentials are sent to the remote destination for authentication. There are different secure authentication programme. The secure method of authentication must be used to safeguard the user credentials. If you are using PAP (password Authentication Protocol) for authorizing user credential, the user information is passed in plain clear text which can be captured easily. This is the only time when the user must take utmost care in handling his/her credential from any theft. If for any reason these credentials were captured by the intruder, and then once the user connection is authenticate, the intruder will traps the communication, disconnect the original user and takes control of the connection.

Phase 3: PPP Callback Control The Microsoft implementation of PPP includes an optional callback control phase. This phase uses the Callback Control Protocol (CBCP) immediately after the authentication phase. If configured for callback, both the remote client and NAS disconnect after authentication. The NAS then calls the remote client back at a specified phone number. This provides an additional level of security to dial-up connections. The NAS allows connections from remote clients physically residing at specific phone numbers only. Callback is only used for dial-up connections, not for VPN connections.

Phase 4: Invoking Network Layer Protocol(s) Once the previous phases have been completed, PPP invokes the various network control protocols (NCPs) that were selected during the link establishment phase (Phase 1) to configure protocols used by the remote client. For example, during this phase, IPCP is used to assign a dynamic address to the PPP client. In the Microsoft implementation of PPP, the Compression Control Protocol (CCP) is used to negotiate both data compression (using MPPC) and data encryption (using MPPE).

Data-Transfer

Once the four phases of PPP negotiation have been completed, PPP begins to forward data to and from the two peers. Each transmitted data packet is wrapped in a PPP header that is removed by the receiving system. If data compression was selected in phase 1 and negotiated in phase 4, data is compressed before transmission. If data encryption is selected and negotiated, data is encrypted before transmission. If both encryption and compression are negotiated, the data is compressed first, and then encrypted.

Point-to-Point Tunneling Protocol (PPTP)

PPTP encapsulates PPP frames in IP datagram for

transmission over an IP internetwork, such as the Internet. PPTP can be used for remote access and router-to-router VPN connections.

PPTP or Point-to-Point tunneling protocol works over TCP port which is also used for tunnel management and GRE or Generic Routing Encapsulation protocol to encapsulat any PPP frames which will later be used in sending data through the tunnel. Compression or encryption will depend on the tunnel configuration.

VIRTUAL PRIVATE NETWORKS

DEFINITION

Virtual private network (VPN) technologies in Microsoft Windows using the resources on this page. An extension of a private network, a VPN encompasses links across shared or public networks. VPN connections use the connectivity of the Internet plus a combination of tunneling and data encryption technologies, such as the Point-to-Point Tunneling Protocol (PPTP) and Layer Two Tunneling Protocol with Internet Protocol security (L2TP/IPSec), to connect remote clients and remote offices.

A virtual private network (VPN) is a network that uses a public telecommunication infrastructure, such as the Internet, to provide remote offices or individual users with secure access to their organization's network.

A virtual private network can be contrasted with an expensive system of owned or leased lines that can only be used by one organization. The goal of a VPN is to provide the organization with the same capabilities, but at a much lower cost

A VPN works by using the shared public infrastructure while maintaining privacy through security procedures and tunneling protocols such as the Layer Two Tunneling Protocol (L2TP). In effect, the protocols, by encrypting data at the sending end and decrypting it at the receiving end, send the data through a "tunnel" that cannot be "entered" by data that is not properly encrypted. An additional level of security involves encrypting not only the data, but also the originating and receiving network addresses.

AUTHENTICATION

Authentication ensures the identity of all communicating parties. You may have seen the cartoon that appeared in The New Yorker a few years back. A dog sitting in front of a PC turned to his canine friend and said "On the Internet, nobody knows you're a dog." To correctly identify an individual or computing resource, VPNs typically use one or more forms of authentication.

These methods are usually based on password authentication (shared secrets) ordigital certificates. Password authentication is the most prevalent form of user authentication used in computer systems today, but it is also one of the weakest because passwords can be guessed or stolen. Multi-factor authentication is generally a stronger form of authentication and is based on the premise of utilizing something you have in conjunction with something you know. This process is similar to how most ATM cards are used; a user possesses the physical ATM card and "unlocks" it with a password.

For example, many VPNs support SecurID by Security Dynamics, a token card that combines secret key encryption with a one-time password. The password is automatically generated by encrypting a timestamp with the secret key. This one-time password will be valid for a short interval, usually 30 to 60 seconds.

Digital certificates are also becoming more prevalent as an authentication mechanism for VPNs. A digital certificate (based on the X.509 standard) is an electronic document that is issued to an individual by a "Certificate Authority" that can vouch for an individual's identity. It essentially binds the identity of an individual to a public key. A digital certificate will contain a public key, information specific to the user (name, company, etc.), information specific to the issuer, a validity period and additional management information. This information will be used to create a message digest which is encrypted with the Certificate Authority's private key to "sign" the certificate. By utilizing the digital signature verification procedure described above, participants in a conversation can "mutually authenticate" each other. Although this process sounds simple, it involves a complex system of key generation, certification, revocation and management, all part of a Public Key Infrastructure (PKI). A PKI is a broad set of technologies that are utilized to manage public keys, private keys and certificates. The deployment of a PKI solution should not be taken lightly as there are major issues involved with scalability and interoperability.

VPN PROTOCOLS

As a matter of practice, the separate technologies used to provide confidentiality, integrity and authentication in a given implementation are grouped into a broad VPN protocol. Three widely used protocols - IPsec, tunneling and Socks5 - are described below.

IPSEC

The protocol which seems destined to become the de facto standard for VPNs is IPSec (Internet Protocol Security). IPSec is a set of authentication and encryption protocols, developed by the Internet Engineering Task Force (IETF) and designed to address the inherent lack of security for IP-based networks. It is designed to address data confidentiality, integrity, authentication and key management, in addition to tunneling.

The IPSec protocol typically works on the edges of a security domain. Basically, IPSec encapsulates a packet by wrapping another packet around it. It then encrypts the entire packet. This encrypted stream of traffic forms a secure tunnel across an otherwise unsecured network.

The majority of VPN vendors are implementing IPSec in their solutions. The comprehensive nature of the protocol make it ideal for site-to-site VPNs, although there are still interoperability issues that exist across different vendor's implementations. IPSec is a bi-directional protocol, which means that extranet configurations must be carefully designed and implemented. When setting up an extranet VPN, you may not want to give your partners access to your entire network or allow them to access yet another partner through your network.

LAYER 2 TUNNELING PROTOCOL (L2TP)

PPTP is a tunneling protocol which provides remote users encrypted, multi-protocol access to a corporate network over the Internet. Network layer protocols, such as IPX and NetBEUI, are encapsulated by the PPTP protocol for transport over the Internet. Unlike IPSec, PPTP was not originally designed to provide Lan-to-Lan tunneling.

PPTP is built in to NT 4.0, and the client is a free add-on to Windows95. Microsoft's implementation of PPTP has been found to have several problems that make it vulnerable to attacks, and it also lacks scalability in that it only supports 255 concurrent connections per server. The low cost and integration with NT and Windows 95, however, makes PPTP a viable remote access solution where multi-protocol access is needed, heavy-duty encryption and authentication is not needed, and a Microsoft-only solution is appropriate.

PPTP can support only one tunnel at a time for each user. However, its proposed successor, L2TP (a hybrid of PPTP and another protocol, L2F) can support multiple, simultaneous tunnels for each user. L2TP will be incorporated in Windows 2000 and can support IPSec for data encryption and integrity

Socks5

SOCKS version 5 is a circuit-level proxy protocol that was originally designed to facilitate authenticated firewall traversal. It provides a secure, proxy architecture with extremely granular access control, making it an excellent choice for extranet configurations.

SOCKS v5 supports a broad range of authentication, encryption, tunneling and key management schemes, as well as a number of features not possible with IPSec, PPTP or other VPN technologies. SOCKS v5 provides an extensible architecture that allows developers to build system plug-ins, such as content filtering (denying access to Java applets or ActiveX controls, for example) and extensive logging and auditing of users When SOCKS is used in conjunction with other VPN technologies, it's possible to have a more complete security solution than any individual technology could provide.

A user may, for example, incorporate IPSec and SOCKS together. IPSec could be used to secure the underlying network transport, while SOCKS could be used to enforce user-level and application-level access control.

PERFORMANCE AND AVAILABILITY

Most VPN technologies today do not address performance and availability issues, as important as they are. Why? Because the majority of VPN solutions exist on client machines and gateway servers at the extreme ends of the communication path.

They simply cannot consistently affect the performance of the network components in the middle. Unfortunately, this "middle" is exactly where the Internet fits into the architecture. Any cost savings that a VPN provides can be quickly negated if users are forced to sacrifice QoS (quality of service) beyond certain limits. Until a standard QoS mechanism becomes ubiquitous, end-to-end performance guarantees will be hard to implement.

As a partial remedy several Internet Service Providers (ISPs) are offering managed VPN services, which combine security capabilities with QoS guarantees. For example, GE Internetworking provides a managed VPN service that combines an IPSec-based VPN solution from TimeStep Corporation with guaranteed availability of 99.9%, and round-trip latency of less than or equal to 125 milliseconds.

This type of service can be an excellent choice for site-to-site connectivity and is made possible by the fact that ISPs "own the plumbing." Unfortunately, the performance guarantees only apply to traffic within the network controlled by the ISP. Once it passes onto another ISP's portion of the Internet, all bets are off.

OVERVIEW

The term "VPN," or "Virtual Private Network," is one of the most overused buzzwords in the industry today. Proponents claim that VPNs can solve many issues, from extending the enterprise to include strategic business partners and customers, to providing remote users secure multiprotocol access to corporate Intranets, to securing corporate data for transport over the public Internet.

Vendors and consumers alike disagree as to what, exactly, a VPN is. With all the excitement, speculation and competing messages in the press regarding this technology, it's hard to figure out some of the basic questions. What exactly is a VPN? Why do you need a VPN? And what are some of the technologies used in deploying a VPN? This article will attempt to answer some of these questions.

Towards a Connected Planet

While the Internet holds incredible promise as an enabler for eBusiness, there are somemajor stumbling blocks that must be addressed if an organization is truly to conduct mission-critical business functions over the 'net. The Internet's greatest assets are itsopenness and ubiquity. But these characteristics are also its greatest weaknesses.

Historically, organizations built and deployed mission-critical applications over private local- and wide area networks (LANs and WANs), where the infrastructure was a known entity and access was tightly controlled. The end result was a private data communications infrastructure that had somewhat predictable application availability, performance and security.

Enter the 'Net. The types of applications being deployed across the public Internet today are increasingly mission-critical, whereby business success can be jeopardized by poor application performance. We've all heard the horror stories of frantic Internet traders trying desperately to unload stocks as the markets dropped, while bandwidth constraints hampered their attempts. Remember the phrase "form follows function"? It doesn't matter how attractive and potentially lucrative our applications are if they don't function reliably and consistently. The unpredictable nature of Internet traffic can be a major risk factor for e-business.

What about security? As you increase your connectivity, you increase your exposure and therefore your potential security risks. A disconnected stand-alone personal computer with sensitive information is vulnerable only to people who can gain physical access to it. Connect it to the Internet, however, and you drastically increase its exposure and attendant vulnerability.

Furthermore, data in transit across the Internet is subject to such threats as spoofing, session hijacking, sniffing, and man-in-the-middle attacks. The desire to use the Internet for business and the the risk factors associated with doing so have given rise to a new technology niche: Virtual Private Networks (VPN). VPNs typically are IP-based networks (usually the public Internet) that useencryption and tunneling to achieve one or more of the following goals:

- Connect users securely their own corporate network (remote access)
- Link branch offices to an enterprise network (intranet)
- Extend organizations' existing computing infrastructure to include partners, suppliers and customers (extranet).

The idea is to extend trust relationships across an economical public network without sacrificing security. Ideally, a VPN should behave similarly to a private network; it should be secure, highly available and have predictable performance.

Approaches

Many VPN technologies already exist, with more being developed, marketed and deployed each day. Some products are based on standards (usually emergingstandards); others are proprietary. Some address very specific requirements, such as secure remote access over the Internet for mobile users, while others focus more on secure LAN-to-LAN connectivity. Each product and technology has inherent strengths and weaknesses. The trick is to understand the current technology landscape; to understand how to choose the right solutions dependent on the underlying problems that must be addressed; and to understand where the technology will likely head in the future.

Looking at the design goals for a VPN, security is the focus of most solutions available today, and we therefore begin with approaches to ensuring Confidentiality, Integrity and Authentication. Performance and availability, also important goals, are discussed towards the end of the article.

Confidentiality

Confidentiality protects the privacy of information being exchanged between communicating parties. Towards this end, every VPN solution provides encryption of some sort. The two primary cryptographic systems in use today are secret key cryptographyand public key cryptography.

Secret (or private) key cryptography uses a shared key which is used to encrypt and decrypt messages. The major problem with private key cryptography is key exchange. Sending secret keys across the Internet unencrypted is not an option for obvious reasons.

This is where public key cryptography can help. Public key cryptography uses a mathematically linked key pair for each communicating party. This means that data encrypted with one key can be decrypted with the other key in the pair. A sender can encrypt a message with the recipient's public key, which as the name implies is publicly available (on a server, for example). The recipient can then decrypt the message using his or her own private key. Public key systems enable encryption over an unsecured network as well as a mechanism to exchange secret keys.

On the downside, public key cryptography is computationally intensive, and therefore often combined with secret key cryptography to get the best blend of performance and functionality. For example, the Diffie-Hellman public key algorithm can be used in conjunction with the DES secret key algorithm-Diffie-Hellman to produce the secret key and DES to encrypt the traffic.

Integrity

Integrity ensures that information being transmitted over the public Internet is not altered in any way during transit. VPNs typically use one of three technologies to ensure integrity.

One-way Hash Functions

A hash function generates a fixed-length output value based on an arbitrary-length input file. The idea is that it's easy to calculate the hash value of a file but mathematically difficult to generate a file that will hash to that value. To validate the integrity of a file, a recipient would calculate the hash value of that file and compare it to the hash value sent by the sender. Thus, the recipient can be assured that the sender had the file at the time he or she created the hash value. Examples of hash algorithms are MD5, SHA-1 and RIPE-MD-160.

Message-Authentication Codes (MACs)

Simply add a key to hash functions. A sender would create a file, calculate a MAC based on a key shared with the recipient, and then append it to the file. When the recipient receives the file, it is easy to calculate the MAC and compare it to the one that was appended to the file.

Digital Signatures

Can also be used for data integrity purposes. A digital signature is essentially public key cryptography in reverse. A sender digitally "signs" a document with their private key and the recipient can verify the signature via the sender's public key.

SECURE CONNECTIVITY

Improve security and maintain productivity with Cisco VPN technology. Cisco VPNs help securely connect offices, remote users, and business partners. VPNs have become the primary solution for remote connectivity for organizations of all sizes, using affordable, third-party Internet access.

Enhance Productivity and Cut Costs

Cisco VPN solutions provide exceptional security through encryption and authentication technologies that protect data in transit from unauthorized access and attacks. A Cisco VPN helps you.

- Use highly secure communications, with access rights tailored to individual users
- Quickly add new sites or users, without significantly expanding your existing infrastructure
- Improve productivity by extending corporate networks, applications, and collaboration tools
- Reduce communications costs while increasing flexibility

Two VPN technologies are currently in use: site-to-site VPNsand remote access VPNs.

Site-to-Site VPNs

Site-to-site VPNs provide an Internet-based WAN infrastructure to extend network resources to branch offices, home offices, and business partner sites. All traffic between sites is encrypted using IPsec protocol and integrates network features such as routing, quality of service, and multicast support. Cisco VPNs also offer:

- Reliable and high-quality transport of complex, mission-critical traffic, such as voice and client server applications
- Simplified provisioning and reduced operational tasks for network designs
- Integrated advanced network intelligence and routing for a wide range of network designs

Remote Access VPNs

Remote access VPNs extend almost any data, voice, or video application to the remote desktop, emulating the main office desktop. With this VPN, you can provide highly secure, customizable remote access to anyone, anytime, anywhere, with almost any device. Cisco remote access VPNs:

- Create a remote user experience that emulates working on the main office desktop
- Deliver VPN access safely and easily to a wide range of users and devices

- Support a wide range of connectivity options, endpoints, and platforms to meet your dynamic remote access needs

NETWORK OPERATIONS

DEFINITION

A network operations centre (NOC) is a place from which administrators supervise, monitor and maintain a telecommunications network. Large enterprises with large networks as well as large network service providers typically have a network operations centre, a room containing visualizations of the network or networks that are being monitored, workstations at which the detailed status of the network. The Managed Network Operations solution assumes operational fault management responsibility over all or a subset of a telecom carrier's network through a central NOC (Network Operation Centre), applying state-of-the-art operations processes and tools.

We provide 24 x 7 network surveillance and trouble resolution via our Global Network Operation Centers (GNOCs) that have the capability to cover every fault detection and resolution aspect of running your network operations.

The Managed Network Operations Solution offers telecom carriers targeted fault management operational support when needing to:

- Migrate from legacy to next-generation operations
- Reduce time to market
- Minimize risk involved in new deployment projects
- Improve network key performance indicators and service level agreements
- Ensure optimum service availability, without increasing internal staff and associated costs
- Introduce new technologies in existing environments
- Launch new services

Network Operations Centre (NOC)

A Network Operations Centre, or NOC, is the primary

work space engineers utilize to monitor, manage and trouble-shoot problems on a network.

The Network Operations Centre offers oversight of problems, configuration and change management, network security, performance and policy monitoring, reporting, quality assurance, scheduling, and documentation by utilizing sophisticated network manage-ment, monitoring and analysis tools.

The NOC provides a structured environment that effectively coordinates operational activities with all participants and vendors related to the function of the network. The NOC technicians typically provide support twenty-four hours a day, seven days a week.

Typical daily processes include:

- Monitoring operations of all backbone links and network devices.
- Ensuring continuous operation of servers and services.
- Providing quality support for network users.
- Troubleshooting of all network and system related problems.
- Opening tickets to track and document resolution of problems.
- 24 hours a day, 7 days a week supervised operation by highly skilled network and system engineers.

PTS has experience in designing, building, and installing Command Centers, Control Centers, Network Operation Centers, Network Management Centers, Network Control Centers, Data Centers, Security Operations Centers, Mock Trading Rooms and various other monitoring intensive control facilities.

We can provide a turn-key solution by handling everything you need including space design, console furniture, audio/visual systems, network & support infrastructure monitoring and/or managed services as well as installation including display and video walls.

PTS can help you make the most out of your available space. We start by analyzing your specific needs and goals for the project including the operational requirement, space limitations, time constraints and budget objectives. With your goals in mind, our team of designers and audio/visual experts develop possible configurations. Working closely with you, we make the necessary revisions to initial design concepts to arrive at the best possible solution for your particular operation.

Chapter 5

Network Operating Systems

A network operating system (NOS) is a computer operating system system that is designed primarily to support workstation, personal computer, and, in some instances, older terminal that are connected on a local area network (LAN). Artisoft's LANtastic, Banyan VINES, Novell's NetWare, and Microsoft's LAN Manager are examples of network operating systems. In addition, some multi-purpose operating systems, such asWindows NT and Digital's OpenVMS come with capabilities that enable them to be described as a network operating system.

A network operating system provides printer sharing, common file system and database sharing, application sharing, and the ability to manage a network name directory, security, and other housekeeping aspects of a network. A network operating system (NOS) is a software programme that controls other software and hardware that runs on a network.

It also allows multiple computers, also known as network computers, to communicate with one main computer and each other, so as to share resources, run applications, and send messages, among other things. A computer network can consist of a wireless network, local area network (LAN), a wide area network (WAN), or even two or three computer networks. The heart of any of these networks, however, is the network operating system.

There are different types of operating systems. Most individual computer users run client operating systems, like Windows XP®, which run on a single computer. Personal computers that individuals use at home have a client operating system which manages the interactions and processes between the computer and its peripherals such as the keyboard, mouse, external monitor, and printer. In a sense, this is also a network, though it is different in scale than a network operating system which manages the interactions of many computers.

A network usually consists of many network computers that are connected to a central hub or router. The central hub, in turn, is connected to a larger, main computer. The network may also include other devices like printers, a tape-backup system, and a central storage facility. The main network computer runs all the connected computers and devices with the help of the operating system software.

A network administrator is the person who installs and manages the network and its operating system. He or she may configure the NOS to recognize a wireless network as well. If a WAN is involved, this would probably require more than one network administrator, as the network would likely be located offsite. A network operating system has a menu-driven administration interface.

From this interface, the network administrator may perform a variety of activities. He or she can use the interface to format hard drives, set up security restrictions, or establish log-in information for each user. The interface of a network operating system can also be used to attach shared printers to the network, or configure the system to automatically back data up on a daily basis.

An important component of a network is the file server. A file server is the device where data is stored for use by network computers. It can be a single computer or it can be a cluster of external hard drives hooked up in series to store data. A network operating system helps manage the flow of information between that file server and the network computers.

Examples of network operating systems include UNIX®, Windows 2000 Server ®, and Netware®. Each operating system runs differently, and as such has to be configured to perform the actions the network requires. A good knowledge of each operating system is necessary to work with them.

Network administrators may need to be certified in order to manage particular network operating systems.

EXPLANATION

Network operating systems (NOS) typically are used to run computers that act as servers. They provide the capabilities required for network operation. Network operating systems are also designed for client computers and provide functions so the distinction between network operating systems and stand alone operating systems is not always obvious.

Network operating systems provide the following functions:

- File and print sharing.
- Account administration for users.
- Security.

INSTALLED COMPONENTS

- Client functionality
- Server functionality

FUNCTIONS PROVIDED

- Account Administration for users
- Security
- File and print sharing

NETWORK SERVICES

- File Sharing
- Print sharing
- User administration
- Backing up data

UNIX

DESCRIPTION

Is it possible for an Information Technology [IT] product to be both mature and state-of-the-art at the same time? In the case of the UNIX® system, the answer is an unqualified "Yes." The UNIX system has continued to develop over the past twenty-five years. In millions of installations running on nearly every hardware platform made, the UNIX system has earned its reputation for stability and scalability. Over the years, UNIX system suppliers have steadily assimilated new technologies so that UNIX systems today provide more functionality as any other operating system.

Perhaps the key to the continuing growth of the UNIX system is the free-market demands placed upon suppliers who produce and support software built to open standards. The "open systems" approach is in bold contrast to other operating environments that lock in their customers with resultant high switching costs. UNIX system suppliers, on the other hand, must constantly provide the highest quality systems in order to retain their customers. Those who become dissatisfied with one UNIX system implementation retain the ability to easily move to another UNIX system implementation.

The continuing success of the UNIX system should come as no surprise. No other operating environment enjoys the support of every major system supplier. Mention the UNIX system and IT professionals immediately think not only of the operating system itself, but also of the large family of application software that the UNIX system supports. In the IT marketplace, the UNIX system has been the catalyst for sweeping changes that have empowered consumers to seek the best-of-breed without the arbitrary constraints imposed by proprietary environments.

In a nutshell then, the UNIX system is the users' and suppliers' operating environment of choice. The UNIX system represents the best collective efforts of competing suppliers, the most refined standards in the public domain, and the rock-solid stability that comes from years of quality assurance testing, mission-critical use, and refinement. This white paper examines the UNIX system with a special concern for both its extraordinary past and its equally extraordinary prospects for the future.

THE UNIX SYSTEM

The UNIX system has been around for a long time, and many people may remember it as it existed in the previous decades. Many IT professionals who encountered UNIX systems in the past found it uncompromising. While its power was impressive, its command-line interface required technical competence, its syntax was not intuitive, and its interface was unfriendly. Moreover, in the UNIX system's early days, security was virtually nonexistent. Subsequently, the UNIX system became the first operating system to suffer attacks mounted over the nascent Internet. As the UNIX system matured, however, the organization of security shifted from centralized to distributed authentication and authorization systems. Now, a single Graphical User Interface is shipped and supported by all major vendors has replaced command-line syntax, and security systems, up to and including B1, provide appropriate controls over access to the UNIX system.

THE VALUE OF STANDARDS

The UNIX system's increasing popularity spawned the development of a number of variations of the UNIX operating system in the 1980s, and the existence of these caused a mid-life crisis. Standardization had progressed slowly and methodically in domains such as telecommunications and third-generation languages; yet no one had addressed standards at the operating system level.

For suppliers, the thought of a uniform operating environment was disconcerting. Consumer lock-in was woven tightly into the fabric of the industry. Individual consumers, particularly those with UNIX system experience, envisioned standardized environments, but had no way to pull the market in their direction. However, for one category of consumer - governments- the standardization of the UNIX system was both desirable and within reach.

Governments have clout and are the largest consumers of information technology products and services in the world. Driven by the need to improve commonality, both US and European governments endorsed a shift to the UNIX system. The Institute of Electrical and Electronic Engineers POSIX family of standards, along with standards from ISO, ANSI and others, led the way. Consortia such as the X/Open Company (merged with the Open Software Foundation in 1995 to form The Open Group) hammered out draft standards to accelerate the process. In 1994, the definitive specification of what constitutes a UNIX system was finalized through X/Open Company's consensus process. The Single UNIX Specification was born-not from a theoretical, ivory tower approach, but by analyzing the applications that were in use in businesses across the world.

With the active support of government and commercial buyers alike, vendors began to converge on products that implement the Single UNIX Specification, and now all major vendors have products labeled UNIX 95, which indicates that the vendor guarantees that the product conforms to the Single UNIX Specification.

Vendors continue to add value to the UNIX system, particularly in areas of new technology, however that value will always be built upon a single, consensus standard. Meanwhile, the functionality of the UNIX system was established and the mid-life crisis was resolved. Suppliers today provide UNIX systems that are built upon a single, consensus standard. It is also important to remember that even when variance among UNIX systems was at its worst, IT professionals agreed that migration among UNIX system variants was far easier than migration among the proprietary alternatives.

Now with UNIX 95 branded products available from all major systems vendors, the buyer can for the first time buy systems from different manufacturers, safe in the knowledge that each one is guaranteed to implement the complete functionality of the Single UNIX Specification and will continue to do so UNIX system suppliers can assure customers that they own a standards-based system by registering them to use the Open Brand. Below is a list of suppliers who give users this guarantee.

UNIX 95 REGISTERED PRODUCTS

- *DIGITAL*: Digital UNIX® Version 4.0 running Digital's AlphaStations and Digital's Alpha Servers

- *HITACHI*: Hitachi 3050RX, 3500/3X, 3500/4XX running HI-UX/WE2 Version 06-01 and later HITACHI: Hitachi 3500 running HI-UX/WE2 Version 07-01 and later Hewlett-Packard: HP-UX Release 10.20 and later on all HP9000 Series 700 and 800
- HP-UX Release 11.00 or later (in both 32 and 64-bit configurations) on HP9000 Series (all models)
- *IBM*: IBM POWER, POWER2, and Power PCTM Systems with IBM AIX® Version 4.2 or later IBM: OS/390 Version 1 Release 2 or later with OS/390 V1R2 or later Security Server and OS/390 V1R2 or later C/C++ Compiler on IBM System/390 Processors that support OS/390 Version 1 Release 2 NCR: NCR UNIX System V Release 4 MP-RAS Release 3.02 or later on NCR World Mark Series & System 3000 Series NEC: UX/4800 R12.3 and later on UP4800 and EWS4800 Series SCO: SCO UnixWare Family R2.1.1 and later for single and multiprocessor IntelTM 386/486 or Pentium® PCs conforming to PC/AT architectures
- *SGI*: IRIX 6.5 running on Silicon Graphics systems using the MIPS R4000, R5000, R8000 and R10,000 family of processors
- *SNI*: Business Servers running BS2000/OSD V3.0 and higher.
- *SNI*: Reliant UNIX V5.43 running on RM Server Family, all Models RM200/300/400/600 Siemens Pyramid: Reliant UNIX Version 5.43 running on Reliant RM1000® Cluster Server
- *SUN*: Solaris 2.6 on SPARC based systems
- *SUN*: Solaris 2.6 on x86pc based systems

UNIX AND WINDOWS NT

It is common these days to read analysts' accounts and IS professionals' experiences that compare and contrast the UNIX system with Microsoft Corporation's latest operating system, called Windows NT. Opinions vary, of course, but a number of common themes have emerged. The key differences between these operating environments are as follows.

The UNIX system today is more robust, reliable and scalable. Analysts say this observation, which is widely reported from many different viewpoints, makes practical sense. Engineers at Microsoft are retracing the steps that the UNIX system has completed. How else could it be?

In sharp contrast to the open standards that define the UNIX system, Windows NT technology remains fiercely proprietary. Microsoft remains ambivalent to the world of standards. Choosing NT entangles customers with non standard utilities, directories, and software tools that do not conform to any de jure or consensus standards.

The UNIX system today is available on a wide spectrum of computer hardware. Particularly when high performance is at issue, hardware suppliers suggest the UNIX system, rather than Windows NT. The primary appeal of NT is for low-end, office-centered, departmental applications.

Unit shipment growth rates for Windows NT exceed the rates for the UNIX system, which is to be expected for a new product. However, revenue growth in UNIX systems sales is much higher than NT. It is reasonable to expect Windows NT to take a share in the operating systems market, along with other more specialized operating systems. There is no evidence today to indicate that NT will be dominant; in fact, most IT professionals predict that it will not.

Windows NT Server 4.0 is still not a full-function server operating system. While it does support multi-user computing via third-party add-on tools, it lacks certain fundamental features that the UNIX system is known for providing, such as directory services for managing user access and peripherals over a distributed enterprise network.

The presence of the UNIX system in the marketplace has been good for Windows NT. The UNIX system established the market for cross-platform client and server operating environments that NT seeks to address. In turn, NT will improve the market for UNIX systems in the future. That is, competition among UNIX system providers will be enhanced by competition with NT. The choice between open and proprietary products will be quite crisp.

TODAY'S UNIX SYSTEM

The key to the continuing growth of the UNIX system is the free-market demands placed upon suppliers who produce and support software built to public standards. The "open systems" approach is in bold contrast to other operating environments that lock in their customers with high switching costs. UNIX system suppliers, on the other hand, must constantly provide the highest quality systems in order to retain their customers. Those who become dissatisfied with one UNIX system implementation retain the ability to easily move to another UNIX system implementation.

The continuing success of the UNIX system should come as no surprise. No other operating environment enjoys the support of every major system supplier. Mention the UNIX system and IT professionals immediately think not only of the operating system itself, but also of the large family of hardware and application software that the UNIX system supports. In the IT marketplace, the UNIX system has been the catalyst for sweeping changes that have empowered consumers to seek the best-of-breed without the arbitrary constraints imposed by proprietary environments.

The market's pull for the UNIX system was amplified by other events as well. The availability of relational database management systems, the shift to the client/server architecture, and the introduction of low-cost UNIX system servers together set the stage for business applications to flourish. For client/server systems, the networking strengths of the UNIX system shine. Standardized relational database engines delivered on low-cost high-performance UNIX system servers offered substantial cost savings over proprietary alternatives.

UNIX SYSTEM EXISTENCE

For the last two and a half decades, the UNIX system has upheld a tradition of providing its customers with early access to new technologies. For example:

- UNIX systems provided early access to RISC technology. Applications in CAD/CAM, multimedia, and large-scale publishing that demanded high performance workstations have always used the UNIX system platform.

- The UNIX system provided early access to symmetric multiprocessing [SMP] computers. UNIX system-based SMP parallel processors radically improved the price/performance of midsize and high-range servers.
- The UNIX system first enabled distributed transaction processing in conjunction with TP monitors from independent software suppliers. The server side of client/server technology was launched on the UNIX system.
- The UNIX system launched the Internet and the World Wide Web.

UNIX system suppliers also have a proud tradition of integration with legacy systems as well as innovation to uphold. No other system can ensure that disparate systems - usually proprietary systems - can be integrated, allowing the buyer's investment in data and information to be realized with minimal disruption and reinvestment.

There is every reason to believe that the UNIX system will continue to be the platform of choice for innovative development. In the near term, for example, UNIX system vendors will define the scope of Java and provide the distributed computing environment into which the Network Computer terminal will fit and enable it to thrive and grow.

How will Java and the Network Computer terminal manifest themselves? The exact answer is unknown; however, in open computing, the process for finding that answer is well understood. The UNIX system community has set aside (via consensus standards) the wasteful task of developing arbitrary differences among computing environments. Rather than building proprietary traps, this community is actively seeking ways to add value to the UNIX system with improved scalability, reliability, price/performance, and customer service.

Java and the Network Computer terminal offer several potential advantages for consumers. One key advantage is a smaller, lighter, standards-based client. A second advantage is a specification that is not controlled by one company, but is developed to the benefit of all by an open, consensus process. Thirdly, greater code reuse and a component software market based on Object technology, such as CORBA and Java. All of these options and more are being deployed first by members of the UNIX system community.

INDUSTRIAL STRENGTH UNIX SYSTEM

Today's UNIX system is robust, scalable, and it continues to provide uniform access to a wide variety of computing hardware. For these reasons the UNIX system continues to be the operating system of choice for mission-critical systems. The UNIX system is the key enabler for enterprises that wish to keep switching costs as low as possible. That is, the UNIX system remains the only open alternative to locking in on a proprietary operating system.

Scalability is here today, enabling application to run on small-scale systems through to the largest servers necessary. The UNIX system is available on hardware ranging from low-cost PC-class servers on through parallel architectures that harness together 60 or more processors. This range is wider and the choices of hardware more cost effective than any other system. The UNIX system is the only option for Massively Parallel Processing (MPP).

A robust operating system is tough enough to perform successfully under a variety of different operating conditions. By virtue of its worldwide deployment by an international community of system vendors, the UNIX system has earned the reputation for robustness.

Uniform operating system services are at the heart of the standardized UNIX system. Many enterprise systems are assembled with hardware from several different sources. Atop these different hardware platforms, the UNIX operating system provides a uniform platform for database management systems and application software.

The market for the UNIX system continues to expand. IDC estimates the market at US$ 39 billion in 1996 and forecasts the market to be US$ 50 billion in the year 2000. In addition, the installed base of the UNIX system has an estimated value of US$ 122 billion. These market estimates lead to several conclusions about the UNIX system, as follows:

An annual market of US$ 39 billion is large enough to remain attractive to many suppliers and to provide sufficient revenue to fund continuing high levels of investment in support and product enhancement.

The UNIX system's growth rates, which appear modest in comparison to the unit shipment growth of newer products, are anchored by an enormous installed base. High unit shipment growth rates are typical of new entries in a marketplace.

In key benchmarks and mission-critical applications, the UNIX system consistently performs better. The UNIX system is the dominant software platform for Relational Database Management Systems. Investment in developing and enhancing UNIX system products is significantly larger than in any other operating environment.

SINGLE UNIX SPECIFICATION

Today, The Open Group's UNIX 95 brand may be applied to any operating system product that is guaranteed to meet the Single UNIX Specification. The Single UNIX Specification is designed to give software developers a single set of APIs to be supported by every UNIX system. The most significant consequence of the Single UNIX Specification initiative is that it shifts the focus of attention away from incompatible UNIX system product implementations on to compliance with a single, agreed-upon set of APIs.

If an operating system meets the specification, and commonly available applications can run on it, then it can reliable viewed as open. So, the future looks as though it will be about a set of sturdy and dependable specifications standing as a firm foundation upon which many competing product implementations will be built.

By developing a single specification for the UNIX system, The Open Group and the computer industry have completed the foundation of open systems. The next version of the Single

UNIX Specification, known as Version 2 was announced in March 1997. Products guaranteed to conform to this specification will carry the label UNIX 98.

SINGLE UNIX SPECIFICATION

The Single UNIX Specification, Version 2 contains the following enhancements:

- Year 2000 Alignment - changes to minimize the impact of the Millennium Rollover.
- *Threads*: POSIX 1003.1c-1995. The Threads extensions permit development of applications to make significant performance gains on multiprocessor hardware.
- Large File Summit extensions to permit UNIX systems to support files of arbitrary sizes, this is of particular relevance to database applications.
- *Networking Services*: The specifications are aligned with the POSIX 1003.1g standard.
- *MSE*: The Multibyte Support Extension is now aligned with ISO C amendment 1, 1995.
- Dynamic linking extensions to permit applications to share common code across many applications, and ease maintenance of bug fixes and performance enhancements for applications.
- N-bit cleanup (64 bit and beyond), to remove any architectural dependencies in the Single UNIX Specification. This is of particular relevance with the ongoing move to 64 bit CPUs.
- The real-time extensions are an optional feature group, allowing procurement of X/Open real-time systems with predictable, bounded behaviour.
- Inclusion of the existing specifications for the graphical user interface, CDE as an option in the UNIX 98 brand.

BENEFITS FOR APPLICATION DEVELOPERS

- Improved portability.
- Faster development through the increased number of standard interfaces.

- More innovation is possible, due to the reduced time spent porting applications.

BENEFITS FOR USERS

The Single UNIX Specification will evolve and develop in response to market needs protecting users investment in existing systems and applications. The availability of the UNIX system from multiple suppliers gives users freedom of choice rather than being locked in to a single supplier. And the wide range of applications - built on the UNIX system's strengths of scalability, availability and reliability - ensure that mission critical business needs can be met.

SUMMARY

When the history of the information age is written, the extraordinary dynamics of the UNIX system marketplace will be seen as playing an important role. The UNIX system was developed at just the right time and place to be the critical enabler for a revolution in information technology. Client/server architectures, the Internet, object databases, heterogeneous transaction processing, and Web computing all emerged on the shoulders of the UNIX system.

Most importantly, the UNIX system continues to be a driving force for innovation because of its commitment to standards. When proprietary differences are set aside, and with the wide implementation of the Single UNIX Specification they are set aside, suppliers compete by adding value. This fundamental tenet is the reason that the UNIX system has thrived - and will continue to thrive in the years to come.

HISTORY OF UNIX

Unix was originally developed in the 1960s and 1970s by a group of AT&T employees at Bell Labs. Today, Unix systems are split into different branches which have developed over time by AT&T and by commercial vendors and non-profit organizations. Many variations (usually called "flavors") of Unix and Unix-like Operating Systems were released during the dot com boom of the 1990's. The dot com bust caused many of these to consolidate. As a result, of the dozens of commercial variations of Unix that were developed in the 1980s, only Solaris, HP-UX, and AIX are still doing relatively well in the market. Of these, Solaris currently holds the highest market share.

A system is termed UNIX only if it complies fully with (and is certified by) the Single Unix Specification (SUS) standards. Similar systems that do not comply fully or are not certified are termed "Unix-like" operating systems. Examples of popular Unix-like systems include Linux and Xenix.

INTRODUCTION TO LINUX

Linux is quite possibly the most important free software achievement since the original Space War, or, more recently, Emacs. It has developed into an operating system for business, education, and personal productivity. Linux is no longer only for UNIX wizards who sit for hours in front of a glowing console (although we assure you that many users fall into this category). This book will help you get the most from Linux. Linux (pronounced with a short i, as in LIH-nucks) is a UNIX operating system clone which runs on a variety of platforms, especially personal computers with Intel 80386 or better processors.

It supports a wide range of software, from TeX, to the X Window System, to the GNU C/C++ compiler, to TCP/IP. It's a versatile, bona fide implementation of UNIX, freely distributed under the terms of the GNU General Public License. Linux can turn any 80386 or better personal computer into a workstation that puts the full power of UNIX at your fingertips. Businesses install Linux on entire networks of machines, and use the operating system to manage financial and hospital records, distributed computing environments, and telecommunications.

Universities worldwide use Linux to teach courses on operating system programming and design. Computing enthusiasts everywhere use Linux at home for programming, productivity, and all-around hacking. What makes Linux so different is that it is a free implementation of UNIX. It was and still is developed cooperatively by a group of volunteers, primarily on the Internet, who exchange code, report bugs, and fix problems in an open-ended environment. Anyone is welcome to join the Linux development effort. All it takes is interest in hacking a free UNIX clone, and some programming know-how.

HISTORY OF LINUX

UNIX is one of the most popular operating systems worldwide because of its large support base and distribution. It was originally developed at AT&T as a multitasking system for minicomputers and mainframes in the 1970's, but has since grown to become one of the most widely-used operating systems anywhere, despite its sometimes confusing interface and lack of central standardization. Many hackers feel that UNIX is the Right Thing--the One True Operating System. Hence, the development of Linux by an expanding group of UNIX hackers who want to get their hands dirty with their own system.

Versions of UNIX exist for many systems, from personal computers to supercomputers like the Cray Y-MP. Most versions of UNIX for personal computers are expensive and cumbersome. At the time of this writing, a one-machine version of UNIX System V for the 386 runs about US$1500. Linux is a free version of UNIX developed primarily by Linus Torvalds at the University of Helsinki in Finland, with the help of many UNIX programmers and wizards across the Internet. Anyone with enough know-how and gumption can develop and change the system.

The Linux kernel uses no code from AT&T or any other proprietary source, and much of the software available for Linux was developed by the GNU project of the Free Software Foundation in Cambridge, Massachusetts, U.S.A. However, programmers from all over the world have contributed to the growing pool of Linux software.

Linux was originally developed as a hobby project by Linus Torvalds. It was inspired by Minix, a small UNIX system developed by Andy Tanenbaum. The first discussions about

Linux were on the Usenet newsgroup, comp.os.minix. These discussions were concerned mostly with the development of a small, academic UNIX system for Minix users who wanted more. The very early development of Linux mostly dealt with the task-switching features of the 80386 protected-mode interface, all written in assembly code. Linus writes,

``After that it was plain sailing: hairy coding still, but I had some devices, and debugging was easier. I started using C at this stage, and it certainly speeds up development. This is also when I started to get serious about my megalomaniac ideas to make `a better Minix than Minix.' I was hoping I'd be able to recompile gcc under Linux someday...

``Two months for basic setup, but then only slightly longer until I had a disk driver (seriously buggy, but it happened to work on my machine) and a small file system. That was about when I made 0.01 available (around late August of 1991): it wasn't pretty, it had no floppy driver, and it couldn't do much of anything. I don't think anybody ever compiled that version. But by then I was hooked, and didn't want to stop until I could chuck out Minix."

No announcement was ever made for Linux version 0.01. The 0.01 sources weren't even executable. They contained only the bare rudiments of the kernel source and assumed that you had access to a Minix machine to compile and experiment with them. On October 5, 1991, Linus announced the first ``official" version of Linux, which was version 0.02. At that point, Linus was able to run bash (the GNU Bourne Again Shell) and gcc (the GNU C compiler), but not much else.

Again, this was intended as a hacker's system. The primary focus was kernel development--user support, documentation, and distribution had not yet been addressed. Today, the Linux community still seems to treat these issues as secondary to ``real programming"--kernel development. After version 0.03, Linus bumped up the version number to 0.10, as more people started to work on the system.

After several further revisions, Linus increased the version number to 0.95 in March, 1992, to reflect his expectation that the system was ready for an ``official" release soon. (Generally, software is not assigned the version number 1.0 until it is theoretically complete or bug-free.). Almost a year and a half later, in late December of 1993, the Linux kernel was still at version 0.99.pl14--asymptotically approaching 1.0. At the time of this writing, the current stable kernel version is 2.0 patchlevel 33, and version 2.1 is under development.

Most of the major, free UNIX software packages have been ported to Linux, and commercial software is also available. More hardware is supported than in the original kernel versions. Many people have executed benchmarks on 80486 Linux systems and found them comparable with mid-range workstations from Sun Microsystems and Digital Equipment Corporation. Who would have ever guessed that this ``little'' UNIX clone would have grown up to take on the entire world of personal computing?

SYSTEM FEATURES

Linux supports features found in other implementations of UNIX, and many which aren't found elsewhere. In this section, we'll take a nickel tour of the features of the Linux kernel. Linux is a complete multitasking, multiuser operating system, as are all other versions of UNIX. This means that many users can log into and run programmes on the same machine simultaneously.

The Linux system is mostly compatible with several UNIX standards (inasmuch as UNIX has standards) at the source level, including IEEE POSIX.1, UNIX System V, and Berkely System Distribution UNIX. Linux was developed with source code portability in mind, and it's easy to find commonly used features that are shared by more than one platform. Much of the free UNIX software available on the Internet and elsewhere compiles under Linux ``right out of the box.'' In addition, all of the source code for the Linux system, including the kernel, device drivers, libraries, user programmes, and development toois, is freely distributable.

Other specific internal features of Linux include POSIX job control (used by shells like csh and bash), pseudoterminals (pty devices), and support for dynamically loadable national or customized keyboard drivers. Linux supports virtual consoles that let you switch between login sessions on the same system console. Users of the screen programme will find the Linux virtual console implementation familiar.

The kernel can emulate 387-FPU instructions, and systems without a math coprocessor can run programmes that require floating-point math capability. Linux supports various file systems for storing data, like the ext2 file system, which was developed specifically for Linux. The Xenix and UNIX System V file systems are also supported, as well as the Microsoft MS-DOS and Windows 95 VFAT file systems on a hard drive or floppy. The ISO 9660 CD-ROM file system is also supported.

Linux provides a complete implementation of TCP/IP networking software. This includes device drivers for many popular Ethernet cards, SLIP (Serial Line Internet Protocol) and PPP (Point-to-Point Protocol), which provide access to a TCP/IP network via a serial connection, PLIP (Parallel Line Internet Protocol), and NFS (Network File System).

The Linux kernel is developed to use protected-mode features of Intel 80386 and better processors. In particular, Linux uses the protected-mode, descriptor based, memory-management paradigm, and other advanced features. Anyone familiar with 80386 protected-mode programming knows that this chip was designed for multitasking systems like UNIX. Linux exploits this functionality.

The kernel supports demand-paged, loaded executables. Only those segments of a programme which are actually in use are read into memory from disk. Also, copy-on-write pages are shared among executables. If several instances of a programme are running at once, they share physical memory, which reduces overall usage. When the system requires more physical memory, it swaps inactive pages to disk, letting you run larger applications and support more users. However, swapping data to disk is no substitute for physical RAM, which is much faster.

The Linux kernel also implements a unified memory pool for user programmes and disk cache. All free memory is used by the cache, which is reduced when running large programmes. Executables use dynamically linked, shared libraries: code from a single library on disk. This is not unlike the SunOS shared library mechanism. Executable files occupy less disk space, especially those which use many library functions. There are also statically linked libraries for object debugging and maintaining ``complete'' binary files when shared libraries are not installed. The libraries are dynamically linked at run time, and the programmer can use his or her own routines in place of the standard library routines.

To facilitate debugging, the kernel generates core dumps for post-mortem analysis. A core dump and an executable linked with debugging support allows a developer to determine what caused a programme to crash.

SOFTWARE FEATURES

Virtually every utility one would expect of a standard UNIX implementation has been ported to Linux, including basic commands like ls, awk, tr, sed, bc, and more. The familiar working environment of other UNIX systems is duplicated on Linux. All standard commands and utilities are included. (Novice UNIX or Linux users should introduction to basic UNIX commands.)

Many text editors are available, including vi, ex, pico, jove, and GNU emacs, and variants like Lucid emacs, which incorporates extensions of the X Window System, and joe. The text editor you're accustomed to using has more than likely been ported to Linux. The choice of a text editor is an interesting one. Many UNIX users prefer ``simple'' editors like vi. (The original author wrote this book with vi.) But vi has many limitations due to its age, and modern editors like emacs have gained popularity. emacs supports a complete, Lisp based macro language and interpreter, powerful command syntax, and other extensions.

There are emacs macro packages which let you read electronic mail and news, edit directory contents, and even engage in artificially intelligent psychotherapy sessions (indispensible for stressed-out Linux hackers). Most of the basic Linux utilities are GNU software. GNU utilities support advanced features that are not found in the standard versions of BSD and UNIX System Vprograms. For example, the GNU vi clone, elvis, includes a structured macro language that differs from the original implementation. However, GNU utilities are intended to remain compatible with their BSD and System V counterparts. Many people consider the GNU versions to be superior to the originals.

A shell is a programme which reads and executes commands from the user. In addition, many shells provide features like job control, managing several processes at once, input and output redirection, and a command language for writing shell scripts. A shell script is a programme in the shell's command language and is analogous to a MS-DOS batch file.

. Many types of shells are available for Linux. The most important difference between shells is the command language. For example, the C SHell (csh) uses a command language similar to the C programming language. The classic Bourne S Hell sh uses another command language. The choice of a shell is often based on the command language it provides, and determines, to a large extent, the qualities of your working environment under Linux.

The GNU Bourne Again Shell (bash) is a variation of the Bourne Shell which includes many advanced features like job control, command history, command and filename completion, an emacs-like interface for editing command lines, and other powerful extensions to the standard Bourne Shell language. Another popular shell is tcsh, a version of the C Shell with advanced functionality similar to that found in bash. Other shells include zsh, a small Bourne-like shell; the Korn Shell (ksh); BSD's ash; and rc, the Plan 9 shell.

If you're the only person using the system and refer to use vi and bash exclusively as your editor and shell, there's no reason to install other editors or shells. This ``do it yourself'' attitude is prevalent among Linux hackers and users.

TextProcessing and Word Processing

Almost every computer user needs a method of preparing documents. In the world of personal computers, word processing is the norm: editing and manipulating text in a ``What-You-See-Is-What-You-Get" (WYSIWYG) environment and producing printed copies of the text, complete with graphics, tables, and ornamentation.

Commercial word processors from Corel, Applix, and Star Division are available in the UNIX world, but text processing, which is quite different conceptually, is more common. In text processing systems, text is entered in a page-description language, which describes how the text should be formatted. Rather than enter text within a special word processing environment, you can modify text with any editor, like vi or emacs. Once you finish entering the source text (in the typesetting language), a separate programme converts the source to a format suitable for printing. This is somewhat analogous to programming in a language like C, and ``compiling" the document into printable form.

Many text processing systems are available for Linux. One is groff, the GNU version of the classic troff text formatter originally developed by Bell Labs and still used on many UNIX systems worldwide. Another modern text processing system is TeX, developed by Donald Knuth of computer science fame. Dialects of TeX, like LaTeX, are also available.

Text processors like TeX and groff differ mostly in the syntax of their formatting languages. The choice of one formatting system over another is based upon what utilities are available to satisfy your needs, as well as personal taste.

Many people consider groff's formatting language to be a bit obscure and use find TeX more readable. However, groff produces ASCII output which can be viewed on a terminal more easily, while TeX is intended primarily for output to a printing device. Various add-on programmes are required to produce ASCII output from TeX formatted documents, or convert TeX input to groff format.

Another programme is texinfo, an extension to TeX which is used for software documentation developed by the Free Software Foundation. texinfo can produce printed output, or an online-browsable hypertext ``Info" document from a single source file. Info files are the main format of documentation used in GNU software like emacs. Text processors are used widely in the computing community for producing papers, theses, magazine articles, and books. (This book is produced using LaTeX.) The ability to process source language as a text file opens the door to many extensions of the text processor itself. Because a source document is not stored in an obscure format that only one word processor can read, programmers can write parsers and translators for the formatting language, and thus extend the system.

What does a formatting language look like? In general, a formatted source file consists mostly of the text itself, with control codes to produce effects like font and margin changes, and list formatting.

Programming Languages and Utilities

Linux provides a complete UNIX programming environment which includes all of the standard libraries, programming tools, compilers, and debuggers which you would expect of other UNIX systems.

Standards like POSIX.1 are supported, which allows software written for Linux to be easily ported to other systems. Professional UNIX programmers and system administrators use Linux to develop software at home, then transfer the software to UNIX systems at work.

This not only saves a great deal of time and money, but also lets you work in the comfort of your own home. (One of the authors uses his system to develop and test X Window System applications at home, which can be directly compiled on workstations elsewhere.) Computer Science students learn UNIX programming and explore other aspects of the system, like kernel architecture.

With Linux, you have access to the complete set of libraries and programming utilities and the complete kernel and library source code. Within the UNIX software world, systems and applications are often programmed in C or C++. The standard C and C++ compiler for Linux is GNU gcc, which is an advanced, modern compiler that supports C++, including AT&T 3.0 features, as well as Objective-C, another object-oriented dialect of C. Besides C and C++, other compiled and interpreted programming languages have been ported to Linux, like Smalltalk, FORTRAN, Java, Pascal, LISP, Scheme, and Ada (if you're masochistic enough to programme in Ada, we aren't going to stop you).

In addition, various assemblers for writing protected-mode 80386 code are available, as are UNIX hacking favorites like Perl (the script language to end all script languages) and Tcl/Tk (a shell-like command processing system which has support for developing simple X Window System applications). The advanced gdb debugger can step through a programme one line of source code at a time, or examine a core dump to find the cause of a crash.

The gprof profiling utility provides performance statistics for your programme, telling you where your programme spends most of its execution time. As mentioned above, the emacs text editor provides interactive editing and compilation environments for various programming languages. Other tools include GNU make and imake, which manage compilation of large applications, and RCS, a system for source code locking and revision control.

Finally, Linux supports dynamically linked, shared libraries (DLLs), which result in much smaller binaries. The common subroutine code is linked at run-time. These DLLs let you override function definitions with your own code. For example, if you wish to write your own version of the malloc() library routine, the linker will use your new routine instead of the one in the libraries.

X Window System

The X Window System, or simply X, is a standard graphical user interface (GUI) for UNIX machines and is a powerful environment which supports many applications. Using the X Window System, you can have multiple terminal windows on the screen at once, each having a different login session. A pointing device like a mouse is often used with X, although it isn't required. Many X-specific applications have been written, including games, graphics and programming utilities, and documentation tools. Linux and X make your system a bona fide workstation. With TCP/IP networking, your Linux machine can display X applications running on other machines.

The X Window System was originally developed at the Massachusetts Institute of Technology and is freely distributable. Many commercial vendors have distributed proprietary enhancements to the original X Window System as well. The version of X for Linux is XFree86, a port of X11R6 which is freely distributable. XFree86 supports a wide range of video hardware, including VGA, Super VGA, and accelerated video adaptors. XFree86 is a complete distribution of the X Windows System software, and contains the X server itself, many applications and utilities, programming libraries, and documents.

Standard X applications include xterm, a terminal emulator used for most text-based applications within a window, xdm, which handles logins, xclock, a simple clock display, xman, a X-based manual page reader, and xmore. The many X applications available for Linux are too numerous to mention here, but their number includes spreadsheets, word processors, graphics programmes, and web browsers like the Netscape Navigator. Many other applications are available separately. Theoretically, any application written for X should compile cleanly under Linux.

The interface of the X Window System is controlled largely by the window manager. This user-friendly programme is in charge of the placement of windows, the user interface for resizing and moving them, changing windows to icons, and the appearance of window frames, among other tasks. XFree86 includes twm, the classic MIT window manager, and advanced window managers like the Open Look Virtual Window Manager (olvwm) are available. Popular among Linux users is fvwm--a small window manager that requires less than half the memory of twm.

It provides a 3-dimensional appearance for windows and a virtual desktop. The user moves the mouse to the edge of the screen, and the desktop shifts as though the display were much larger than it really is. fvwm is greatly customizable and allows access to functions from the keyboard as well as mouse. Many Linux distributions use fvwm as the standard window manager. A version of fvwm called fvwm95-2 offers Microsoft Windows 95-like look and feel.

The XFree86 distribution includes programming libraries for wily programmers who wish to develop X applications. Widget sets like Athena, Open Look, and Xaw3D are supported. All of the standard fonts, bitmaps, manual pages, and documentation are included. PEX (a programming interface for 3-dimensional graphics) is also supported.

Many X application programmers use the proprietary Motif widget set for development. Several vendors sell single and multiple user licenses for binary versions of Motif. Because Motif itself is relatively expensive, not many Linux users own it. However, binaries statically linked with Motif routines can be freely distributed. If you write a programme using Motif, you may provide a binary so users without the Motif libraries can use the programme.

A major caveat to using the X Window System is its hardware requirements. A 80386-based CPU with 4 megabytes of RAM is capable of running X, but 16 megabytes or more of physical RAM is needed for comfortable use. A faster processor is nice to have as well, but having enough physical RAM is much more important. In addition, to achieve really slick video performance, we recommend getting an accelerated video card, like a VESA Local Bus (VLB) S3 chipset card. Performance ratings in excess of 300,000 xstones have been achieved with Linux and XFree86. Using adequate hardware, you'll find that running X and Linux is as fast, or faster, than running X on other UNIX workstations.

Networking

Would you like to communicate with the world? Linux supports two primary UNIX networking protocols: TCP/IP and UUCP. TCP/IP (Transmission Control Protocol/Internet Protocol) is the networking paradigm which allows systems all over the world to communicate on a single network, the

Internet. With Linux, TCP/IP, and a connection to the Internet, you can communicate with users and machines via electronic mail, Usenet news, and FTP file transfer.

Most TCP/IP networks use Ethernet as the physical network transport. Linux supports many popular Ethernet cards and interfaces for personal computers, including pocket and PCMCIA Ethernet adaptors.

However, because not everyone has an Ethernet connection at home, Linux also supports SLIP (Serial Line Internet Protocol) and PPP (Point-to-Point Protocol), which provide Internet access via modem. Many businesses and universities provide SLIP and PPP servers. In fact, if your Linux system has an Ethernet connection to the Internet and a modem, your system can become a SLIP or PPP server for other hosts.

NFS (Network File System) lets your system seamlessly share file systems with other machines on the network. FTP (File Transfer Protocol) lets you transfer files with other machines. sendmail sends and receives electronic mail via the SMTP protocol; C-News and INN are NNTP based new systems; and telnet,rlogin, and rsh let you log in and execute commands on other machines on the network. finger lets you get information about other Internet users.

The full range of mail and news readers is available for Linux, including elm, pine, rn, nn, and tin. Whatever your preference, you can configure a Linux system to send and receive electronic mail and news from all over the world. The system provides a standard UNIX socket programming interface.

Virtually any programme that uses TCP/IP can be ported to Linux. The Linux X server also supports TCP/IP, and applications running on other systems may use the display of your local system.

UUCP (UNIX-to-UNIX Copy) is an older mechanism to transfer files, electronic mail, and electronic news between UNIX machines. Historically, UUCP machines are connected over telephone lines via modem, but UUCP is able to transfer data over a TCP/IP network as well. If you do not have access to a TCP/IP network or a SLIP or PPP server, you can configure your system to send and receive files and electronic mail using UUCP.

Telecommunications and BBS Software

If you have a modem, you'll be able to communicate with other machines via telecommunications packages available for Linux. Many people use telecommunications software to access bulletin board systems (BBS's) as well as commercial, online services like Prodigy, CompuServe, and America Online. People use modems to connect to UNIX systems at work or school. Modems can send and receive faxes.

A popular communications package for Linux is seyon, which provides a customizable, ergonomic interface undex X and has built-in support for the Kermit and ZModem file transfer protocols. Other telecommunications programmes include C-Kermit, pcomm, and minicom. These are similar to communications programmes found on other operating systems, and are quite easy to use.

If you do not have access to a SLIP or PPP server (see the previous section), you can use term to multiplex your serial line. The term programme allows you to open more than one login session over a modem connection. It lets you redirect X client connections to your local X server via a serial line. Another software package, KA9Q, implements a similar, SLIP-like interface.

Operating a Bulletin Board System (BBS) is a favorite hobby and means of income for many people. Linux supports a wide range of BBS software, most of which is more powerful than that available for other operating systems. With a phone line, modem, and Linux, you can turn your system into a BBS and provide dial-in access for users worldwide. BBS software for Linux includes XBBS and UniBoard BBS packages.

Most BBS software locks the user into a menu based system where only certain functions and applications are available. An alternative to BBS access is full UNIX access, which lets users dial into your system and log in normally. This requires a fair amount of maintenance by the system administrator, but providing public UNIX access is not difficult. In addition to TCP/IP networking, you can make electronic mail and news access available on your system.

If you do not have access to a TCP/IP network or UUCP feed, Linux lets you communicate with BBS networks like FidoNet, which let you exchange electronic news and mail over a telephone line.

World Wide Web

It is worth noting that Linux includes web server software as well as web browsers. The most common server is Apache. Thousands of Linux systems run Apache on the Internet today,including theLinuxResource ssite,www.linuxresources.com. Linux distributions include different web browsers, and other browsers can be downloaded from the Internet. Available browsers include Lynx, Mosaic, Netscape, Arena, and Amaya. Linux provides complete support for Java and CGI applets, and Perl is a standard tool in the Linux programming environment.

Interfacing and MS-DOS

Various utilities exist to interface with MS-DOS. The most well-known application is the Linux MS-DOS Emulator, which lets you run MS-DOS applications directly from Linux. Although Linux and MS-DOS are completely different operating systems, the 80386 protected-mode environment allows MS-DOS applications to behave as if they were running in their native 8086 environment.

The MS-DOS emulator is still under development, but many popular applications run under it. Understandably, MS-DOS applications that use bizarre or esoteric features of the system may never be supported, because of the limitations inherent in any emulator. For example, you shouldn't expect to run programmes that use 80386 protected-mode features, like Microsoft Windows (in 386 enhanced mode, that is).

Standard MS-DOS commands and utilities like PKZIP.EXE work under the emulators, as do 4DOS, a COMMAND.COM replacement, FoxPro 2.0, Harvard

Graphics, MathCad, Stacker 3.1, Turbo Assembler, Turbo C/ C++, Turbo Pascal. Microsoft Windows 3.0 (in real mode), and WordPerfect 5.1.

The MS-DOS Emulator is meant mostly as an ad-hoc solution for those who need MS-DOS for only a few applications and use Linux for everything else. It's not meant to be a complete implementation of MS-DOS. Of course, if the Emulator doesn't satisfy your needs, you can always run MS-DOS as well as Linux on the same system. Using the LILO boot loader, you can specify at boot time which operating system to start. Linux can also coexist with other operating systems, like OS/2.

Linux provides a seamless interface to transfer files between Linux and MS-DOS. You can mount a MS-DOS partition or floppy under Linux, and directly access MS-DOS files as you would any file.

Currently under development is WINE--a Microsoft Windows emulator for the X Window System under Linux. Once WINE is complete, users will be able to run MS-Windows applications directly from Linux. This is similar to the commercial WABI Windows emulator from Sun Microsystems, which is also available for Linux.

Other Applications

A host of miscellaneous programmes and utilities exist for Linux, as one would expect of such a hodgepodge operating system. Linux's primary focus is UNIX personal computing, but this is not the only field where it excels. The selection of business and scientific software is expanding, and commercial software vendors have begun to contribute to the growing pool Linux applications.

Several relational databases are available for Linux, including Postgres, Ingres, and Mbase. These are full-featured, professional, client/server database applications, similar to those found on other UNIX platforms. Many commercial database systems are available as well.

Scientific computing applications include FELT (finite element analysis); gnuplot (data plotting and analysis); Octave (a symbolic mathematics package similar to MATLAB); xspread (a spreadsheet calculator); xfractint (an X-based port of the popular Fractint fractal generator); and xlispstat (statistics). Other applications include SPICE (circuit design and analysis) and Khoros (image and digital signal processing and visualization). Commercial packages like Maple and MathLab are available.

Many more applications have been ported to Linux. If you absolutely cannot find what you need, you can attempt to port the application from another platform to Linux yourself. Whatever your field, porting standard UNIX applications to Linux is straightforward. Linux's complete UNIX programming environment is sufficient to serve as the base for any scientific application.

Linux also has its share of games. These include classic text based dungeon games like Nethack and Moria; MUDs (multi-user dungeons, which allow many users to interact in a text-based adventure) like DikuMUD and TinyMUD; and a slew of X games like xtetris, netrek, and xboard, the X11 version of gnuchess. The popular shoot-em-up, arcade-style game, Doom, has also been ported to Linux.

For audiophiles, Linux supports various sound cards and related software, like CDplayer, which makes a CD-ROM drive into an audio CD player, MIDI sequencers and editors, which let you compose music for playback through a synthesizer or other MIDI controlled instrument, and sound editors for digitized sounds.

Can't find the application you're looking for? The Linux Software Map, described in Appendix A, lists software packages which have been written or ported to Linux. Another way to find Linux applications is to look at the INDEX files found on Linux FTP sites, if you have Internet access.

Most freely-distributable, UNIX based software will compile on Linux with little difficulty. If all else fails, you can write the application yourself. If you're looking for a commercial application, there may be a free ``clone" available. Or, you can encourage the software company to consider releasing a binary version for Linux. Several individuals have contacted software companies and asked them to port their applications to Linux, with various degrees of success.

COPYRIGHT ISSUES

Linux is covered by what is known as the GNU General Public License, or GPL. The GPL was developed for the GNU project by the Free Software Foundation and specifies several provisions for the distribution and modification of free software. Free, in this sense, refers to distribution, not cost. The GPL has always been subject to misinterpretation. We hope that this summary will help you understand the extent and goals of the GPL and its effect on Linux. A complete copy of the GPL is printed in Appendix C.

Originally, Linus Torvalds released Linux under a license more restrictive than the GPL, which allowed the software to be freely distributed and modified, but prevented any money from changing hands for its distribution and use. On the other hand, the GPL allows people to sell and profit from free software, but does not allow them to restrict another's right to distribute the software in any way.

First, it should be explained that free software that is covered by the GPL is not in the public domain. Public domain software by definition is not copyrighted and is literally owned by the public. Software covered by the GPL, on the other hand, is copyrighted by the author. The software is protected by standard international copyright laws, and the author is legally defined. The GPL provides for software which may be freely distributed but is not in the public domain.

GPL-licensed software is also not shareware. Generally, shareware is owned and copyrighted by an author who requires users to send in money for its use. Software covered by the GPL may be distributed and used free of charge. The GPL also lets people take, modify, and distribute their own versions of the software.

However, any derived works of GPL software must also be covered by the GPL. In other words, a company may not take Linux, modify it, and sell it under a restrictive license. If the software is derived from Linux, that software must be covered under the GPL also. The GPL allows free software to be distributed and used free of charge. It also lets a person or organization distribute GPL software for a fee, and even make a profit from its sale and distribution.

However, a distributor of GPL software cannot take those rights away from a purchaser. If you purchase GPL software from a third-party source, you may distribute the software for free, and sell it yourself as well. This may sound like a contradiction.

Why sell software when the GPL allows you to get it for free? Let's say that a company decided to bundle a large amount of free software on a CD-ROM and distribute it. That company would need to charge for the overhead of producing and distributing the CD-ROM, and may even decide to profit from the sales of the software.

This is allowed by the GPL. Organizations that sell free software must follow certain restrictions set forth in the GPL. They cannot restrict the rights of users who purchase the software. If you buy a CD-ROM that contains GPL software, you can copy and distribute the CD-ROM free of charge, or resell it yourself.

Distributors must make obvious to users that the software is covered by the GPL. Distributors must also provide, free of charge, the complete source code to the software distributed. This permits anyone who purchases GPL software to make modifications to that software.

Allowing a company to distribute and sell free software is a good thing. Not everyone has access to the Internet and the ability to download software for free. Many organizations sell Linux on diskette, tape, or CD-ROM via mail order, and profit from the sales. Linux developers may never see any of this profit; that is the understanding reached between the developer and the distributor when software is licensed by the GPL.

In other words, Linus Torvalds knew that companies may wish to sell Linux, and that he might not see a penny of the profits. In the free software world, the important issue is not money. The goal of free software is always to develop and distribute fantastic software and allow anyone to obtain and use it. In the next section, we'll discuss how this applies to the development of Linux.

DESIGNING OF LINUX

New users often have a few misconceptions and false expectations about Linux. It is important to understand the philosophy and design of Linux in order to use it effectively. We'll start by describing how Linux is not designed. In commercial UNIX development houses, the entire system is developed under a rigorous quality assurance policy that utilizes source and revision control systems, documentation, and procedures to report and resolve bugs.

Developers may not add features or change key sections of code on a whim. They must validate the change as a response to a bug report and subsequently ``check in'' all changes to the source control system, so that the changes may be reversed if necessary. Each developer is assigned one or more parts of the system code, and only that developer can alter those sections of the code while it is ``checked out'' (that is, while the code is under his or her control).

Organizationally, a quality assurance department runs rigorous tests on each new version of the operating system and reports any bugs. The developers fix these bugs as reported. A complex system of statistical analysis is used to ensure that a certain percentage of bugs are fixed before the next release, and that the operating system as a whole passes certain release criteria.

The software company, quite reasonably, must have quantitative proof that the next revision of the operating system is ready to be shipped; hence, the gathering and analysis of statistics about the performance of the operating system. It is a big job to develop a commercial UNIX system, often large enough to employ hundreds, if not thousands, of programmers, testers, documenters, and administrative personnel. Of course, no two commercial UNIX vendors are alike, but that is the general picture. The Linux model of software development discards the entire concept of organized development, source code control systems, structured bug reporting, and statistical quality control. Linux is, and likely always will be, a hacker's operating system. (By hacker, I mean a feverishly dedicated programmer who enjoys exploiting computers and does interesting things with them. This is the original definition of the term, in contrast to the connotation of hacker as a computer wrongdoer, or outlaw.)

There is no single organization responsible for developing Linux. Anyone with enough know-how has the opportunity to help develop and debug the kernel, port new software, write documentation, and help new users. For the most part, the Linux community communicates via mailing lists and Usenet newsgroups.

Several conventions have sprung up around the development effort. Anyone who wishes to have their code included in the ``official'' kernel, mails it to Linus Torvalds. He will test and include the code in the kernel as long as it doesn't break things or go against the overall design of the system. The system itself is designed using an open-ended, feature-minded approach.

The number of new features and critical changes to the system has recently diminished, and the general rule is that a new version of the kernel will be released every few weeks. Of course, this is a rough figure. New release criteria include the number of bugs to be fixed, feedback from users testing pre-release versions of the code, and the amount of sleep Linus Torvalds has had this week.

Suffice it to say that not every bug is fixed, nor is every problem ironed out between releases. As long as the revision appears to be free of critical or recurring bugs, it is considered to be stable, and the new version is released. The thrust behind Linux development is not to release perfect, bug-free code: it is to develop a free UNIX implementation. Linux is for the developers, more than anyone else.

Anyone who has a new feature or software application generally makes it available in an alpha version--that is, a test version, for those brave users who want to hash out problems in the initial code. Because the Linux community is largely based on the Internet, alpha software is usually uploaded to one or more Linux FTP sites and a message is posted to one of the Linux Usenet newsgroups about how to obtain and test the code. Users who download and test alpha software can then mail results, bug fixes, and questions to the author. After the initial bugs have been fixed, the code enters a beta test stage, in which it is usually considered stable but not complete. It works, but not all of the features may be present. The software may also go directly to a final stage, in which the software is considered complete and usable.

Keep in mind that these are only conventions--not rules. Some developers may feel so confident of their software that they decide it isn't necessary to release alpha or test versions. It is always up to the developer to make these decisions. You might be amazed at how such an unstructured system of volunteers who programme and debug a complete UNIX system gets anything done at all. As it turns out, this is one of the most efficient and motivated development efforts ever employed. The entire Linux kernel is written from scratch, without code from proprietary sources. It takes a huge amount of work to port all the free software under the sun to Linux. Libraries are written and ported, file systems are developed, and hardware drivers are written for many popular devices--all due to the work of volunteers.

Linux software is generally released as a distribution, a set of prepackaged software which comprises an entire system. It would be difficult for most users to build a complete system from the ground up, starting with the kernel, adding utilities, and installing all of the necessary software by hand. Instead, many software distributions are available which include everything necessary to install and run a complete system. There is no single, standard distribution--there are many, and each has its own advantages and disadvantages. We describe installation of the various Linux distributions starting on .

LINUX AND OTHER OPERATING SYSTEMS

It is important to understand the differences between Linux and other operating systems, like MS-DOS, OS/2, and the other implementations of UNIX for personal computers. First of all, Linux coexists happily with other operating systems on the same machine: you can run MS-DOS and OS/2 along with Linux on the same system without problems. There are even ways to interact between various operating systems, as we'll see.

Why use Linux

Why use Linux, instead of a well known, well tested, and well documented commercial operating system? We could give you a thousand reasons. One of the most important, however, is that Linux is an excellent choice for personal UNIX computing. If you're a UNIX software developer, why use MS-DOS at home? Linux allows you to develop and test UNIX software on your PC, including database and X Window System applications. If you're a student, chances are that your university computing systems run UNIX. You can run your own UNIX system and tailor it to your needs. Installing and running Linux is also an excellent way to learn UNIX if you don't have access to other UNIX machines.

But let's not lose sight. Linux isn't only for personal UNIX users. It is robust and complete enough to handle large tasks, as well as distributed computing needs. Many businesses--especially small ones--have moved their systems to Linux in lieu of other UNIX based, workstation environments. Universities have found that Linux is perfect for teaching courses in operating systems design. Large, commercial software vendors have started to realise the opportunities which a free operating system can provide.

Linux vs. MS-DOS

It's not uncommon to run both Linux and MS-DOS on the same system. Many Linux users rely on MS-DOS for applications like word processing. Linux provides its own analogs for these applications, but you might have a good reason to run MS-DOS as well as Linux. If your dissertation is written using WordPerfect for MS-DOS, you may not be able to convert it easily to TeX or some other format. Many commercial applications for MS-DOS aren't available for Linux yet, but there's no reason that you can't use both. MS-DOS does not fully utilize the functionality of 80386 and 80486 processors. On the other hand, Linux runs completely in the processor's protected mode, and utilizes all of its features. You can directly access all of your available memory (and beyond, with virtual RAM). Linux provides a complete UNIX interface which is not available under MS-DOS. You can easily develop and port UNIX applications to Linux, but under MS-DOS you are limited to a subset of UNIX functionality.

Linux and MS-DOS are different entities. MS-DOS is inexpensive compared to other commercial operating systems and has a strong foothold in the personal computer world. No other operating system for the personal computer has reached the level of popularity of MS-DOS, because justifying spending $1,000 for other operating systems alone is unrealistic for many users. Linux, however, is free, and you may finally have the chance to decide for yourself.

You can judge Linux vs. MS-DOS based on your expectations and needs. Linux is not for everybody. If you always wanted to run a complete UNIX system at home, without the high cost of other UNIX implementations for personal computers, Linux may be what you're looking for.

Linux vs. The Other Guys

A number of other advanced operating systems have become popular in the PC world. Specifically, IBM's OS/2 and Microsoft Windows have become popular for users upgrading from MS-DOS. Both OS/2 and Windows NT are full featured multitasking operating systems, like Linux. OS/2, Windows NT, and Linux support roughly the same user interface, networking, and security features. However, the real difference between Linux and The Other Guys is the fact that Linux is a version of UNIX, and benefits from contributions of the UNIX community at large.

What makes UNIX so important? Not only is it the most popular operating system for multiuser machines, it is a foundation of the free software world. Much of the free software available on the Internet is written specifically for UNIX systems. There are many implementations of UNIX from many vendors. No single organization is responsible for its distribution. There is a large push in the UNIX community for standardization in the form of open systems, but no single group controls this design. Any vendor (or, as it turns out, any hacker) may develop a standard implementation of UNIX.

OS/2 and Microsoft operating systems, on the other hand, are proprietary. The interface and design are controlled by a single corporation, which develops the operating system code. In one sense, this kind of organization is beneficial because it sets strict standards for programming and user interface design, unlike those found even in the open systems community. Several organizations have attempted the difficult task of standardizing the UNIX programming interface. Linux, in particular, is mostly compliant with the POSIX.1 standard. As time goes by, it is expected that the Linux system will adhere to other standards, but standardization is not the primary goal of Linux development.

Linux vs. Other Implementations of UNIX

Several other implementations of UNIX exist for 80386 or better personal computers. The 80386 architecture lends itself to UNIX, and vendors have taken advantage of this. Oher implementations of UNIX for the personal computer are similar to Linux. Almost all commercial versions of UNIX support roughly the same software, programming environment, and networking features. However, there are differences between Linux and commercial versions of UNIX.

Linux supports a different range of hardware than commercial implementations. In general, Linux supports most well-known hardware devices, but support is still limited to hardware which the developers own. Commercial UNIX vendors tend to support more hardware at the outset, but the list of hardware devices which Linux supports is expanding continuously. We'll cover the hardware requirements for Linux in Section. Many users report that Linux is at least as stable as commercial UNIX systems. Linux is still under development, but the two-pronged release philosophy has made stable versions available without impeding development. The most important factor for many users is price. Linux software is free if you can download it from the Internet or another computer network. If you do not have Internet access, you can still purchase Linux inexpensively via mail order on diskette, tape, or CD-ROM.

Of course, you may copy Linux from a friend who already has the software, or share the purchase cost with someone else. If you plan to install Linux on a large number of machines, you need only purchase a single copy of the software--Linux is not distributed with a ``single machine'' license.

The value of commercial UNIX implementations should not be demeaned. In addition to the price of the software itself, one often pays for documentation, support, and quality assurance. These are very important factors for large institutions, but personal computer users may not require these benefits. In any case, many businesses and universities have found that running Linux in a lab of inexpensive personal computers is preferable to running a commercial version of UNIX in a lab of workstations.

Linux can provide workstation functionality on a personal computer at a fraction of the cost. Linux systems have travelled the high seas of the North Pacific, and manage telecommunications and data analysis for an oceanographic research vessel. Linux systems are used at research stations in Antarctica. Several hospitals maintain patient records on Linux systems. Other free or inexpensive implementations of UNIX are available for the 80386 and 80486.

One of the best known is 386BSD, an implementation of BSD UNIX for the 80386. The 386BSD package is comparable to Linux in many ways, but which one is better depends on your needs and expectations. The only strong distinction we can make is that Linux is developed openly, and any volunteer can aid in the development process, while 386BSD is developed by a closed team of programmers. Because of this, serious philosophical and design differences exist between the two projects. The goal of Linux is to develop a complete UNIX system from scratch (and have a lot of fun in the process), and the goal of 386BSD is in part to modify the existing BSD code for use on the 80386.

NetBSD is another port of the BSD NET/2 distribution to several machines, including the 80386. NetBSD has a slightly more open development structure, and is comparable to 386BSD in many respects.

Another project of note is HURD, an effort by the Free Software Foundation to develop and distribute a free version of UNIX for many platforms. Contact the Free Software Foundation (the address is given in Appendix C) for more information about this project. At the time of this writing, HURD is still under development.

Other inexpensive versions of UNIX exist as well, like Minix, an academic but useful UNIX clone upon which early development of Linux was based. Some of these implementations are mostly of academic interest, while others are full fledged systems.

HARDWARE REQUIREMENTS

You must be convinced by now of how wonderful Linux is, and of all the great things it can do for you. However, before you rush out and install Linux, you need to be aware of its hardware requirements and limitations.

Keep in mind that Linux is developed by users. This means, for the most part, that the hardware supported by Linux is that which the users and developers have access to. As it turns out, most popular hardware and peripherals for personal computers are supported. Linux supports more hardware than some commercial implementations of UNIX. However, some obscure devices aren't supported yet.

Another drawback of hardware support under Linux is that many companies keep their hardware interfaces proprietary. Volunteer Linux developers can't write drivers for the devices because the manufacturer does not make the technical specifications public. Even if Linux developers could develop drivers for proprietary devices, they would be owned by the company which owns the device interface, which violates the GPL. Manufacturers that maintain proprietary interfaces write their own drivers for operating systems like MS-DOS and Microsoft Windows. Users and third-party developers never need to know the details of the interface.

In some cases, Linux programmers have attempted to write hackish device drivers based on assumptions about the interface. In other cases, developers work with the manufacturer and try to obtain information about the device interface, with varying degrees of success.

In the following sections, we attempt to summarize the hardware requirements for Linux. The Linux Hardware HOWTO contains a more complete listing of hardware supported by Linux.

Disclaimer: Much hardware support for Linux is in the development stage. Some distributions may or may not support experimental features. This section lists hardware which has been supported for some time and is known to be stable. When in doubt, consult the documentation of your Linux distribution. for more information about Linux distributions.

Linux is available for many platforms in addition to Intel 80x86 systems. These include Macintosh, Amiga, Sun SparcStation, and Digital Equipment Corporation Alpha based systems. In this book, however, we focus on garden-variety Intel 80386, 80486, and Pentium processors, and clones by manufacturers like AMD, Cyrix, and IBM.

Motherboard and CPU Requirements

Linux currently supports systems with the Intel 80386, 80486, or Pentium CPU, including all variations like the 80386SX, 80486SX, 80486DX, and 80486DX2. Non-Intel clones work with Linux as well. Linux has also been ported to the DEC Alpha and the Apple PowerMac.

If you have an 80386 or 80486SX, you may also wish to use a math coprocessor, although one isn't required. The Linux kernel can perform FPU emulation if the machine doesn't have a coprocessor. All standard FPU couplings are supported, including IIT, Cyrix FasMath, and Intel. Most common PC motherboards are based on the PCI bus but also offer ISA slots. This configuration is supported by Linux, as are EISA and VESA-bus systems. IBM's MicroChannel (MCA) bus, found on most IBM PS/2 systems, is significantly different, and support has been recently added.

Memory Requirements

Linux requires very little memory, compared to other advanced operating systems. You should have 4 megabytes of RAM at the very least, and 16 megabytes is strongly recommended. The more memory you have, the faster the system will run.

Some distributions require more RAM for installation. Linux supports the full 32-bit address range of the processor. In other words, it uses all of your RAM automatically. Linux will run with only 4 megabytes of RAM, including bells and whistles like the X Window System and emacs. However, having more memory is almost as important as having a faster processor. For general use, 16 megabytes is enough, and 32 megabytes, or more, may be needed for systems with a heavy user load.

Most Linux users allocate a portion of their hard drive as swap space, which is used as virtual RAM. Even if your machine has more than 16 megabytes of physical RAM, you may wish to use swap space. It is no replacement for physical RAM, but it can let your system run larger applications by swapping inactive portions of code to disk. The amount of swap space that you should allocate depends on several factors;

Hard Drive Controller Requirements

It is possible to run Linux from a floppy diskette, or, for some distributions, a live file system on CD-ROM, but for good performance you need hard disk space. Linux can co-exist with other operating systems--it only needs one or more disk partitions.

Linux supports all IDE and EIDE controllers as well as older MFM and RLL controllers. Most, but not all, ESDI controllers are supported. The general rule for non-SCSI hard drive and floppy controllers is that if you can access the drive from MS-DOS or another operating system, you should be able to access it from Linux. Linux also supports a number of popular SCSI drive controllers. This includes most Adaptec and Buslogic cards as well as cards based on the NCR chip sets.

Hard Drive Space Requirements

Of course, to install Linux, you need to have some amount of free space on your hard drive. Linux will support more than one hard drive on the same machine; you can allocate space for Linux across multiple drives if necessary. How much hard drive space depends on your needs and the software you're installing.

Linux is relatively small, as UNIX implementations go. You could run a system in 20 megabytes of disk space. However, for expansion and larger packages like X, you need more space.

If you plan to let more than one person use the machine, you need to allocate storage for their files. Realistic space requirements range from 200 megabytes to one gigabyte or more. Each Linux distribution comes with literature to help you gauge the precise amount of storage required for your software configuration.

Monitor and Video Adaptor Requirements

Linux supports standard Hercules, CGA, EGA, VGA, IBM monochrome, Super VGA, and many accelerated video cards, and monitors for the default, text-based interface. In general, if the video card and monitor work under an operating system like MS-DOS, the combination should work fine under Linux. However, original IBM CGA cards suffer from ``snow'' under Linux, which is not pleasant to view.

Graphical environments like X have video hardware requirements of their own. Rather than list them here, we relegate that discussion to Section Popular video cards are supported and new card support is added regularly.

Miscellaneous Hardware

You may also have devices like a CD-ROM drive, mouse, or sound card, and may be interested in whether or not this hardware is supported by Linux.

Mice and Other Pointing Devices

Typically, a mouse is used only in graphical environments like X. owever, several Linux applications that are not associated with a graphical environment also use mice. Linux supports standard serial mice like Logitech, MM series, Mouseman, Microsoft (2-button), and Mouse Systems (3-button). Linux also supports Microsoft, Logitech, and ATIXL bus mice, and the PS/2 mouse interface. Pointing devices that emulate mice, like trackballs and touchpads, should work also.

CD-ROM Drives

Many common CD-ROM drives attach to standard IDE controllers. Another common interface for CD-ROM is SCSI. SCSI support includes multiple logical units per device so you can use CD-ROM ``jukeboxes." Additionally, a few proprietary interfaces, like the NEC CDR-74, Sony CDU-541 and CDU-31a, Texel DM-3024, and Mitsumi are supported. Linux supports the standard ISO 9660 file system for CD-ROMs, and the High Sierra file system extensions.

Tape drives

Any SCSI tape drive, including quarter inch, DAT, and 8MM are supported, if the SCSI controller is supported. Devices that connect to the floppy controller like floppy tape drives are supported as well, as are some other interfaces, like QIC-02.

Printers

Linux supports the complete range of parallel printers. If MS-DOS or some other operating system can access your printer from the parallel port, Linux should be able to access it, too. Linux printer software includes the UNIX standard lp and lpr software. This software allows you to print remotely via a network, if you have one. Linux also includes software that allows most printers to handle PostScript files.

Modems

As with printer support, Linux supports the full range of serial modems, both internal and external. A great deal of telecommunications software is available for Linux, including Kermit, pcomm, minicom, and seyon. If your modem is accessible from another operating system on the same machine, you should be able to access it from Linux with no difficulty.

Ethernet Cards

Many popular Ethernet cards and LAN adaptors are supported by Linux. Linux also supports some FDDI, frame relay, and token ring cards, and all Arcnet cards. A list of supported network cards is included in the kernel source of your distribution.

SOURCES OF LINUX INFORMATION

Many other sources of information about Linux are available. In particular, a number of books about UNIX in general will be of use, especially for readers unfamiliar with UNIX. We suggest that you peruse one of these books before attempting to brave the jungles of Linux. Information is also available online in electronic form. You must have access to an online network like the Internet, Usenet, or Fidonet to access the information. A good place to start is If you do not, you might be able to find someone who is kind enough to give you hard copies of the documents.

Online Documents

Many Linux documents are available via anonymous FTP from Internet archive sites around the world and networks like Fidonet and CompuServe. Linux CD-ROM distributions also contain the documents mentioned here. If you are can send mail to Internet sites, you may be able to retrieve these files using one of the FTP e-mail servers that mail you the documents or files from the FTP sites. for more information on using FTP e-mail servers.

Linux on World Wide Web

The Linux Documentation Project Home Page is on the World Wide Web at http://sunsite.unc.edu/LDP This web page lists many HOWTOs and other documents in HTML format, as well as pointers to other sites of interest to Linux users, like ssc.com, home of the Linux Journal, a monthly magazine.

WINDOWS

INTRODUCTION

Windows is the operating system sold by the Seattle-based company Microsoft. Microsoft, originally christened "Traf-O-Data" in 1972, was renamed "Micro-soft" in November 1975, then "Microsoft" on November 26, 1976. Microsoft entered the marketplace in August 1981 by releasing version 1.0 of the operating system Microsoft DOS (MS-DOS), a 16-bit command-line operating system

The first version of Microsoft Windows (Microsoft Windows 1.0) came out in November 1985. It had a graphical user interface, inspired by the user interface of the Apple computers of the time. Windows 1.0 was not succesful with the public, and Microsoft Windows 2.0, launched December 9, 1987, did not do much better. After minor revisions of Microsoft Windows 95, named Windows 95A OSR1, Windows 95B OSR2, Windows 95B OSR2.1 and Windows 95C OSR2.5, Microsoft released the next version of Windows on June 25, 1998: Windows 98. Windows 98 natively supported features other than those of MS-DOS but was still based upon it.

What's more, Windows 98 suffered from poor memory handling when multiple applications were running, which could cause system malfunctions. A second edition of Windows 98 came out on February 17, 2000; it was named Windows 98 SE (for "Second Edition"). On September 14, 2000, Microsoft released Windows Me (for Millennium Edition), also called Windows Millennium. Windows Millennium was based largely on Windows 98 (and therefore on MS-DOS), but added additional multimedia and software capabilities. Furthermore, Windows Millennium included a system-restore mechanism for returning to a previous state in the event of a crash. Concurrent with these releases, Microsoft had been selling (since 1992) an entirely 32-bit operating system (which therefore was not based on MS-DOS) for professional use, at a time when business primarily used mainframes. It was Windows NT (for Windows "New Technology"). Windows NT was not a new version of Windows 95 or an improvement on it, but an entirely different operating system. On May 24, 1993, the first version of Windows NT was released. It was called Windows NT 3.1, and was followed by Windows NT 3.5 in September 1994 and Windows 3.51 in June 1995. With Windows NT 4.0, launched for sale on August 24, 1996, Windows NT finally became a true success. In July 1998, Microsoft released Windows NT 4.0 TSE (Terminal Server Emulation), the first Windows system that allowed terminals to be plugged into a server, i.e. use thin clients to open a session on the server.

ICONS

On the desktop screen you will see several small pictures. These pictures are called "Icons." The "My Computer" picture below is an example of an icon. Double clicking the left mouse button on an Icons will start the programmes it represents. Another way to start programmes is by using the "Start" button.

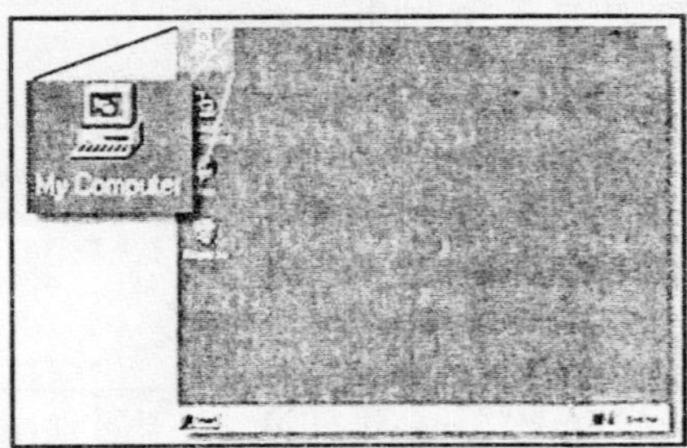

THE "START" BUTTON

The "Start" button is probably the most used part of the Windows Desktop. The start button is where you access all the programmes on the computer. When you click on the"Start" button you will be shown a menu of the major computer headings. These headings provide access to the major programmes on your computer.

Quick Tip: If the desktop does not show the gray bar with the "Start" button on it, simply move your mouse (cursor) to the bottom edge of the screen and the task bar will appear.

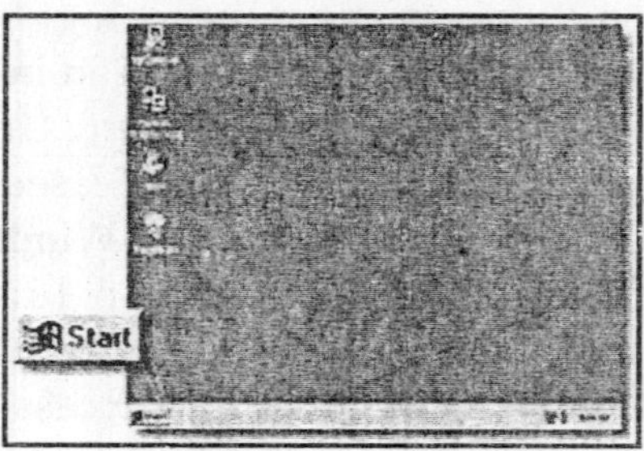

MENU

When you click on the "Start" button a menu with options will appear. Moving the mouse over the items in the menu causes them to highlight. Clicking on a highlighted item will open that programme.

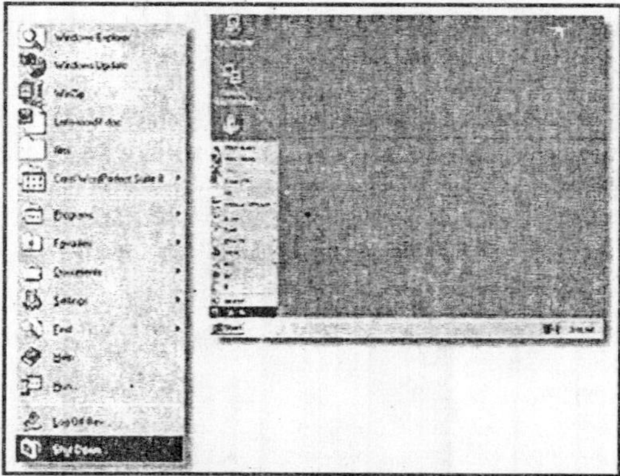

To close the "Start" menu click on the screen anywhere other then the menu

FINDING A PROGRAMME

Moving the mouse over a menu item marked with an arrow as shown below will open another list with more options.

To see all the programmes available for you to use on your computer clickon the Start button and in the menu that appears, highlight the item named "Programmes."

A new list will appear that holds more selections. Explore these lists to see all the programmes available to you. When you have found the programme that you want to use click on its icon

THE TASKBAR

Windows has the ability to run several programmes at once and to easily switch back and forth between running programmes. All programmes currently running are shown on the windows "taskbar." The taskbar is a gray bar with pictures on in it that runs across the very bottom of the screen. The taskbar can be recognized by the "Start" button located on its left hand side and the clock on its right. To switch between programmes that are running at the same time, click on the programme buttons shown on the taskbar. This is demonstrated below.

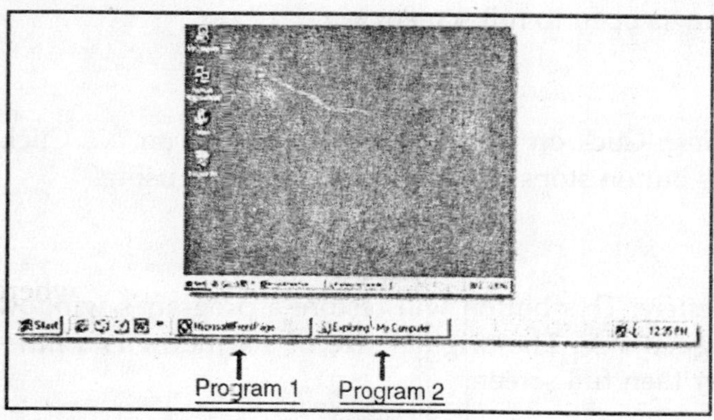

ADJUSTING A WINDOW'S SIZE

Most Windows programmes share the same look and feel which makes switching between and learning new programmes easier. Common to all Windows programmes is the ability to adjust the shape and size of the window you are working in. Some of the ways you can change a window includes; moving, closing, maximizing, minimizing and restoring it.

The following diagram and chart explains how to adjust a window:

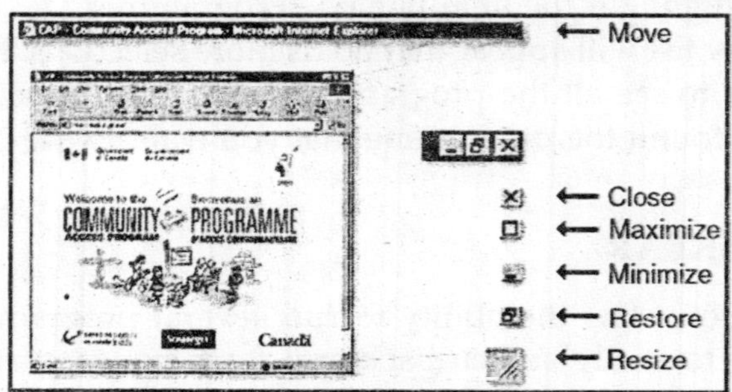

How to Adjust a Window

Move: Click and hold down the mouse button on the coloured bar at the top of any programme window. While holding down the mouse button drag the window to where you would like it on the screen. This cannot be done when a window is open to full screen.

Close: Click on the button marked with an "x." Clicking on this button stops the programme you are using.

Restore: This button will restore a program's window to its original size. The original size of a window is a little bit smaller then full screen.

Maximize: This button opens a program's window so that it fills the screen as much as it can.

Minimize: This button puts a programme on hold and places it on the taskbar at the bottom of your screen. To re-open a programme that is on the taskbar click on the box which represents the programme you want to open.

Resizing: When the mouse (cursor) is positioned over this part of the programme window, a set of arrows appears. You will now be able to stretch the programme window in any direction. The "My Computer" programme is a tool that lets you see everything that is stored on your computer. It is useful for finding, organizing and storing files on your computer. Files represent stored information that you have named. Think of "My Computer" as a filing cabinet for your computer. You can open the "My Computer" programme by double clicking on the "My Computer" icon on the "desktop" as shown below.

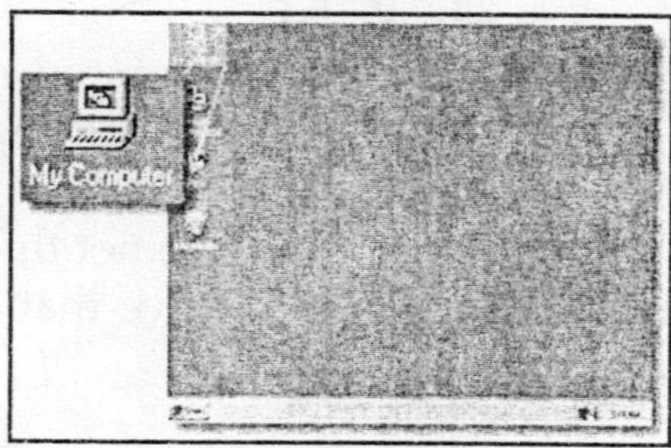

Once you have double clicked on the icon, the following window will appear.

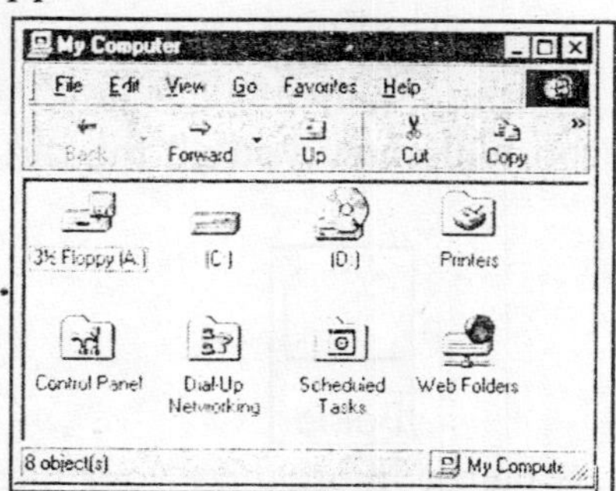

The icons in the" My Computer" window represent all the drives, folder and files on your computer. The following describes the icons that you will use the most as a new computer user.

Drives

Drives are like filing cabinets for computer files. To see what is stored on a drive double click on its icon and a list of files and folders will appear. These files and folders will be arranged alphabetically. To open any of these files double click on them.

The A: drive icon opens files saved on a floppy disk. You may only open this drive when you have put a floppy disk into the drive slot of the computer.

The C: drive icon on most home computers represents the hard drive. This is the drive where all the programmes that your computer runs are stored. You can also store files that you have created on this drive. If you do not think that the C: drive is your hard drive, look for a drive that has the same picture for an icon.

The D: drive icon represents the CD-ROM drive. Double clicking on this icon will show you all the files stored on a CD-ROM.

Folders: Folders help you organize your files by dividing

up a drive into alphabetically organized sections. Double clicking on a folder will open it. Each folder can also hold other folders and files.

Files: Files are information stored by a programme. For example a file created in "WordPerfect" will be saved with the ending ".wpd." Double clicking on a file will open it.

Chapter 6

Mobile Communication

In a mobile communication terminal for starting and simultaneously using a plurality of applications, one desired application starts fast to improve the operability when the number of started applications reaches a present limiting number of applications. An application start determining unit searches a list of started applications in response to the instruction of the start of application to obtain the number of started applications, and determines that the application cannot start when the number of started applications reaches a preset limiting number of applications.

An ending-application selecting unit selects, as an ending application to be ended, the application with the low priority from the start applications based on the preset priority of application when the application start determining unit determines that the application cannot start. An application ending unit performs the ending processing of the ending application selected by the ending-application selecting unit and deletes the selected ending application from the list of started applications.

A mobile communication terminal for starting and simultaneously using a plurality of applications, comprising: application start determining means which compares the number of started applications with a preset numerical value that is a maximum number of simultaneously used applications, determines that the application can start when the number of started applications is less than the numerical value, and determines that the application cannot start when the number of started applications reaches the numerical value;

ending-priority list creating means which calculates values indicating the using situation of the started applications in response to the determination of the application start determining means that the application cannot start and creates a list of ending priority indicating the order of applications with low influence in the case of ending the application; ending-application selecting means which selects the ending application based on the list of ending priority in response to the determination of the application start determining means that the application cannot start and clears the list of ending priority; application ending means which performs the ending processing of the ending application selected by the ending-application selecting means; application starting means which starts the application instructed by a user in response to the determination of the application start determining means that the application starts; and wherein the ending-priority list creating means collects data on evaluation items indicating the using situations including the total time displayed after starting the application, the number of switching times for display operation, and the last display time, obtains the order of started applications every evaluated item, multiplies the order by a weighting coefficient preset every evaluated item and every type of application, adds the multiplied result every application, calculates the values indicating the using situations, sorts the applications in order of the larger values, and creates the list of ending priority.

An application starting control method of a mobile communication terminal for starting and simultaneously using a plurality of applications, comprising the steps of: presetting a numerical value that is a maximum number of simultaneously used applications; selecting, from started applications, an ending application to be ended based on a priority when the number of simultaneously used applications will exceed the numerical value; newly allowing to start an application after ending the selected ending application; and collecting data for the started applications, including a total time displayed after starting the application, the number of switching times for display operation, and the last display time, determining an order of the respective data for each of the started applications, multiplying each determined order by respective weighting coefficients for each of the started applications, adding the multiplied results for each of the started applications, and creating the priority by sorting the applications based on the added results. A mobile communication terminal for starting and simultaneously using a plurality of applications, comprising: application start determining means which compares the number of started applications with a preset numerical value that is a maximum number of simultaneously used applications, determines that the application can start when the number of started applications is less than the numerical value, and determines that the application cannot start when the number of started applications reaches the numerical value; selecting means which selects an ending application to be ended on the basis of low priority from the started applications, in response to the determination of the application start determining means that the application cannot start; application ending means which performs ending processing of the ending application selected by the ending application selecting means; application starting means which starts the application instructed by a user in response to the determination of the application start determining means that the application can start; and ending-priority list creating means for collecting data on evaluation items indicating the using situations including the total time displayed after starting the application, the number of switching times for display operation, and the last display time, obtaining the order of started applications every evaluated item, multiplying the order by a weighting coefficient preset every evaluated item and every type of application, adding the multiplied result every application, calculating the values indicating the using situations, sorting the applications in order of the larger values, and creating a priority list.

INVENTION

The present invention relates to a mobile communication

terminal and an application starting control method thereof. More particularly, the present invention relates to a mobile communication terminal for starting and simultaneously using a plurality of applications and an application starting control method thereof. Recently, one type of mobile phones is sold to start a plurality of applications and simultaneously use a plurality of functions similarly to a personal computer or the like, under the improvement of CPU processing capacity. Such a mobile phone terminal enables a user to send an email while viewing a site screen on the Internet or to check the schedule by a scheduler while having a call.

However, the mobile phone terminal does not have a sufficient memory capacity or power capacity. Therefore, if many applications simultaneously start similarly to the personal computer, a malfunction is caused in the communication function or the started application operation becomes unstable. An unnecessary application must terminate without continuously staying resident in memory when the number of simultaneously-used applications reaches a predetermined limiting number.

Preferably, the unnecessary application automatically ends. As disclosed in the above-mentioned publication, the degree of importance is set to the application so as to use the application with the high degree of importance for a long time when the remaining amount of battery is reduced while a plurality of applications start, and the application with the low degree of importance ends when the remaining amount of battery reduces. However, when the number of applications to be started is over a predetermined number, the application to be ended does not automatically end.

DETAILS

It is an object of the present invention to provide a mobile communication terminal and an application starting control method thereof, for fast starting a desired application and improving the operability by automatically selecting and ending the application to be ended when the number of started applications reaches a predetermined limiting number upon starting the application. According to the present invention, there is provided an application starting control method of a mobile communication terminal for starting and simultaneously using a plurality of applications, comprising the steps of presetting a limiting number of simultaneously used applications; selecting, from started applications, an ending application to be ended based on the priority when applications over a limiting number are going to be started; and newly allowing to start an application after ending the selected ending application.

The priority may be preset or may be determined based on a using situation of the started application. The selected ending application may be displayed on a screen in response to the selection of the ending application. In this case, the selected ending application is ended in response to the approval operation of a user.

According to the present invention, there is also provided a mobile communication terminal for starting and simultaneously using a plurality of applications, comprising application start determining means which compares the number of started applications with a preset limiting number of simultaneously used applications, determines that the application can start when the number of started applications is less than the limiting number, and determines that the application cannot start when the number of started applications reaches the limiting number; selecting means which selects an ending application to be ended on the basis of low priority from the started applications in response to the determination of the application start determining means that the application cannot start; application ending means which performs ending processing of the ending application selected by the ending application selecting means; and application starting means which starts the application instructed by a user in response to the determination of the application start determining means that the application can start.

The application starting means may start the application instructed by the user in response to the ending processing of the application ending means. The application start determining means may determine whether or not the application starts in response to the instruction to start the application from the user.

The mobile communication terminal may have a list of started applications indicating the started applications. In this case, the application start determining means searches the list of started application to obtain the number of started applications. The application ending means deletes the selected ending application from the list of started applications. The application starting means starts the application determined as the start by the application start determining means and registers the started application to the list of started applications. The mobile communication terminal may further comprises means for receiving the approval of the user before the ending processing of the ending application in response to the selection of the ending application by the ending application selecting means.

According to the present invention, there is also provided a mobile communication terminal for starting and simultaneously using a plurality of applications, comprising application start determining means which compares the number of started applications with a preset limiting number of simultaneously used applications, determines that the application can start when the number of started applications is less than the limiting number, and determines that the application cannot start when the number of started applications reaches the limiting number; ending-priority list creating means which calculates values indicating the using situation of the started applications in response to the determination of the application start determining means that the application cannot start and creates a list of ending priority indicating the order of applications with low influence in the case of ending the application; ending-application selecting means which selects the ending application based on the list of ending priority in response to the determination of the application start determining means that the application cannot start and clears the list of ending priority; application ending means which performs the ending processing of the ending application selected by the ending-application selecting means; and application starting means which starts the application instructed by a user in response to the determination of the application start determining means that the application starts. The ending-priority list creating means may collect data on evaluation items indicating the using situations including the total time displayed after starting the application, the number of switching times for display operation, and the last display time, place a number to each of started applications in the order of their magnitude every evaluated item, multiply the number by a weighting coefficient preset every evaluated item and every type of application, add the multiplied results every application, calculate the values indicating the using situations, sort the applications in order of the larger values, and create the list of ending priority.

The mobile communication terminal may have a list of started applications indicating the started application. In this case, the application start determining means searches the list of started applications and obtains the number of started applications; the application ending means deletes the selected ending application from the list of started applications, and the application starting means starts the application determined as the start by the application start determining means and registers the started application to the list of started applications. According to the present invention, the limiting number (maximum number) of applications for simultaneous use is set and when the start of a new application amounts to the number of applications over the limiting number, the application for ending is automatically determined and is ended in accordance with the priority from among the using applications. Thus, in case that the number of applications reaches the limiting number, the new application is started quickly and the operability upon starting the application is improved.

WIRELESS COMMUNICATIONS

Wireless communications is a rapidly growing segment of the communications industry, with the potential to provide high-speed high-quality information exchange between portable devices located anywhere in the world. Potential applications enabled by this technology include multimedia Internet-enabled cell phones, smart homes and appliances, automated highway systems, video teleconferencing and distance learning, and autonomous sensor networks, to name just a few. However, supporting these applications using wireless techniques poses a significant technical challenge.

This course will cover advanced topics in wireless communications for voice, data, and multimedia. We begin with a brief overview of current wireless systems and standards. We then characterize the wireless channel, including path loss for different environments, random log-normal shadowing due to signal attenuation, and the flat and frequency-selective properties of multipath fading. Next we examine the fundamental capacity limits of wireless channels and the characteristics of the capacity-achieving transmission strategies. These strategies are typically not practical. Thus, our next focus will be on practical digital modulation techniques and their performance under wireless channel impairments, including flat and frequency selective fading. The next part of the course is spent investigating techniques to improve the speed and performance of wireless links.

We will investigate the design and performance of adaptive modulation and diversity techniques to compensate for flat-fading. Three techniques to combat frequency-selective fading are then examined: adaptive equalization, multicarrier modulation, and spread spectrum. We will also study the multiple access capabilities of spread spectrum with multiuser detection. The course concludes with a brief overview of wireless networks, including multiple and random access techniques, WLANs, cellular system design, and ad-hoc network design.

Applications for these systems, including the evolution of cell phones and PDAs, smart homes and appliances, sensor networks, and automated highways and skyways, will also be discussed. Presenting comprehensive coverage of this fast moving field, Wireless Communications and Mobile

Computing provides the R&D communities working in academia and the telecommunications and networking industries with a forum for sharing research and ideas. The convergence of wireless communications and mobile computing is bringing together two areas of immense growth and innovation. This is reflected throughout the journal by strongly focusing on new trends, developments, emerging technologies and new industrial standards. Under the guidance of an international editorial and advisory board drawn from academia and industry, this high quality, peer-reviewed journal, provides leading edge coverage of the opportunities and challenges driving the research and development of mobile communication systems.

All you need to stay ahead :

- High calibre survey papers
  Written by leading experts in the wireless and networking communities.
- Rapid publication times
  Due to electronic review and submission of original research papers
- Special Issues
  Addressing key topics of interest and managed by high profile editors
- An international forum for the sharing of research and ideas
  Key topics presented by leading individuals at the cutting edge of new technologies.

BANDWIDTH

In computer networks, bandwidth is often used as a synonym for data transfer rate - the amount of data that can be carried from one point to another in a given time period (usually a second). This kind of bandwidth is usually expressed in bits (of data) per second (bps). Occasionally, it's expressed as bytes per second (Bps). A modem that works at 57,600 bps hastwice the bandwidth of a modem that works at 28,800 bps. In general, a link with a high bandwidth is one that may be able to carry enough information to sustain the succession of images in a video presentation. It should be remembered that a real communications path usually consists of a succession of links, each with its own bandwidth. If one of these is much slower than the rest, it is said to be a bandwidth bottleneck.

In electronic communication, bandwidth is the width of the range (orband) of frequencies that an electronic signal uses on a given transmission medium. In this usage, bandwidth is expressed in terms of the difference between the highest-frequency signal component and the lowest-frequency signal component. Since the frequency of a signal is measured in hertz (the number of cycles of change per second), a given bandwidth is the difference in hertz between the highest frequency the signal uses and the lowest frequency it uses. A typical voice signal has a bandwidth of approximately three kilohertz (3 kHz); an analog television (TV) broadcast video signal has a bandwidth of six megahertz (6 MHz) -- some 2,000 times as wide as the voice signal.

BANDWIDTH MONITOR PRO

Do you ever wonder how much bandwidth you are using?
How fast you are downloading or uploading?
Or if you're closing in on your monthly transfer limit?
If so Bandwidth Monitor Pro is the utility for you!

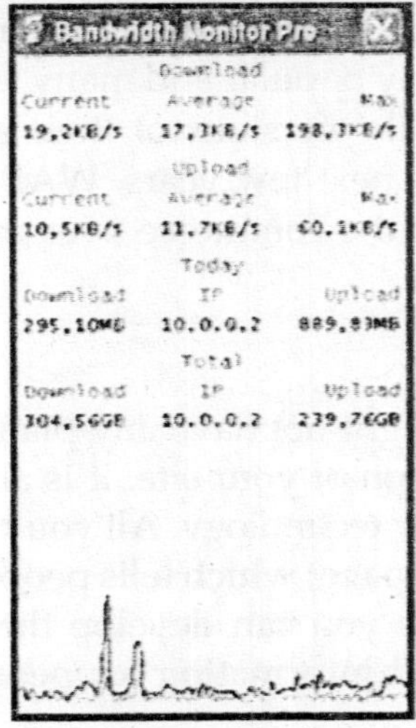

Detailed Logging

Supports logging of all your network adapters at once with separate statistics for each adapter. You can go back and check your daily, weekly, monthly, yearly or total transfer.

Always Control

With the small transfer graph placed in the system tray you always have control of your bandwidth usage.

Highly Customizable

Bandwidth Monitor Pro can be customized to display the information you want. You can also change the graph type and colours.

Advanced Alert System

You can set up rules with various actions and conditions.

Lets say that you have a monthly transfer limit of 30GB.

You can then set up Bandwidth Monitor Pro to alert you when your approaching that limit.

MOBILE INTERNET WML

WML (Wireless Markup Language) is the new web language for making sites on mobile phones. Over the past few months new WAP (Wireless Applications Protocol) phones have become extremely popular and many large websites have created special 'mobile' versions of their site. Many people predict that, over the next few years, WAP sites will become even morepopular and e-commerce over mobile phones will be widely available.

USING WML

Although you might not have any plans immediately for creating a WAP version of your site, it is always a good idea to get involved in new technology. All you need to do is make a small site (even one page) which tells people a bit about your website. In the future you can develop the site further with things like e-mail and information for people to get directly off their phones.

The main sites which will benefit from WAP are ones providing a service like e-mail, live sports scores or a calendar service etc. but there are many other uses. For example, a site giving music reviews could put their reviews on a WAP site. People could then read the reviews on their mobile phone while browsing through the CDs in a shop.

HAVING WAP PHONE

To create a WAP site you don't need a WAP enabled phone. You can get a WAP simulator for a PC. This is a piece of software which will give you a WAP phone on your desktop. You can then type in the URLs of WAP sites and can view them on your PC. You can get a very good free WAP simulator from YourWAP

COMPARING SITES

WAP sites are not like standard web sites at all. As an example, you are looking at part of the Gowansnet web site. Here is a screenshot of the Gowansnet WAP site (http://gowansnet.waphosts.net):

As you can see, sites written in WML are monochrome, very limited and there is very little screen space. Because of this you must be very careful when you are designing a WAP site as it is nothing like a web site.

BEGINNING WAP SITE

After reading the introduction you should understand about WAP sites, WML and what you can do with them so I will go straight into how to create a site. Note that you should really either have a WAP phone or a WAP simulator so that you can view your site and a knowledge of HTML is useful.

Finding A WML Host

Unfortunately WML cannot be run on all web hosts. For WML content to be run, a web host must make some changes to the configuration of their web server. If your host cannot do this for you, you can try WAPHosts.net. They can provide you with a server which will support WML.

Declaring A WML Document

Cards

Instead of having pages, WAP sites have cards. These are what is displayed on the screen at one time, just like a page. More than one card can be inserted in each WML document. To declare a card, insert the following:

```
<card id="index" title="My WAP Site"
newcontext="true">
```

This will make a card with the ID index (used for linking) and will display the text:

My WAP Site at the top of the screen.

Closing Tags

Unlike with HTML, it is extremely important to close WML tags. If you do not, a page will certainly not work. You must close both the <card> and <wml> tags:

```
</card>
</wml>
```

ADDING TEXT

In the last part I showed you how to create the basic file which will contain your WAP site. In this part I am going to show you how to insert text and how to format it.

The <p> Tag

Just like in HTML the <p> tag is used to show where a

paragraph begins and ends. Unlike HTML, though, all text on a WML page must be inside these tags. You are not allowed to nest these tags either. One important thing to remember about WML is that, unlike HTML where a page will still display even if there is bad code, a WAP phone will just reject a page if there is and code it doesn't understand.

As with HTML you use the tags as follows:

```
<p>
information
</p>
```

Aligning Text

Aligning text in WML is nearly exactly the same as in HTML, except you can't use the centre tag. All aligning must be done using the following <p> tags:

Centre:

```
<p align="centre">
```

Right:

```
<p align="right">
```

The
 Tag

In WML (as mentioned earlier) all tags must be closed. This causes problems when using old HTML tags (like <Br>) which have no closing tag. To get around this, some tags have had a / put on the end e.g.

```
<Br />
```

This, like in HTML will make a line break.

Text

In WML there is actually no font tag (as you can only display text in the phone's default font in black). To show text all you need to do is put it in between the <p> and </p> tags. Here is an example of a full WML document:

```
<?xml version="1.0"?>
<!DOCTYPE wml PUBLIC "-//WAPFORUM//DTD WML 1.1/
/EN" "http://www.wapforum.org/DTD/wml_1.1.xml">
<wml>
<card id="index" title="My WAP Site"
```

```
newcontext="true">
<p align="centre">
```

Welcome to my new WAP site. You can view this on your mobile phone anywhere in the world!

It is amazing!

```
</p>
</card>
</wml>
```

HYPERLINKS & IMAGES

In part 3 I showed you how to create a basic WAP site with one page and some text. This week I will show you how you can make this better by adding extra parts, linking to them (and other sites) and how to add images to your site.

More Cards

As I explained in the second part of this tutorial, WAP sites have cards instead of pages. They are really the same as pages except they can all be written in one file. To add another card, all you need to do is put in another <card> tag with a different ID to the others. For example:

```
<card title="About Me" id="about">
  information
</card>
```

would be added below the first card but before the </wml> tag.

Linking

There are three ways to link to another WAP site, file or card. Just like in HTML these can either be the full path to a file or a relative link.

To link to a WAP site you use the following:

```
<a href="http://gowansnet.waphosts.net/">
  Gowansnet</a>
```

in your text. To link to another file on your site you would use:

```
<a href="links.wml">My Links</a>
```

and to link to another card in the same page you use:

```
<a href="#about">About Me</a>
```

Index

P

R

S

T

U

V

W